INSIDE THE NAZI WAR MACHINE

OTHER BOOKS BY BEVIN ALEXANDER

How the South Could Have Won the Civil War:
The Fatal Errors That Led to
Confederate Defeat

How America Got It Right: The U.S. March to
Military and Political Supremacy

How Wars Are Won: The 13 Rules of War
from Ancient Greece to the War on Terror

How Hitler Could Have Won World War II:
The Fatal Errors That Led to Nazi Defeat

Robert E. Lee's Civil War

Korea: The First War We Lost

Lost Victories: The Military Genius of
Stonewall Jackson

How Great Generals Win

The Future of Warfare

INSIDE THE NAZI WAR MACHINE

HOW THREE GENERALS UNLEASHED HITLER'S BLITZKRIEG UPON THE WORLD

Bevin Alexander

NAL
CALIBER

NAL Caliber
Published by New American Library, a division of
Penguin Group (USA) Inc., 375 Hudson Street,
New York, New York 10014, USA
Penguin Group (Canada), 90 Eglinton Avenue East, Suite 700, Toronto,
Ontario M4P 2Y3, Canada (a division of Pearson Penguin Canada Inc.)
Penguin Books Ltd., 80 Strand, London WC2R 0RL, England
Penguin Ireland, 25 St. Stephen's Green, Dublin 2,
Ireland (a division of Penguin Books Ltd.)
Penguin Group (Australia), 250 Camberwell Road, Camberwell, Victoria 3124,
Australia (a division of Pearson Australia Group Pty. Ltd.)
Penguin Books India Pvt. Ltd., 11 Community Centre, Panchsheel Park,
New Delhi - 110 017, India
Penguin Group (NZ), 67 Apollo Drive, Rosedale, North Shore 0632,
New Zealand (a division of Pearson New Zealand Ltd.)
Penguin Books (South Africa) (Pty.) Ltd., 24 Sturdee Avenue,
Rosebank, Johannesburg 2196, South Africa

Penguin Books Ltd., Registered Offices:
80 Strand, London WC2R 0RL, England

First published by NAL Caliber, an imprint of New American Library,
a division of Penguin Group (USA) Inc.

First Printing, September 2010
10 9 8 7 6 5 4 3 2 1

LIBRARY OF CONGRESS CATALOGING-IN-PUBLICATION DATA:

Alexander, Bevin.
Inside the Nazi war machine: how three generals unleashed Hitler's Blitzkrieg upon the world/
Bevin Alexander.
p. cm.
Includes bibliographical references and index.
ISBN 978-0-451-23120-8
1. World War, 1939–1945—Campaigns—France. 2. Lightning war—History—20th century.
3. Rommel, Erwin, 1891–1944. 4. Manstein, Erich von, 1887–1973. 5. Guderian, Heinz, 1888–1954.
6. Military art and science—Germany—History—20th century.
7. Strategy—History—20th century. I. Title.
D761.A59 2010
940.54'13430922—dc22   2010016063

Set in Adobe Caslon
Designed by Patrice Sheridan

Printed in the United States of America

CONTENTS

MAPS

INSIDE THE NAZI WAR MACHINE

Adolf Hitler, accompanied by two Luftwaffe enlisted men, in front of the Eiffel Tower, June 1940.

INTRODUCTION

This is the story of how three low-ranking German generals—Erich von Manstein, Heinz Guderian, and Erwin Rommel—shattered the armies of France, Belgium, Holland, and Great Britain, forced the abject surrender of France, and evicted Britain from the Continent, all within the space of six weeks in 1940. The effects were world-shaking.

These three generals handed the German dictator, Adolf Hitler, the keys to the domination of Europe, North Africa, and the Middle East; the neutralization of the British Empire; and the reduction of the Soviet Union to subservience.

The campaign in the West in 1940 was the most complete military triumph in modern times. But it could have been an even vaster victory that could have abruptly transformed the political structure of the world. That this did not happen is because Hitler reacted in panic and disbelief to the stunning success that was unfolding. Instead of recognizing the gift that the generals had presented him, he frantically put the brakes on the advance. At precisely the moment when German forces were about to seize the port of Dunkirk, Hitler ordered the tanks to stop and allowed the entire British Expeditionary Force (BEF) to escape.

This was the single most devastating military mistake in modern times. If the BEF had been forced to surrender, virtually the entire British professional army with nearly all of its top commanders would have become captives. General Alan Brooke, later chief of the Imperial General Staff, who himself escaped from Dunkirk, said that, if the BEF had not returned to England, "it is hard to see how the army could have recovered from the blow." The British, with virtually no land forces, would have been almost as vulnerable to aerial invasion as the Dutch had been when German airborne troops seized the heart of Holland and forced its surrender in just five days. Avoiding invasion and liberating their troops would have almost surely been decisive factors in forcing the British to end the war.

If Britain had been forced to make peace in June 1940, the choking blockade of the Royal Navy would have been lifted, the world's raw materials would have flowed freely into Europe, and Germany would have become supreme on the Continent. It would have had the choice of attacking the Soviet Union without fear of its rear, or of so intimidating the Soviets that Joseph Stalin would have acquiesced to nearly all German demands. In other words, Germany would have instantly become the heart of a great European empire that could have dictated world events.

Yet even after the gross mistake of allowing the British to escape from Dunkirk, Hitler still could have achieved a virtually invincible empire. Only a single understrength British armored division in Egypt barred him from occupying North Africa, Suez, and the Middle East. Seizing these regions would have forced the Royal Navy to abandon the Mediterranean, given Hitler unlimited oil, and placed German armies within striking distance of the Soviet oilfields in the Caucasus and along the shores of the Caspian Sea. With Soviet oil in peril, Stalin would have gone to any lengths to placate Hitler. Britain would have been forced to use all its limited power to protect its crown jewel, India. Germany would have faced no military danger and, with all of continental Europe's industry in its hands, could have become as powerful as the United States.

But Hitler did not see this opportunity any more than he saw the opportunity at Dunkirk. He paid little attention to North Africa and attacked the Soviet Union headlong in June 1941. These two colossal and almost inconceivable blunders brought about Hitler's own demise and the death of the Third Reich in 1945. But this did not have to be.

Part of this remarkable story is the incapacity of all of the senior generals and politicians—on both the German and the Allied sides—to recognize the transformative impact of two weapons, the tank and the dive-bomber. Because of this, Manstein and Guderian had to overcome immense opposition within the reactionary senior reaches of the German army before and even during the time they, along with Rommel, demonstrated to the equally reactionary senior leaders of the Allies that World War I's method of warfare had been fatally outmoded. The story of the campaign in the West in 1940, therefore, is a double narrative of how a small group of revolutionaries, carrying out a totally new kind of war, overcame not only their unseeing superiors in the German army but also shattered their equally blind opponents in the Allied armies.

There are two kinds of conventional war, static and maneuver. The First World War was the preeminent example of static war, which seeks to achieve victory by firepower, by methodical, measured advances supported by cannons, and by maintaining a solid, continuous, linear front. The victors, France and Britain, believed they possessed the keys to permanent military supremacy by continuing to follow the principles of static war that they had perfected in four years of conflict.

But on May 10, 1940, static warfare was replaced by a modern war of maneuver. Maneuver warfare is the exact opposite of static war. It is a system of such rapid movement that the enemy does not have time to establish a continuous front, and is defeated either by being overridden by fast-moving forces rushing into his rear or by being surrounded in cauldrons and forced to surrender. The two forms of warfare are completely incompatible. The side that conducts static war is not organized to switch over to maneuver war.

The French, therefore, were incapable of reacting when the Germans broke a vast hole in the continuous French front and opened the entire rear to raging torrents of fast-moving German mechanized forces. Shortly after the disaster had struck, General Maxime Weygand, newly appointed supreme commander, told French prime minister Paul Reynaud: "We have gone to war with a 1918 army against a German army of 1939. It is sheer madness." French and British leaders had simply slept through a revolution in warfare.

The campaign in the West in 1940, in addition to being one of the most decisive in history, marked the greatest disparity of force between victor and vanquished that has ever been recorded, including the hitherto unsurpassed victories of Alexander the Great's small Macedonian army over the vast hosts of the ancient Persian Empire. In 1940, four corps, consisting of 164,000 men, less than 8 percent of the German army—and fewer than 60,000 of these men were at the critical point where the actual victory was won—brought about the complete rout of the better-equipped and much more heavily armed Allied armies totaling 3,300,000 men.

There were two keys to the battlefield victories achieved by this small fragment of the German army. The most important was the concept that Heinz Guderian insisted upon—that all tanks must be concentrated in armored or panzer divisions. Guderian was following a long-standing maxim, enunciated by Napoleon Bonaparte: "The art of warfare can be boiled down to a single principle: concentrate a greater mass than the enemy at a single point."

Guderian preached that massed tanks could break through almost anywhere because the Allies spread their more numerous and more heavily armored tanks in "penny packets" all along the battle line. The French general Charles Delestraint summarized the difference with only a bit of hyperbole: "We had three thousand tanks and so did the Germans. We used them in a thousand packs of three, the Germans in three packs of a thousand."

At no place were the defending Allied tanks and antitank guns numerous enough to stop a massed panzer attack. Therefore, the panzers could break through and spread like a flood into the Allied rear, cutting supply lines, scattering reinforcements, and destroying the equilibrium of the main line of resistance. Erwin Rommel described the new concept quite well: "We must view today's war from the cavalry viewpoint—we must lead panzer units like cavalry squadrons; we must issue commands from the panzers as they race along, just as commands were given out in earlier days from the saddle."

Allied to this concept of massing tanks at a single *Schwerpunkt,* or center of main effort, was the second key to German success: the first aerial artillery in history. It was delivered by the Stuka dive-bomber, a slow aircraft already obsolescent that could drop bombs with pinpoint accuracy on particular enemy targets. The Stuka ensured that the panzers did not have to wait for artillery to come forward in order to neutralize enemy fortifications or centers of resistance. Diving from the sky, the Stuka served the same role that artillery had served in previous wars, and could do it far more quickly. Moreover, the Stuka pilots turned on a loud siren they called "the trumpet of Jericho" when they dived. The high-pitched scream of the siren aroused intense fear and panic among the Allied soldiers and did more than bombs to break up resistance.

The highly mobile panzers and the Stukas made it possible for the Germans to advance deep into enemy territory, and to move with such stunning speed that the Allies could never set up a barrier in front of them and could organize only weak, isolated attacks on the flanks that struck merely glancing blows.

There was one strategic or broad theater-wide factor that made the 1940 campaign overwhelming. It was conceived by Erich von

Manstein. He saw that the Allies expected the Germans to attack into northern Belgium because they could not succeed in a direct attack through the Maginot Line, a massive series of interlocking fortifications built by the French along the German frontier in the 1930s. To block this anticipated advance, the Allies were certain to rush their mobile formations at full speed into Belgium the moment the Germans crossed the Belgian frontier.

Manstein accordingly drew on an ancient axiom of warfare, stated as early as 400 B.C. by the great Chinese strategist Sun Tzu: "Make an uproar in the east, but strike in the west." The Germans, Manstein insisted, must stage a huge "uproar" in northern Belgium and Holland with as noisy and as obvious threats as possible to convince the Allies that the main attack was coming there, just as they expected. This would cause the Allies to push up to the Dyle River, a little east of Brussels, to meet the onrushing German army.

Meanwhile, the *true* German offensive, led by seven of the ten panzer divisions the Germans possessed, would proceed inconspicuously through the heavily wooded Ardennes mountains of Luxembourg and eastern Belgium, a region the French had declared to be impassable. Shielded on the north by two panzer divisions, one commanded brilliantly by Erwin Rommel, the panzer corps led by Guderian would emerge from the Ardennes and cross the Meuse River at Sedan. Guderian would now be *behind* the Allied front, and could strike out directly west for the English Channel, 160 miles away, against virtually no opposition, and thereby could cut off all of the mobile Allied armies in Belgium and force either their surrender or swift evacuation by sea.

Despite unrelenting opposition from the German high command, this is how the campaign finally developed. It happened because Manstein and his supporters got the attention of Hitler almost at the last minute, and Hitler agreed to the concept, though, as it turned out, he really didn't understand its significance.

The campaign in the West in 1940, therefore, was not only the most decisive in modern history, but it also was one of the most remarkable ever recorded. It turned all previous views of warfare upside down, showed that the supposedly wisest leaders of armies and states were completely wrong, and demonstrated that ancient axioms of warfare and new methods of combat, when they are correctly applied together, can shatter armies and nations and change the world.

Hitler marks a map while his German staff officers look on.

CHAPTER 1

BREAKFAST AT HITLER'S

It was one of the oddest get-togethers in World War II, a "working breakfast" of the German führer Adolf Hitler with five newly appointed army corps commanders and Erwin Rommel, just named chief of the new 7th Panzer (or Armored) Division. It was held on February 17, 1940, in Hitler's quarters in the giant white New Reich Chancellery building in Berlin. There was no precedent or logic for such an event. Hitler didn't customarily break bread with low-ranking generals or, for that matter, with high-ranking generals. So there was something quite incompatible and conspiratorial about the whole affair.

There was, in fact, a secret being kept, but the organization that was being deceived was the German army's headquarters and General Staff, the *Oberkommando des Heeres* or OKH, the organization entrusted with planning a campaign against France and Great Britain and the organization that should have been privy to all the German Reich's military secrets.

The OKH was being left out of the loop for a very special reason. The commander of the German army, General Walther von Brauchitsch, and the chief of the General Staff, Lieutenant General Franz Halder, for months had been defiantly refusing to consider a proposed plan for defeating the British and the French, a

9

plan that was radically different from the one they themselves had concocted.

This alternative plan, so despised by Brauchitsch and Halder, focused on the town of Sedan in northern France, a place distant from northern Belgium and Holland where OKH was concentrating, and thus it was irremediably discordant, contrary, and subversive to the official line.

It had been offered by Major General Erich von Manstein, the fifty-three-year-old chief of staff of Army Group A. His memorandums to OKH over the past three months had become so insistent that Halder, in exasperation, pulled off a bureaucratic maneuver to get rid of him. Manstein, Halder explained to the army group commander, General Gerd von Rundstedt, really was past due for promotion. An officer junior to Manstein had been named commander of a panzer or armored corps, and it wouldn't be fair to deprive Manstein of a higher post as well. Accordingly, Manstein was removed from his position as chief adviser to Rundstedt and sent off to command the 38th Infantry Corps, which had not even been organized, and which, Halder knew, had only a walk-on role in the upcoming campaign in the West. That, Halder assumed, would take care of Manstein and his nagging, disconcerting ideas.

But there was a revolt in the ranks back at Army Group A's headquarters at the lovely old city of Koblenz, originally *Confluentes*, Latin for the confluence of the Rhine and Moselle rivers, where Julius Caesar built a bridge across the Rhine in 55 B.C. Two of Manstein's assistants, Colonel Günther Blumentritt and Major Henning von Tresckow, were strong advocates of Manstein's plan, and were deeply angered by Halder's ploy. When Hitler's chief military aide, Colonel Rudolph Schmundt, came to Koblenz on a visit in late January 1940, they laid Manstein's whole idea out to him. Schmundt was especially attentive. He and Tresckow were old friends, and Schmundt thought the plan contained the same ideas

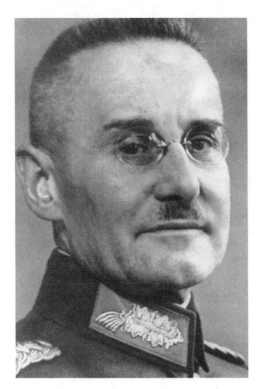

Franz Halder, chief of staff of the German army.

that Hitler had been expressing to him, but in a more precise manner. Shortly thereafter, Blumentritt—with both Manstein's and Rundstedt's approval—sent Schmundt a copy of Manstein's last proposal to the OKH (dated January 12, 1940).[1]

Back in Berlin, Schmundt explained Manstein's ideas to Hitler on February 2, probably using the copy Blumentritt had sent him for reference. Hitler had been thinking about Sedan for a long time, but was never able to formulate any coherent idea about a strike there. In Manstein's arguments, he found the broad concept that was missing. This was the day that he decided to make a decisive change in the offensive plan.[2]

But Hitler did not think through the situation. He was aiming at the tactical problem of getting on the opposite bank of the Meuse

General Walther von Brauchitsch, commander of the German army during the 1940 campaign in France.

River at Sedan. It's clear from how the campaign developed that he did not comprehend Manstein's strategic plan, which was vastly bigger than crossing the river at Sedan, and was aimed at producing total victory over France and a forced peace with Britain.

Schmundt realized that getting Hitler's approval on February 2 was not enough. Manstein had not been heard from directly, and Schmundt felt he should have the chance to put his cards on the table, most especially to tell Hitler that the great bulk of Germany's limited panzer and motorized *Schnell Truppen,* or fast troops, must be committed to this main effort and not dissipated among the separate armies, as the OKH planned to do. That's how he got the bright idea of a "working breakfast" with five new corps commanders, including Manstein, along with Rommel, who was a favorite of Hitler's. A get-acquainted breakfast would keep Halder from having any suspicions, and would protect Manstein from being accused of going over Halder's head to the German dictator.

The breakfast was convivial, with friendly, casual conversations. When it was over, Hitler asked Manstein to follow him back to his private office. Only Schmundt and Brigadier General Alfred Jodl, chief of operations for the Wehrmacht or armed forces, came along. There Hitler listened as if transfixed to Manstein's complete argument. He agreed with all of Manstein's conclusions.[3] Manstein departed to his new corps command at Stettin, east of Berlin.

The next day, February 18, Hitler summoned Brauchitsch and ordered him to implement the main elements contained in Manstein's plan. His key decision was to place "the bulk of the panzers" under Army Group A.[4] But Hitler didn't indicate that the ideas came from anyone but himself. Brauchitsch and Halder meanwhile had received some intimations of a sea change in Hitler's thinking, probably from backstairs informants, and were ready on the eighteenth with revisions that mirrored Manstein's proposals. These were presented, of course, without hinting to Hitler that they had dusted off Manstein's ideas.

It is probable that Halder and Brauchitsch didn't originally

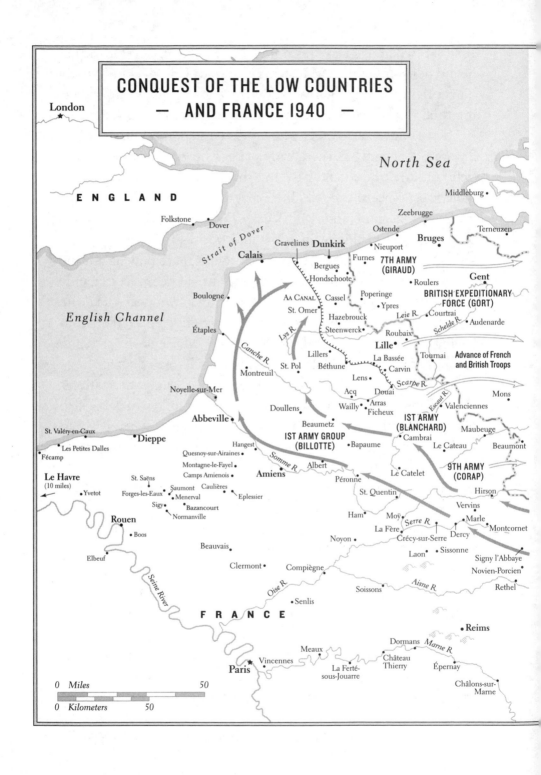

CONQUEST OF THE LOW COUNTRIES
— AND FRANCE 1940 —

London

ENGLAND

North Sea

Middleburg

Folkstone Dover

Zeebrugge

Strait of Dover

Ostende Terneuzen

Gravelines Dunkirk Bruges

Calais Nieuport

Bergues Furnes 7TH ARMY
Hondschoote (GIRAUD)

Boulogne AA CANAL Cassel Poperinge Roulers Gent

St. Omer Ypres BRITISH EXPEDITIONARY
FORCE (GORT)

English Channel Hazebrouck Leie R. Courtrai

Étaples Steenwerck Roubaix Schelde R. Audenarde

Lys R. Lille

Canche R. Lillers La Bassée Tournai Advance of French
and British Troops

St. Pol Béthune Carvin

Noyelle-sur-Mer Montreuil Lens Scarpe R. Mons

Acq Douai Valenciennes

St. Valéry-en-Caux Doullens Wailly Arras 1ST ARMY
Ficheux (BLANCHARD) Maubeuge

Abbeville Beaumetz Bapaume Cambrai Le Cateau Beaumont

Dieppe Hangest 1ST ARMY GROUP
(BILLOTTE)

Les Petites Dalles Quesnoy-sur-Airaines 9TH ARMY
Fécamp Montagne-le-Fayel Somme R. Albert Le Catelet (CORAP)

Le Havre Camps Amienois Amiens Péronne Hirson
(10 miles) St. Saëns Caulières St. Quentin

Yvetot Saumont Eplessier Vervins

Forges-les-Eaux Menerval Ham Moÿ Serre R. Marle

Sigy Bazancourt La Fère Dercy Montcornet

Rouen Normanville Noyon Crécy-sur-Serre

Boos Beauvais Laon Sissonne Signy l'Abbaye

Elbeuf Clermont Compiègne Novien-Porcien

Seine River Oise R. Soissons Aisne R. Rethel

Senlis

FRANCE

Reims

Meaux Dormans Marne R.

Paris Vincennes Château Épernay
La Ferté- Thierry
sous-Jouarre Châlons-sur-
Marne

0 Miles 50

0 Kilometers 50

pass on Manstein's ideas to Hitler not only because they were a direct contradiction and criticism of OKH's own plans, but also because they were sure Manstein's ideas would make Hitler even more eager to carry out his offensive in the West. From the beginning, they had been trying to get the führer to renounce it.[5] Now, faced with Hitler's knowledge of the plan, they pretended they were in favor. Duplicity and dissimulation were spread all around.

Thus it came to pass that the most radical strategic plan in modern times was set in motion. Hitler claimed all the credit for what happened, though he really didn't understand it at all, and the story of how it actually was conceived and who was responsible didn't come out until after the war.

The whole course of events was set in motion on September 27, 1939, when Hitler summoned his top generals to the chancellery and announced that he intended to launch an offensive through Luxembourg, Belgium, and Holland at the earliest possible moment. His aim was to defeat as much of the French army as could be done and to gain territory along the English Channel and North Sea as bases for air and sea operations against Britain.[6] There was no thought of attacking France directly, because the heavily fortified Maginot Line, built by France in the 1930s, covered the German-French frontier from the Swiss border to a point just beyond the southwestern corner of Luxembourg.

Hitler's generals were aghast. The campaign to defeat Poland was concluding, but still ongoing. OKH had no plan whatsoever for an offensive in the West. There were nowhere near enough weapons, tanks, aircraft, even ammunition to sustain a campaign against the extremely powerful and well-equipped French army and the British Expeditionary Force of ten mobile divisions. To think of a campaign in the West—and one with such low aspirations— appeared on the verge of madness.[7]

This was especially true because hope lingered that Britain and France, who had declared war on Germany on September 3, would conclude a peace without fighting. The two major Western powers were extremely angry with Hitler, but many thought they might be placated in some way. The world now knew that Adolf Hitler was a dishonest and unscrupulous conniver and a congenital liar, but the full scope of his political aims and his crimes against humanity had not been revealed. Leaders were increasingly fearful of his persecutions of Jews, but did not yet know that they were dealing with one of the most evil monsters ever to appear on earth.[8] Hitler had not commenced the *Endlösung,* or Final Solution, his attempt to kill all of the Jews of Europe, nor the campaign that began in 1941 to starve millions of Slavs in eastern Europe to provide *Lebensraum,* or living space, for Germans. There was still a naive hope, in other words, that through negotiation Europe could reach an equilibrium with a Germany dominant in central Europe and the Balkans, but not a Germany embarked on world conquest.[9]

The world had been stunned when Joseph Stalin concluded a nonaggression pact with Hitler on August 23, 1939. World leaders did not know that Stalin had made this step out of despair. Europe's fear of Soviet Communism—and Stalin's homicidal lust for world power—was almost as intense as its fear of Nazi Germany and Hitler. Accordingly, Britain, France, and Poland had been unwilling to form an alliance with the Soviet Union to stop Germany militarily. Stalin thus was trying to reach at least a temporary accommodation with Hitler, who had often threatened to destroy the Soviet state.

The agreement sealed the fate of Poland. Within days it was invaded from all sides. Western leaders soon confirmed that the pact contained an agreement to partition Poland and to divide up eastern Europe into German and Soviet spheres of influence. Russia occupied all of eastern Poland as part of the agreement with Nazi Germany.

So eastern Europe was being carved up. Britain and France could do nothing about it. What, reasonable persons might ask, could Britain and France hope to achieve by continuing the war?

True, British and French leaders were thoroughly disabused of any trust of Adolf Hitler. They had tried for six years to appease the German dictator by allowing him to rearm, to reoccupy the Rhineland, which had been demilitarized by the Treaty of Versailles of 1919, and to seize and absorb Austria in March 1938. They had even accepted his firm assurances at Munich in September 1938 that all he wanted from Czechoslovakia was the Sudetenland region, occupied by ethnic Germans. It was only on March 15, 1939, that the scales fell from their eyes. On that date Hitler, despite his promises, seized the Czech portions of Bohemia and Moravia, and turned Slovakia into a satellite state. Only then did the British prime minister, Neville Chamberlain, the arch appeaser of Hitler, realize that he had been deceived, and only then did he decide to guarantee the integrity of Poland, pulling a reluctant France along with him.

But now Poland also had fallen. There was no possibility that British and French forces could reclaim Poland's independence, except by a direct attack on Germany. And even if this did happen—and it would take years—what chances would the Western powers have of regaining eastern Poland held by the Soviet Union, or of stopping other likely aggressions by Joseph Stalin? Answer: none.

Therefore, a peace offensive aimed at working out some arrangement with the West seemed to many persons, not least the senior generals in the German army, to be the proper course for Germany to follow. Hitler had said he had no territorial ambitions in western Europe, and it was plain that neither Britain nor France really wanted to fight Germany.

So it was an utter shock to the top military leadership that Hitler had arrived at a diametrically opposite conclusion: He wanted to defeat the Western powers, not work out a reasonable compromise with them. But, perhaps because he had been a front-line soldier who had experienced firsthand the unbelievably deadly and indecisive battles along the Western Front in World War I, Hitler had little faith in the ability of Germany to humble either power completely. Thus his aspirations were extremely modest.

Although Brauchitsch and Halder were very much set against a campaign in the West, they obediently produced a plan and presented it to Hitler on October 19, 1939. It was simply a reiteration of the instructions Hitler had given them. The *Schwerpunkt*, or center of main effort, was to be delivered by the army's right wing, Army Group B, facing Holland and northern Belgium. Three field armies, plus the bulk of the panzer or armored forces, were to thrust on both sides of Brussels toward Bruges to seize the Belgian portion of the channel coast. It was an improvisation, devoid of any ideas, and gave rise to the question whether either Brauchitsch or Halder really wanted to produce a workable plan.

Despite the fact that Hitler had gotten the plan he called for, he was not pleased, and sent it back to be reworked. Halder produced a second directive on October 29, but it contained no new ideas either. It did add an additional thrust with panzers passing south of Liège. But this merely provided for two *Schwerpunkten* instead of one, and was directly contrary to German military doctrine, which called for concentration on a single point of emphasis, not on a diffused set of objectives.

Hitler's entire military experience had been as an infantryman in the trenches. He never rose above the grade of corporal, and was untrained in military theory. He did not see the contradiction of two centers of effort, which has the effect of halving the strength of the blow at both places. Consequently, he thought he had improved the plan when he ordered a third main thrust to be made even farther south. He directed that an armored or panzer corps and a motorized infantry force should thrust toward Sedan by way of southern Luxembourg. Sedan was in northern France just south of the Ardennes forest of eastern Belgium and Luxembourg. He selected Sedan for no other reason than he thought it would be the easiest place to cross the north-flowing Meuse River, which constituted a major barrier to any strike west. But now the German plan had three *Schwerpunkten.* The main points of effort were everywhere and nowhere.

Meanwhile Hitler had been setting and postponing dates for the offensive to start. Now he postponed the date once more. Although he gave the worsening weather as the reason, the actual cause was that he was becoming more and more uncertain about the plan.

Then on January 10, 1940, a totally unexpected incident took place. Major Hellmuth Reinberger, a general staff officer in the Luftwaffe, the German air force, had orders to travel from Münster to Cologne. In the officers' club he encountered a friend, Major Erich Hoenmanns, a pilot, who offered to fly him to Cologne. Rail traffic was slow and Reinberger took him up on the offer. But on the trip a fog bank arose and Hoenmanns lost sight of the Rhine River. As he was trying to find it, his engine cut out. The plane made a crash landing on a snow-covered meadow next to the Meuse River near Mechelen-sur-Meuse, in Belgium. Reinberger tried to burn the document he was bearing, but Belgian gendarmes arrested him before he could finish the job. The secret orders were plans for *Fall Gelb,* or Case Yellow, the latest directive that Halder had produced for the invasion of the West.

Although Belgium was trying to maintain its neutrality, authorities passed on the information to French and British chiefs. The orders looked authentic, but Allied officers suspected they might be a plant to deceive the Allies as to German intentions. Even so, the orders, as well as Allied intelligence reports from various sources, indicated an almost immediate attack by the Germans, though in fact the date had been pushed off indefinitely.

The Belgians rushed into quick talks with the British and French authorities, with the aim of inviting Allied troops in if Germany attacked. General Maurice Gamelin, commander in chief of French forces, held an emergency meeting of senior generals at supreme headquarters at Château de Vincennes just east of Paris. They decided French mobile forces should be ready in an instant to carry out the advance into Belgium that they had planned if the Germans invaded. On January 13, the Belgians, on reports from their embassy in Berlin, informed the French foreign ministry at the Quai d'Orsay in Paris that they expected an invasion two days later. At sunup on January 14, French lookouts discovered that all barriers at crossings into Belgium had been removed. This set off hurried movements of French soldiers up to and, in a few cases, over the frontier. But at sunup on January 15, the French discovered that the barriers were back in place. The invasion had not come, after all, and Belgium reverted to its neutral status.[10]

The frantic movements of French troops up to and over the frontier were not lost on German reconnaissance pilots or spies in European capitals. The movements confirmed to Hitler and the OKH what they had already surmised from other intelligence sources—that the Allies would enter Belgium the moment they suspected a German invasion. The mistaken landing of a German airplane on a Belgian field had given the Allied game plan away. From now on, it was certain that the Allies would advance to the most logical defensive line in Belgium, the Dyle River east of Brussels, when the Germans struck.

This fact had a profound effect in bringing about a radical change in German strategy, for a hurried movement of the Allies into Belgium was crucial to the success of the extremely different plan that Erich von Manstein had been pushing for from the moment he saw the original OKH directive on October 21, 1939.

But change was not in the minds of Brauchitsch and Halder. Despite knowing that *Fall Gelb* had been discovered by the Allies, they had no alternative, and they were still stonewalling

Erich von Manstein,
chief of staff of
Army Group A.

Manstein. OKH's third deployment directive, issued on January 30, also contained no new ideas. The three *Schwerpunkten* were still there. The only thing new was that German forces were to attack on only twenty-four hours' notice. This meant that troops had to move up closer to the frontiers.

It was in this environment of mounting crisis and decision that Blumentritt and Tresckow revealed the ideas of their former boss, Manstein, to Hitler's military aide, Colonel Schmundt, and set in motion a secret program to force a change in the OKH directive.

Born in Berlin in 1887, Erich von Manstein was a scion of an aristocratic Junker family that had produced a number of high-ranking officers in the Prussian army. Wounded in Russia in November 1914, he served the remainder of the First World War as a staff officer. During the interwar years he helped rebuild the German army and was widely regarded as one of its most brilliant officers.

The Allies knew that the Germans were bound to attack through Belgium, because it was the only way around the Maginot Line. Manstein felt the Allies were accordingly bound to go into Belgium to meet them, because they wanted to fight as far from France as possible. This would lead to a frontal clash. At best the Germans could achieve only a partial success, and any gains would be accomplished by brute force and at heavy cost. There was little hope of doing more than driving the French and British back to the Somme River in northern France, where they could build a strong defensive line and probably stop further German advances.

Manstein wrote later that to strive after the limited objectives in the OKH order justified neither the political hazards of violating three countries' neutrality nor the military stakes involved. "The offensive capacity of the German army was our trump card," he wrote, "and to fritter it away on half-measures was inadmissible."[11]

Besides, the certainty that the Allies would rush into Belgium opened a stunning opportunity that had not occurred to Halder and the OKH. Manstein saw that the Germans should encourage this advance by staging as loud and convincing a decoy attack into Holland and northern Belgium as possible, for the surer the Allies were that the main German attack was coming there, the farther they would advance to meet it, and the more easily they could be cut off and forced to surrender. This was because the Germans could make the actual center of their attack, their real *Schwerpunkt*, by using *Schnell Truppen* to rush through the heavily wooded Ardennes mountains to the south.

It was no secret that the Allies anticipated no main blow there. In 1933 Marshal Henri-Philippe Pétain, then minister of war and a hero of World War I, told the French Senate that the Ardennes could not be crossed by substantial German forces.[12] Two ideas had become articles of faith in the French army: "*Les Ardennes sont imperméables aux chars* (the Ardennes are impenetrable by tanks)" and "*La Meuse est infranchissable* (the Meuse cannot be crossed)." General Gamelin had called the Meuse "Europe's best tank obstacle." The French thought it would take the Germans two weeks, even if they did get through the Ardennes, before they could try to cross the Meuse, and by that time powerful French defenses could be erected to stop them.[13]

But Manstein didn't believe the Ardennes were impassable for tanks nor the Meuse uncrossable. Right next to the elegant Hotel Riesen-Fürstenhof beside the Rhine, where he was staying in Koblenz, was lodged an officer who could tell him whether he was correct. This officer was Lieutenant General Heinz Guderian, commander of the 19th Panzer (or Armored) Corps, and the father of the German armored force. Guderian, from a family of Prussian landed gentry, had served most of the First World War as a radio and signals officer on the Western front. He took part in the initial attack through the Ardennes in 1914 and had attended a General Staff school at Sedan in 1918 while the town was occupied by Germans. Thus, he was intimately acquainted with the Ardennes and Sedan. After the war he was assigned as a motor transport officer, and became absorbed in studies of armored warfare. He convinced the army to combine tanks, infantry, artillery, and engineers into fast-moving panzer divisions, an idea that he summarized in his highly acclaimed 1937 book, *Achtung-Panzer!*

Manstein, Guderian wrote, "asked me to examine the plan of his from the point of view of a tank man. After a lengthy study of maps and making use of my own memories of the terrain from the First World War, I was able to assure Manstein that the operation he had planned could in fact be carried out. The only condition I attached was that a sufficient number of armored and motorized divisions must be employed, if possible all of them."[14]

This was precisely the answer that Manstein was looking for. The best chance for Germany, he said, "consisted in launching a surprise attack through the Ardennes," where the Allies would not be expecting any armor because of the broken terrain.[15] He saw a situation that could take advantage of two recently developed weapons—fast tanks and dive-bombers—that Halder and the OKH were failing to appreciate fully.[16]

Mobility and the capacity to crack through opposition quickly were absolute preconditions of Manstein's plan to cross the Meuse at Sedan and then strike for the English Channel. The absence of mobility accounted for the failure of German offensives in World War I. In 1915, lower-ranking German officers figured a way to break holes in the solid Western front by laying down heavy fire on a particular point of an enemy trench, while one or more teams of eight to twelve *Stosstruppen*, or storm troopers, infiltrated the trench line and "rolled it up" with grenades and small-arms fire. This fire-and-maneuver system overcame Allied guns and fortifications, and became the fundamental method of small-unit engagements employed by all armies down to the present day.[17]

Manstein followed *Stosstrupp* tactics in calling for a break-through (*Durchbruch*) of the enemy line, preferably by an immediate attack while still on the move. Despite the experience of *Stosstruppen* in World War I, the idea of a breakthrough and quick exploitation remained alien to German doctrine. At the turn of the twentieth century, Chief of Staff Count Alfred von Schlieffen argued for encircling the enemy to create a giant pocket or cauldron. To him an exposed flank—as was inherent in Manstein's and Guderian's thinking—was an absolute taboo. Schlieffen could visualize a victory only as a compact turning movement of one wing of an army. But Manstein and Guderian wanted the panzers to push through to the enemy rear completely isolated, like a wedge.[18]

Guderian summarized the concept as follows: "After the breakthrough, it is a matter of decisive importance to push ahead as far as the fuel will permit, regardless of the threat to the flank, making full use of engines, without rest or breaks, marching day and night. Neutralizing enemy flank attacks is the mission of all following corps."[19]

This concept was essentially a motorized version of the *Stosstrupp* development of World War I. In contrast to the linear thinking of Allied commanders, who required units to advance uniformly next to one another in precise lines at precise times in coordination with precisely advancing artillery fire, *Stosstruppen* attacked independently, without regard for their exposed flanks. Later the English strategist Basil H. Liddell Hart described the concept as an "expanding torrent." He saw the assault teams as being like water that always seeks the easiest path to the sea. *Stosstruppen* also advanced along the lines of least resistance.

While the Allies concentrated their reserves at the point of strongest resistance, the Germans concentrated their reserves at the point of weakest resistance. The first wave of *Stosstruppen* was

A flight of Stuka dive-bombers, which, with bombs dropped on pinpoint targets, could knock out hostile guns and fortifications deep in enemy territory, permitting German panzer forces to penetrate fast and far without having to wait for supporting artillery.

trained to go around centers of resistance and leave them to be dealt with by following troops. The objective was to push deep into enemy territory as quickly as possible. Teams were not concerned with engaging and annihilating the enemy. Instead, they pushed past them deep into the rear, where they threatened enemy supply lines, command centers, and lines of retreat. *Stosstruppen* often created panic because Allied soldiers were fixated on maintaining a continuous line.

But the *Stosstrupptaktik* (storm troop or infiltration tactics) had not won the First World War for the Germans. The reason was that the soldiers moved on foot and the Allies were always able to bring up reinforcements by rail in time to seal the breaches. By 1940, Guderian had been preaching for ten years that this fatal flaw could be solved by using fast-moving tanks both to create holes in an enemy line and to rush through the holes into the enemy's rear, where they could spread chaos and disintegration. The speed of the tank advance would be too great for heavy artillery to follow, but the Stuka dive-bomber, developed by the Luftwaffe in the 1930s, could serve as aerial artillery and break up any enemy strongpoints that the tanks could not overcome.

The Stuka was the Junker 87B, with nonretractable landing gear, an 1,100-pound bomb load, and a top speed of only 240 miles per hour. It was already obsolescent in 1940, but the Stuka (short for *Sturzkampfflugzeug,* or dive battle aircraft) could make pinpoint attacks on enemy targets. Since the Luftwaffe expected to gain air superiority quickly with its excellent fighter, the Messerschmitt 109, the Stuka would have the sky largely to itself. The Allied air forces had not seen a need for such a plane, and concentrated primarily on area bombing, which was much less effective on the battlefield.

Guderian had built the panzer arm on the teachings of two English experts, J. F. C. Fuller and Basil H. Liddell Hart, whose ideas of concentrating armor in large units had been largely ignored in their own country.[20] The German high command was as hidebound as the British leadership, and fought Guderian's ideas. It was Hitler's enthusiasm for tanks that gave Guderian the opening he needed to establish an army doctrine of putting all armor into panzer divisions, instead of dividing it into small detachments parceled out to infantry divisions, as remained the practice in the French and British armies.

Erwin Rommel produced the best one-sentence description of blitzkrieg warfare: "The art of concentrating strength at one point, forcing a breakthrough, rolling up and securing our flanks on either side before the enemy has time to react, and then penetrating like lightning deep into his rear."[21]

This was a revolutionary idea. Most leaders thought tanks should be used as they had been employed in World War I—to assist infantry in carrying out assaults *on foot* against enemy objectives. For this reason, the best Allied tanks, like the British Matilda and the French Char B, were heavily armored monsters that could deflect most enemy fire but could move scarcely faster than an infantryman could walk. German tanks, on the other hand, were "fast runners" with less armor, but able to travel at around 25 miles an hour and designed for quick penetration of an enemy line and fast exploitation of the breakthrough thereafter into the enemy rear.

Guderian pointed out with disarming logic that if one side had 2,100 tanks and dispersed them evenly across a 300-mile front to support infantry divisions, the tank density would be seven per mile, not enough to be decisive except in local engagements. If the other side had the same number of tanks and concentrated them at a single *Schwerpunkt*, or center of attack, the density would be as many tanks as could physically be fitted onto the roads and fields in the sector. Such a density would be bound to break through. Defending tanks and antitank guns would be too few to destroy all the attacking armor, leaving the remainder to rush into the rear, with other motorized forces following to exploit the victory. This would inevitably destroy the equilibrium of the main line of resistance and force the entire front to disintegrate.

Nevertheless, the British and French armies persisted in spreading most of their tanks among their infantry divisions. Both remained under the delusion that battles would be fought all along a continuous line, and that they could move tanks and guns to block any point where a few enemy tanks achieved a breakthrough. They did not comprehend the effect of massing large numbers of tanks for a decisive penetration at a single point.[22]

Guderian insisted that the tanks and the dive-bombers could achieve what the *Stosstruppen* had been unable to do in World War I. Halder, at a war game at Koblenz on February 7, 1940, pronounced Guderian's ideas "senseless." He thought it might be possible for panzers to reach the Meuse and even secure bridgeheads across it. But he maintained that they could not break out until the infantry armies could catch up and then launch a "unified attack" on the ninth or tenth day of the campaign. Guderian contradicted him strongly: "The essential was that we use all of the available limited offensive power of our armor in one surprise blow at one decisive point; to drive a wedge so deep and wide that we need not worry about our flanks; and then immediately to exploit any successes gained without bothering to wait for the infantry corps."[23]

Manstein saw an even greater potential. Once the panzers reached the English Channel, 160 miles west of Sedan,[24] all of the Allied troops who had moved into Belgium would be encircled in a giant cauldron. If these troops were lost, Britain would be left with no army, and France would have so few forces remaining that it could not defend the rest of the country. Manstein saw that crossing the Meuse at Sedan could produce a total victory, forcing the complete surrender of France and making it probable that the British would conclude a peace treaty in order to free their army from captivity and avoid an invasion of their islands.

Manstein also pointed out a potentially destructive weakness in the OKH plan. An offensive across Belgium would proceed straight westward, leaving a vast and ever-growing space to the south where the Allies could launch a counterblow that could drive into the exposed flank of the German army and cut it off from its supplies and perhaps force it to surrender. In other words, the OKH plan exposed Army Group B to the very danger that a movement by the Allies into Belgium would expose the British and French armies to. Manstein didn't think the French high command would have the audacity to launch such a deadly counteroffensive, but "the possibility could still not be discounted."[25]

With the approval of the Army Group A commander, General von Rundstedt, Manstein sent the OKH seven memorandums outlining his alternative plan between October 31, 1939, and January 12, 1940. None got any response.

Manstein presented a direct intellectual challenge to Halder. It was a challenge that Halder took personally, because he and Manstein were intense professional rivals. This explains in part Halder's extreme reluctance to accept Manstein's proposed revisions in *Fall Gelb*.

Manstein had compiled an outstanding record as a combat leader and staff officer in World War I, and in 1936, already noted throughout the army for his intelligence, he became the deputy to Ludwig Beck, chief of the General Staff.[26] He was seen as Beck's successor, when Beck, as everyone expected, rose to command of the army.

But Beck was deeply opposed to Hitler's aggressive foreign policy, and Hitler instead chose the lower-rated and much weaker Brauchitsch, a man he could control, as army commander, in 1938. At the same time, Beck's ally Manstein was ordered to Liegnitz in Silesia to command a division, and Franz Halder was put in his place. When Beck resigned in protest, it was Halder who became chief of the General Staff on September 1, 1938, not Manstein.

There was a marked difference in the personalities of the two officers. Halder, three years older than Manstein, from a distinguished Bavarian military family, looked like a university professor, and was known for his methodical, systematic way of thinking and his relentless logic. For relaxation he did mathematical exercises. Manstein was the opposite, noted for quick, intuitive decisions and unorthodox thinking. For Manstein, the logical solution might not be the best solution, because the enemy might be thinking along the same lines. An illogical solution was likely to take the enemy by surprise. It was this turn of Manstein's mind that caused him to conceive of putting the main effort in the difficult Ardennes with the bulk of the panzers—because the orthodox Allied generals manifestly would not come to this conclusion.

With Hitler's order on February 18, 1940, OKH produced the final plan for *Fall Gelb*. The most important change was to move the *Schwerpunkt* of the attack from Army Group B southward to Army Group A, which was to advance through Belgium and Luxembourg south of the line Liège-Charleroi. Army Group B was to attack north of this line to draw as many Allied elements toward it as possible.

The key was the allocation of seven of Germany's ten panzer divisions to the main effort. Heinz Guderian's 19th Corps with three panzer divisions had the primary task of thrusting through the Ardennes to emerge at Sedan on the fourth day of the attack. Major General Georg-Hans Reinhardt's 41st Panzer Corps with two panzer divisions was to strike Monthermé on the Meuse a few miles north of Sedan. Lieutenant General Hermann Hoth's 15th Panzer Corps with two panzer divisions, one of them Erwin Rommel's 7th, was to cross the Meuse at Dinant about thirty miles north of Sedan, with the aim of shielding any effort by the Allies to strike southward.

But the final OKH directive still did not embody Manstein's

General Gerd von Rundstedt,
commander of Army Group A.

and Guderian's injunctions that the panzers must push for the
English Channel immediately after crossing the Meuse. Halder
and almost the entire general officers corps considered it indispensable first to secure bridgeheads over the Meuse by moving up
infantry divisions after the panzers crossed. The thrust was to be
continued only after buildup of an adequate screen on the southern flank of the bridgeheads.

Halder dared not venture the big leap to the channel in one
swift move. But delaying ran the risk of giving away the opportunity of encircling the Allied wing in Belgium. Manstein wanted a
total decision and was willing to accept total risk. The great moment would come when Guderian crossed the Meuse. Would he
follow the orders of his superiors or would he follow his and Manstein's instincts and strike hell-for-leather for the channel?

Meanwhile an immense amount of opposition arose to the new

directive from orthodox, conservative German generals. To the astonishment of Guderian, Halder suddenly became the plan's only advocate in the higher command. Halder came to this epiphany because he saw that it was the only chance for a major victory, and now he had to face vehement critics. The most vocal was General Fedor von Bock, commander in chief of Army Group B.

"You will be creeping past within ten miles of the Maginot Line with the flank of your breakthrough and hope the French will watch inertly," he complained. "You are cramming the mass of the tank units together into the sparse roads of the Ardennes mountain country, as if there were no such thing as air power. And you then hope to be able to lead an operation as far as the coast with an open southern flank 200 miles long, where stands the mass of the French army." He said this transcended "the frontiers of reason."

Rundstedt also began to have doubts. Halder had replaced Manstein as his chief of staff with Major General Georg von Sodenstern, a very conservative officer, who did everything he could to frustrate Manstein's plan. The moment Manstein was removed, headquarters of Army Group A began to plan a blitzkrieg in slow motion.

Sodenstern became the central opposition figure. He convinced Rundstedt that the panzers and the motorized forces should not spearhead the offensive. He wanted to use them only after a tactical breakthrough had been achieved by infantry divisions at Sedan and other targets on the Meuse. Sodenstern was not convinced that the panzers and motorized infantry could force crossings of the Meuse with the breadth necessary. Even if they did, Sodenstern complained, they would be so exhausted they could not then drive deep into enemy areas.

Halder rejected Sodenstern's argument. "We must resort to extraordinary means and bear the attendant risk," he said.

Halder saw that Hitler's go-for-broke political moves had

placed Germany in a catastrophic situation. There was only one way out, he concluded—*Flucht nach vorn,* or flight forward, toward a radical military solution. The offensive in the West in 1940 was an act of desperation for Germany to escape from a strategically perilous impasse.[27]

Manstein leads a dinner with his staff. It was he who conceived the idea of concentrating German armor for a strike through the Ardennes Forest of eastern Belgium and Luxembourg, while mounting a massive decoy offensive through Holland and northern Belgium. It produced the greatest military triumph in modern times.

CHAPTER 2

UPROAR IN THE NORTH

It's doubtful whether Erich von Manstein knew much if anything about Sun Tzu, the Chinese military sage who lived around 400 B.C. His maxims deeply influenced Oriental warfare for millennia, but became widely known in the West only around the time of the Vietnam War. However, Manstein's mind operated very much along the astute lines of Sun Tzu's mind. Thus he arrived on his own at one of Sun Tzu's most fundamental concepts—"make an uproar in the east, but attack in the west."

This rule embodies the military truth that deception—to give the impression, for example, that one is going to attack at one place but actually to attack at another—is the surest way of achieving victory. For with deception one can induce the enemy to misdirect his strongest forces to defend a place that appears to be the primary target but is not, thereby leaving the actual point of attack ill defended or not defended at all. This truth makes clear Sun Tzu's most profound statement: "The way to avoid what is strong is to strike what is weak."

Manstein, therefore, insisted that the Germans stage an extremely loud and convincing sham attack into Holland and northern Belgium, so as to bring forward the strongest and most mobile Allied forces, leaving only weak formations to guard the actual point of the German attack to the south—the difficult mountainous and wooded region of the Ardennes and the town of Sedan just beyond.

This was the concept that Adolf Hitler accepted in his directions to OKH on February 18, 1940, and it was the aim of Halder and Brauchitsch in assigning forces and targets. Manstein's idea became known in the German army as the *Sichelschnitt*, or sickle-cut plan, an apt description signifying that a strong armored thrust would swing easily like a sickle all the way around the Allied armies in Belgium, and harvest them like a sheaf of grain cut from its stalks.

However, all great strategic plans require an enemy who is gullible enough to fall into a trap. The great Carthaginian commander Hannibal carried out the greatest battle of annihilation in history at Cannae in southern Italy in 216 B.C. But he never could have done this except for the Roman consul, Caius Terentius Varro, who perceived as a weakness the fact that Hannibal's poorest infantry were pushed forward in the center of the battle line. Varro attacked straight into this advanced center, pushing the poor infantry far backward. But he ignored the strong Carthaginian infantry that Hannibal had stationed on either flank, and he was overwhelmed when these forces fell on both sides of the Romans while Hannibal's cavalry closed off their rear. The result was a massacre.

It is not enough to come up with a wonderful theory. To be successful, a great general must have an opponent who believes others think along the same unimaginative lines as he does. Such a commander is mystified when the great general does something totally unexpected. Both the French and the British leaders believed they were countering the ideas of the German commanders when they resolved to rush into northern Belgium. It never occurred to the Allied generals that the Germans might have another plan altogether.

Troops of the British Expeditionary Force move in Bren gun carriers shortly before the start of the campaign in the West in May 1940.

This lack of imagination is also shown in the fact that the Allied commanders did not realize the anticipated German drive straight westward in Belgium would present them with a marvelous opportunity to remain precisely where they were along the French frontier, and to drive directly into the southern flank of the Germans as they advanced. Manstein saw this danger very clearly, and used it as an argument to strike through the Ardennes. The thought never crossed the minds of the Allied commanders.

There are many cautionary tales to warn leaders not to be deceived or tricked by seeming mistakes or concessions of the enemy. The most famous is the myth of the Trojan horse, which the Greeks left as a present outside the gate of Troy. When the Trojans pulled the wooden horse inside their walls, warriors hidden inside the horse's body descended at night and opened the gate to the Greek army. This lesson was taken up by Virgil (70–19 B.C.) in

General Maurice Gamelin, commander in chief of the French army.

the *Aeneid*: "Do not trust the horse, Trojans . . . I fear the Greeks even when they bring gifts."

The French had been committed almost from the start to going into Belgium to meet an expected German attack. With the agreement of the British, General Maurice Gamelin, the French commander in chief, called for motorized French and British Expeditionary Force troops to move to the Dyle River east of the Belgian capital of Brussels. The new line would run along the Meuse from Givet, France, to Namur, Belgium, cross the 33-kilometer (20-mile) "Gembloux Gap" between the Meuse and the Dyle, and follow the Dyle up to Antwerp.

The "Cavalry Corps" of two light armored divisions under General René-Jacques-Adolphe Prioux was to rush eastward past the Dyle and the Gembloux Gap to meet the enemy, giving the other Allied troops time to secure the Dyle line.[1]

Early in 1940, General Gamelin became fixated on a new idea. He decided that the 7th Army should move over close to the English Channel and, the moment the Germans struck, it should rush straight to Antwerp and then across the Dutch frontier to Breda, where it could join up with Dutch forces to create a continuous front.

But Breda was twice as far from the French border as it was from the German border, and the idea that the French could beat the Germans to it was an illusion. Breda threatened instead to become a trap for the 7th Army.

The so-called "Breda plan" aroused the immediate opposition of General Alphonse-Joseph Georges, commander in chief of the northeastern front covering Belgium and the Ardennes. The 7th Army, made up of six infantry divisions including two fully motorized divisions under Henri Giraud, was part of the central reserve held in readiness around Reims. Manstein had cited this city as the precise point whence a massive counterattack might be launched against Sedan, once the Meuse had been breached. And here was Gamelin removing the only large mobile reserve of the French army from the key central position and sending it to the extreme western fringe of the line.

"That is an adventure," Georges protested. "If the enemy should only be feigning in Belgium, then he can maneuver elsewhere. We should therefore not employ our reserves for this operation. This is nothing but a dream."[2]

But Gamelin overruled Georges and on March 20, 1940, ordered that the 7th Army was to push for Breda. The same day he made another grave mistake. Originally only ten French and five British divisions were to carry out the Dyle plan. The remaining forces were to remain on the frontier to await developments. But Gamelin raised the movement to thirty divisions, including nearly every motorized and partly mechanized elite unit. Now virtually all the forces along the Belgian frontier were going to rush into a vast cauldron.

Despite this planned rapid move, the French and British remained committed to static warfare. Static war seeks to achieve victory by firepower, especially from heavy cannon, and by maintaining an inviolable, continuous, linear front that is so long and powerful that it cannot be flanked or broken. If the enemy somehow manages to penetrate this front, doctrine calls for sealing off the penetration by moving up reserves to close the breach. During World War I on the Western front, the preeminent example of static war, the front line ran from the coast of Belgium to the Swiss frontier. This same concept was in the minds of the French and British generals. By moving up to the Dyle line, they expected to re-create another unbroken line that would connect with the Maginot Line a few miles east of Sedan.[3]

It had not dawned on the senior generals that the Germans were about to challenge them with maneuver warfare. The French generals especially possessed a sovereign sense of superiority that looked down as if from a great height upon any ideas that contradicted their own doctrines. Winston Churchill wrote: "No one can understand the decisions of that period without realizing the immense authority wielded by the French military leaders and the belief of every French officer that France had the primacy in the military art."[4]

But in fact the French command system was hopelessly obsolete. There was not a single radio or Teletype machine in General Gamelin's supreme headquarters in the Château de Vincennes just east of Paris. When Gamelin wanted to contact General Georges, the northeastern front commander, he normally got into his staff car and was driven to Georges's headquarters at La Ferté-sous-Jouarre. This involved a 60-kilometer ride and two hours round-trip. Because the phone network broke down again and again, motorcycle messengers delivered many dispatches. It generally took 48 hours before an order reached a unit at the front.

French doctrine was geared to planning all operations in detail in advance. This required the drafting of interminable orders in which every particular was prescribed for subordinate units.[5] By the time an order reached a field unit, it was usually outdated. In the campaign to come, the French never seized the initiative. They were rarely able to take any action on their own, and most of their reactions came too late.[6]

The British command system was similar. After much experience with the British, Erwin Rommel wrote: "Their unwieldy and rigidly methodical technique of command, their over-systematic issuing of orders down to the last detail, leaving little latitude to the junior commander, and their poor adaptability to the changing course of the battle were to blame for the British failures."[7]

German doctrine stood at precisely the opposite pole. Erich von Manstein wrote that in the German army "individual leadership was fostered on a scale unrivaled in any other army, right down to the most junior NCO or infantryman, and in this lay the secret of our success."[8]

The German system of command was based on the *Auftragstaktik* that came out of the Prussian army. This system left a large measure of freedom of action to subordinate commanders. The mission regulated only *what* was to be done, not *how* it was to be done. This tradition of individual leadership motivated German commanders, even senior generals, to lead from the very front. In the campaign to come, senior leaders were usually with the foremost tanks or in the first boats in an assault river crossing.[9] The French officers and to a lesser extent the British officers, on the other hand, generally operated from command posts far in the rear. In the campaign in the West in 1940, action was so fast and so dynamic that only the leader at the focal point of events could take advantage of favorable moments by making lightninglike decisions. For the panzer leaders, assessing a situation, forming a plan, and issuing orders as a rule occurred on the spot with a direct view of the actual events. This was the single most important factor in German success.[10]

British and French leaders were aware that technological developments had taken place in the 1920s and 1930s. Aircraft and motor vehicles especially became much more effective as platforms for weapons. But the Allied generals used these improvements mainly to make static warfare more efficient. For example, they created the "infantry" tank, a heavily armored, extremely slow vehicle with a very short range to help the infantry break through enemy trench lines and fortifications. They built long-range offensive bombers designed to strike the factories and cities of the enemy in the belief that this would cause his entire war effort to collapse.[11] But they also built defensive fighter aircraft to shoot down such enemy "strategic bombers" before they could do damage to their own cities and factories. *Plus ça change, plus c'est la même chose*—the more things change, the more they remain the same.

A few renegades thought the changes pointed to entirely different conclusions. J. F. C. Fuller and Basil H. Liddell Hart foresaw tanks' ability to create maneuver warfare. Some aircraft visionaries doubted whether enemy populations could be brought to submission by the threat of bombs, and wanted to develop instead aerial weapons that could help win tactical engagements on the battlefield itself.

Neither of these alternative uses for improved vehicles modified the thinking of British and French leaders. But the Germans did not want to repeat the static war methods that had defeated them, and, seeking a return to mobility and maneuver, they adopted fast tanks, in the form of panzer divisions, and battlefield aircraft, in the form of the Stuka dive-bomber.[12]

While the certainty of rapid advance into Belgium implied that some French forces must be mobile and fast-moving, the army remained deeply committed to defense, not offense. The 1936 field service regulations, *Instruction sur l'emploi tactique des grandes unités*, emphasized the continuity of the battle line, and directed that no offensive action could occur without heavy superiority of artillery. Tanks were to be used to assist the infantry. All tactics were methodical and slow. A war of movement was out. A course for divisional and regimental commanders at the Centre des Hautes Études devoted 75 percent of the time to defensive methods.[13]

Meanwhile the situation in the Allied camp was changing dramatically. Allied forces were so inactive on the Western front that the fall and winter of 1939–1940 became known in the British Empire and the United States as the "phony war," in France as the *drôle de guerre*, and in Germany as the *Sitzkrieg*.

The Soviet Union took advantage of its pact with Germany to demand from Finland large cessions of territory as a buffer around the city of Leningrad (St. Petersburg) and elsewhere. The Finns refused and Soviet troops invaded on November 30, 1939. The Finns performed brilliantly in the "winter war," but Soviet power was too great. Russians breached the main Finnish defensive line on February 11, 1940, and Finland capitulated on March 12, ceding the land Russia wanted.

The French parliament was particularly angry with Premier Édouard Daladier because the Allies had done nothing to help Finland, while the Germans were massing on the frontiers of the Low Countries. The deputies didn't know of the fatal mistake General Gamelin was making in committing virtually all available mobile forces to a headlong rush into Belgium, but opinion was widespread that he was incapable of directing the war. His greatest

French premier Paul Reynaud.

strength seemed to be his ability to pacify all sides, not to make correct decisions. As the historian Nicole Jordan wrote, Gamelin's "inveterate habit was to tell interlocutors whatever he sensed that they wanted to hear."[14] Daladier could not summon the courage to fire Gamelin, however, and this spelled his ouster. On March 20, 1940, Daladier lost a vote of confidence in the Chamber of Deputies. Paul Reynaud formed a new government, but had so little general support that he was obliged to accept Daladier as minister of defense, and Daladier held on to Gamelin.

Reynaud's acceptance of office was a serious error. Though his motives were respectable, and he had many virtues—intelligence, industry, courage, and candor—he lacked authority. Reynaud had never had a party behind him and he had no party now, and not much support within the Chamber of Deputies. The future of the government was thus precarious. But there really was no alternative. France at the moment of its highest need found itself saddled with a weak and indecisive government, and with an incompetent general in command.[15]

On March 27, 1940, Reynaud, with the ministers of marine and air, flew to London and the next day they signed a Franco-British declaration. It was a mutual agreement not to negotiate or conclude an armistice or treaty of peace without common consent.[16]

At this time Britain and France saw a chance to damage the German war economy by mining the territorial waters of Norway to prevent shipment of iron ore from northern Sweden during the winter through the Norwegian port of Narvik. This ore was vital to the German war effort, but could not be moved by way of the Baltic Sea during the winter because the Gulf of Bothnia froze over. At the same time Hitler coveted the deep fjords of Norway as protected places to launch German surface ships, aircraft, and submarines against British supply lines. Both sides began plans to occupy Norway.

Hitler struck first, seizing Denmark in a swift coup de main and occupying key ports of Norway on April 9, 1940. The Allies contested the occupation of Norway and scored some successes, especially at sea. But German efforts were more ordered and decisive, and Allied forces soon withdrew.

In Britain, Prime Minister Neville Chamberlain could not present a convincing explanation for the Norwegian fiasco to the House of Commons, and his support, already weak because of his appeasement of Hitler, evaporated. On the evening of May 9, 1940, Labour Party leaders Arthur Greenwood and Clement Attlee refused to form a unified government under the Conservatives so long as Chamberlain remained chief of the Conservative Party. This forced his resignation.

The next day, May 10, 1940, the very day the Germans attacked in the West, Winston Churchill—the strongest and most eloquent voice against Hitler—seized the rudder of a unity government.

Chamberlain belonged to it as lord president, a job with little power, while Churchill demanded for himself the newly formed Ministry of Defense. From then on, he could make agreements with the military chiefs of staff over the head of the minister of war. Thus, Britain at last possessed strong and resolute leadership, but France remained with a weak and unfocused government.

OKH set up a new "panzer group" of five armored and three motorized divisions under General Ewald von Kleist containing Heinz Guderian's 19th Panzer Corps, Hans Reinhardt's 41st Corps, and Gustav von Wietersheim's 14th Motorized Corps. They were to be *der Sturmbock*, or the battering ram, of Army Group A to breach the Meuse around Sedan. Also allocated was the 15th Corps under Hermann Hoth, whose two panzer divisions were to cross the Meuse farther north at Dinant and shield Kleist's main effort on that flank. Each of the *Schnell Divisionen*, or fast divisions, had an average of 16,700 men, including attached units.[17] OKH allocated 2nd Army to help protect Army Group A's southern flank. OKH thus transferred the main weight to the southern wing.

At the same time Fedor von Bock's Army Group B remained strong enough, with two armies, to attack into northern Belgium and Holland. Bock had the remaining three panzer divisions— two in the 16th Corps under Erich Hoepner to lead his assault, and one (the 9th under Alfred Hubicki) assigned to the Holland operation.

Early on the morning of May 10, 1940, the greatest concentration of armor in the history of warfare burst across the frontiers of the Low Countries. Of a total of 2,400 tanks, 1,800 were in seven panzer divisions that struck through the Ardennes for the Meuse River. The remaining 600 were the leading edges of Fedor von Bock's enormous decoy offensive to the north.

But it was not tanks that stunned the world that momentous morning in May. People all over the globe were riveted to radios, from which frenzied reports poured of sensational landings by paratroops in seemingly hundreds of places all over Belgium and Holland. Actual landings were numerous enough, but the Germans also dropped dummies in parachutes over wide areas. Everything was in utter chaos. No one knew much more than that a massive, unprecedented offensive had opened in northern Belgium and Holland. It was precisely as the Allied generals had expected—the Germans, they said, were making their bid to defeat France.

In contrast to the wild reports of paratroop landings "everywhere," the real German aerial assault was dramatic enough. In the first great airborne invasion in history, 4,000 paratroops of Kurt Student's 7th Airborne Division descended from the early morning sky into "Fortress Holland" around the Hague, Rotterdam, Utrecht, and Moerdijk. The paratroops seized key bridges and four airfields, allowing Theodor von Sponeck's 22nd Infantry Air-Landing Division of 12,000 men to begin arriving by transport aircraft.

The Dutch stopped with heavy losses an effort by the paratroops to seize the Hague and the government by a coup de main, and they hoped to defend this region for a couple of weeks, long enough for the French 7th Army to join them at Breda and establish a continuous line. But the Germans quickly got hold of the key bridges in the Dordrecht-Moerdijk-Rotterdam area and held them until the 9th Panzer Division broke through the frontier and rushed to the bridges on May 13, eliminating all possibility of resistance.

Other dramatic scenarios played out at the bridges over the Maas (Meuse) River and the Albert Canal around Maastricht, fifteen miles inside the Dutch frontier. The bridges there were vital to the Germans to get their panzers into the open plains of Belgium beyond. Special detachments of German spies failed to grab the Maas bridges in the town of Maastricht, and the Dutch blew them.

The most spectacular event took place at the Belgian fort of Eben Emael about five miles south of Maastricht. It guarded the Albert Canal and the parallel Maas just to the east. Eben Emael, constructed of reinforced concrete and housing casemated 75mm and 120mm guns, had been completed in 1935 and was regarded as virtually impregnable.

Early on the morning of May 10, twenty ten-man gliders drawn by Junker 52 transports pulled off from fields near Cologne under the command of Captain Albert Koch. Over Aachen at 8,000 feet, the gliders unhooked and slowly descended over Dutch territory, ten landing beside four key bridges on the Albert Canal, and nine landing right on the flat roof of Eben Emael.

The ropes that were pulling the glider bearing the commander of the Eben Emael detachment, Lieutenant Rudolf Witzig, snapped and his vessel had to be retrieved by another Ju-52. Before Witzig arrived, Sergeant Helmut Wenzel took command and set explosive charges in the gun barrels, casemates, and exit passages of the fort. In moments the German engineers had incapacitated the fort and sealed the 650-man garrison inside. The next day the fort surrendered to German infantry, who had crossed the Maas and the canal in rubber boats.[18]

Meanwhile, engineers under Captain Koch landed at the vital bridges over the Albert Canal at Vroenhoven, Veldwezelt, and Briegden just west of Maastricht and seized them before the Belgians could blow them. The Belgians counterattacked the next day and destroyed the bridge at Briegden, but the Germans held the other three.

It took well over a day to construct military bridges across the Maas at Maastricht, but when these opened, Erich Hoepner's 16th Panzer Corps rushed over and smashed a wide path for Walther von Reichenau's following 6th Army.

Immediately upon hearing that the German offensive had opened, General Gamelin ordered the main Allied force on the left wing, the 1st Group of Armies under Gaston Billotte, to rush to the Dyle River. Included in this force was the "Cavalry Corps" of two light mechanized divisions under General Prioux with 200 tanks apiece. On the left of this army group was the British Expeditionary Force of nine infantry divisions under John Standish, Lord Gort. The British moved to the line Louvain-Wavre south of the Belgian army, while the French swung in below the British from Wavre southward to Namur and Dinant on the Meuse, and then on southward to Givet, just inside the French frontier. Meanwhile Gamelin directed the French cavalry—motorized forces, armored cars, and horse brigades—to penetrate into the Ardennes and hold up the Germans.

Gamelin also ordered the 7th Army under General Giraud to rush, as planned, up to Breda, about thirty miles southeast of Rotterdam and just north of Antwerp, to link up with the Dutch army. But on May 13, the Germans carried out the first aerial atrocity of World War II. Their aircraft rained bombs down on the undefended center of Rotterdam, killing about a thousand civilians and terrorizing the country. Two days later, the Dutch capitulated. Their army had scarcely been engaged. With no Dutch army to join, and in danger of being surrounded by advancing Germans, Giraud withdrew his 7th Army back to Antwerp.

To serve as a hinge around Sedan between the Maginot Line and the armies that had swept northeastward, Gamelin relied on two French armies (the 2nd and 9th) of four cavalry divisions and twelve infantry divisions, composed mostly of older reservists. This Sedan sector was the least fortified portion of the French frontier. The cavalry, which were sent ahead into the Ardennes, were useless against tanks, and the infantry possessed few antitank or antiaircraft guns.

Meanwhile, the German Luftwaffe allowed the Allied rush to the Dyle line to proceed unhindered. German aircraft concentrated rather on beating down Allied defenses in the rear and knocking out Allied aircraft still lined up on the ground. The Germans were successful to a large degree. The Dutch and Belgian fighters were generally inferior to the Messerschmitt 109s, but the French fighters, especially the Dewoitine 520, the Bloch 152, and the American-built Curtiss Hawk, were more or less comparable. However, the French did not deploy many of these fighters in the battle zone, and the Luftwaffe was able to achieve air superiority very quickly.[19] Also, the British Royal Air Force deployed on the Continent a few Hawker Hurricane fighters, which were roughly comparable to the Messerschmitt, but held back in England its Supermarine Spitfire, which was somewhat superior.

Over the Ardennes, the Luftwaffe kept only fighter planes that pounced on any Allied reconnaissance aircraft that they could find. But they did not have to worry about bombers, because the Allies thought the movements through this forest were only subordinate efforts, and made no attempt to bomb them.

Behind Hoepner's panzers (3rd and 4th Divisions), the 6th Army advanced quickly, encircling the Belgian fortress of Liège, and pressing the Allies and Belgians back to Antwerp and toward the Dyle line. Georg Küchler's 18th Army, which had moved into Holland, turned on Antwerp as soon as the Dutch surrendered, and seized the city on May 18. The French cavalry that had advanced into the Ardennes made little impression on the German forward elements, and withdrew behind the main Allied positions.

Now occurred the first great tank battle in the history of the world.

The French lined up six elite divisions and several independent tank battalions along the 33-kilometer Gembloux Gap. *La trouée de Gembloux* was not protected by any natural obstacles. The Belgians had built some defenses, but not many. Eight kilometers in front of the gap was an extended tank obstacle, *le barrage de Coin-*

tet, running for 23 kilometers northwest and southeast of the village of Perwez. It consisted of a heavy iron grille of steel T-beams positioned on rollers, 2.5 meters high and 3 meters deep, reinforced by concrete blocks, barbed wire, and mines. However, there were numerous gaps in this line.

A positive defense of the line was provided by Prioux's Cavalry Corps of two light mechanized divisions (2nd and 3rd), sent out 30 kilometers (18 miles) to the northeast of Gembloux around the village of Hannut to meet the onrushing panzers.

Prioux wanted to retreat even before the fight started. He felt extremely exposed out at Hannut. On May 11, getting reports that the panzers were approaching, Prioux phoned the 1st Army commander, General Georges Blanchard, to tell him that the Dyle line must be abandoned, and all the Allied forces had to move back to the Escaut (Schelde) River, 75 kilometers (45 miles) west. The Belgians were falling back as fast as they could, Prioux complained. His Cavalry Corps would be unable to delay the panzers, and there was not enough time for the 1st Army to establish itself along the Dyle and the Gembloux Gap. Blanchard passed Prioux's fears on to 1st Army Group commander Billotte, who responded that any change in the Dyle plan could only be disastrous, and ordered Prioux to remain in place and to meet the German attack.[20]

Prioux's formation was huge, comparable to a panzer corps. It contained 239 Hotchkiss tanks mounting 37mm guns, and 176 Somua tanks carrying 47mm guns, the best tank cannon in the world at the time. Prioux's orders were to hold off the panzers until at least the fifth day of the campaign to give the infantry time to improve their positions along the gap.

The French tanks were waiting when Hoepner's panzers came up to Hannut on May 12. The French were much superior, in part because, at first, only the 4th Panzer Division was on hand. Just one bridge was made available to the panzers over the Albert Canal, forcing the 3rd Panzer Division to follow behind. It did not arrive until later in the day. When the 4th Panzer attacked, it was soundly defeated. A few panzer commanders tried to tackle the French tanks too boldly. In duels, especially with the French Somuas, the Germans lost in a shocking fashion. The Somuas had 55mm of armor and the Hotchkiss tanks had 45mm, compared to 30mm on both the Panzer IIIs and IVs. Many experts considered the Somua the most modern and best battle tank at the time.[21]

The German Panzer III crews discovered that their 37mm projectiles bounced off the armor of both the Hotchkiss and Somua tanks. Only the Panzer IVs' low-velocity 75mm cannons could penetrate them, and they had to get at close range to do so. Even so, the Germans made progress, primarily because Stuka dive-bombers arrived, and made effective hits on the French tanks, and because of the rigid battle tactics of the French.

General Prioux, in orthodox French fashion, had placed his tanks in static positions and had strung them out in long lines. Also, few of the French tanks had working radios, and officers sometimes had to dismount and go from tank to tank to give orders. In addition, the French tanks had room in the turret for only one man. Thus the tank commander had to be tactical leader, gunner, and assistant gunner, all at once. The two-man German turrets, however, allowed the tank commander to occupy himself fully with his command tasks. The German tanks, all equipped with interconnecting radios, were able to concentrate their efforts and moved constantly from one point of attack to another.

The next day, May 13, was even worse for the French. Prioux lined up his armor like a string of pearls for miles between Tirlemont on the north and Huy on the Meuse River on the south. The line lacked depth and Prioux created no reserve for a counterthrust. In doing this Prioux violated one of the fundamental maxims of his illustrious predecessor, Napoleon Bonaparte. A French marshal once submitted to Napoleon a plan in which the army was positioned in a linear pattern from one end of the border to the other. Napoleon responded sarcastically: "Are you trying to prevent smuggling?"

General Hoepner, like the other panzer generals, followed Napoleon's rule, "concentrate a greater mass than the enemy at a single point."[22] Seeing that Prioux had spread out his tanks, Hoepner concentrated his two divisions on a narrow sector of the 3rd Light Mechanized Division around Hannut and cracked through, destroying 75 Hotchkiss and 30 Somua tanks in the process. The 2nd Mechanized Division on the south simply stood in place and did nothing.

The breakthrough was costly for the Germans. They lost 160 tanks destroyed or disabled, but the penetration at one spot forced the entire Cavalry Corps to abandon the field. When Prioux fell back, he didn't try to delay the German advance. Instead, he withdrew in one swift move, pulling entirely behind the Gembloux Gap line. When the panzer commanders saw this happening, they started in pursuit. *Le barrage de Cointet* scarcely slowed them. In a number of cases they merely followed the retreating French tanks through big gaps, and kept on going.

When the panzers reached the Gembloux line, they tried to break through at once, but were repulsed. General Hoepner, fearing more losses, called off the attack. But the message didn't reach the 3rd Panzer farther north, and its rifle regiment punched all the way through the main line of resistance and the rear stop line by nightfall. The Gembloux Gap had been penetrated.

Once more, rigid French tactics helped the Germans. When Prioux's corps got behind the Gembloux line, 1st Army broke it up and distributed the tank battalions behind the infantry divisions. Yet the Germans had been tremendously weakened in fighting the Cavalry Corps. The 4th Panzer had only 137 armored vehicles on the morning of May 16, and just four Panzer IVs. A quarter of all the tanks in 3rd Panzer, and these mainly

A panzer column halts its advance briefly, but remains in formation.

the Panzer IIIs and IVs, were not operational. The breakup of the powerful Cavalry Corps was incomprehensible, because, if concentrated, it could still have been used for a formidable counterattack.

With the Cavalry Corps gone, the French were no longer able to hold the Gembloux Gap. Hoepner's orders had been to bait the enemy to induce him to move into a trap. He had done his job. The Allies were deep into northern Belgium. Now his corps no longer had a role.

The German high command saw that the clash at Hannut had demonstrated that the French were fighting very poorly, and that further attacks by panzers might cause them to retreat as fast as they had come forward. To prevent this from happening, the German high command placed Hoepner's corps under Army Group A, which moved it south to help in the *real* German attack.[23]

In the midst of the frightening news from the Continent, Winston Churchill stood up in the House of Commons on May 13 and declared: "I have nothing to offer but blood, toil, tears, and sweat . . . You ask, what is our aim? I can answer in one word: Victory. Victory at all costs." His defiant stand united Parliament. The vast majority voted for him as prime minister.

A unit of the 1st Panzer Division prepares for an assault in the move to Sedan on May 12, 1940.

CHAPTER 3

ATTACK IN THE SOUTH

While the world's attention was focused on the awesome battles in Belgium and Holland, the actual *Schwerpunkt,* or center of gravity, of the German offensive plunged almost unnoticed through the Ardennes toward the weakest point of the French line, 60 miles away. Well behind the panzers, the German infantry divisions plodded on foot, their supply wagons and artillery pieces being pulled mostly by horses.

The leading element of Army Group A was the 19th Panzer Corps (1st, 2nd, and 10th Panzer Divisions), commanded by Heinz Guderian. His tanks were targeted at Sedan on the Meuse. Just to the north, Georg Hans Reinhardt's 41st Panzer Corps with three divisions (6th and 8th Panzer and 2nd Motorized) aimed at Monthermé, about 15 miles northwest of Sedan. Each of the five panzer divisions averaged 253 tanks.

About 25 miles north of Reinhardt was Hermann Hoth's 15th Panzer Corps with two divisions, the 5th and 7th (under Erwin Rommel), with a total of 542 tanks. This corps' job was to get across the Meuse at Dinant and keep the Allies in Belgium from interfering with Guderian or Reinhardt in their thrust westward.

Everything depended on speed. The Germans had to cross the Meuse before the Allies woke up to the danger. If they did, they still had time to assemble a massive defensive line along the river and delay the offensive long enough to bring up reinforcements. If that did happen, the French might be able to counterattack through Army Group A and endanger Army Group B to the north, or they might hold the panzers along the Meuse and prevent the campaign of annihilation that Manstein had designed.

The lead element in the advance through the Ardennes was 1st Panzer Division. Guderian had given Neufchâteau as its objective for the day. The town was 62 kilometers (40 miles) west of the German frontier and 34 kilometers (20 miles) northeast of Sedan. The division traversed undefended Luxembourg on the morning of May 10. The leading company of the 1st Motorcycle Battalion and three armored reconnaissance cars were far ahead, and reached Martelange on the Belgian frontier to find the bridge over the Sauer (Sûre) River blown. The Germans drew fire from the Belgian hill opposite. Five minutes later Lieutenant Colonel Hermann Balck, commander of the 1st Rifle Regiment of 1st Panzer, arrived, and ordered the motorcycle company of 100 infantry to cross the river and drive the enemy, of about the same strength, off the hill. The infantrymen had no support because a Belgian T-13 tank with a 47mm gun was on the other side and kept the reconnaissance cars from showing themselves.

The infantry made no preparation whatsoever. They waded the river, rushed through the village of Martelange, and launched an uphill assault across 200 meters of open terrain. When the Germans appeared, the Belgians were so surprised that they immediately evacuated the hill and withdrew with their tank. This first fight set the example for the entire campaign. Balck's recipe for success was speed and surprise.

The infantry pushed on four kilometers west up the Sauer valley to Bodange, a hamlet with a dozen farmsteads on high ground at the junction of the Sauer and the Basseille rivers. A company of the Belgian Ardennes Light Infantry was defending the place. The panzers and other vehicles couldn't start advancing until five thirty p.m., when the engineers finished a pontoon bridge at Martelange. The 1st Motorcycle Battalion decided to attack unaided, in hopes surprise would bring success as at Martelange. But the Belgians spotted the Germans, and halted the assault. It was only after the Germans got an 88mm antiaircraft gun across the Sauer and knocked out strongpoints that infantry captured the hamlet in a house-to-house fight. The Belgians had held up the entire advance for six hours.

So far, not a single tank had played a role in the advance of 1st Panzer Division.

Because of the broken bridge at Martelange, the first tanks of 2nd Panzer Regiment didn't arrive at the edge of Neufchâteau until nine thirty a.m. on May 11. The rest of the division's panzers were strung out single file back down the road to Martelange. The French beat the Germans to the town. The French 5th Light Cavalry Division had set up defensive positions anchored on Neufchâteau and Libramont, nine kilometers north.

When Major General Rudolf Kirchner, commander of 1st Panzer, surveyed the situation, he decided to avoid Neufchâteau, and ordered 2nd Panzer Regiment to swing around south of the town. The leading panzers easily broke through a thin line of resistance three kilometers southeast of Neufchâteau, came up on Petitvoir, six kilometers west of town, overran a French 105mm artillery battery on the outskirts, and sent plunging tank fire from a hill right into the village. The unexpected attack threw the French defense into chaos. Many French soldiers bolted, but the main body held on grimly to Petitvoir because it was on their road of retreat.

By now the 1st Panzer Regiment had come forward. General Kirchner, instead of sending it to help the 2nd Regiment capture Petitvoir, ordered it to push even farther west. Ignoring their flanks, the 1st Regiment tanks rushed on to capture the highway junction of Biourge, four kilometers beyond Petitvoir. The French now found they were cut off from their main road of withdrawal.

Soldiers began streaming rearward in disorder, following any small byway or path they could find. Defense of Neufchâteau collapsed. When a battalion of the 1st Rifle Regiment turned on the town in the afternoon, it was empty of enemy soldiers.

The seizure of Neufchâteau was a classical example of German *Stosstrupp,* or storm troop, tactics of World War I. The panzers followed the same procedure *Stosstruppen* had followed—infiltrating deep into the enemy rear along the line of least resistance. The advance of the tanks caused the French front to collapse, not because of attack, but because of panic.

The sudden onslaught of German forces through the Ardennes, though disregarded by the French high command, caused a huge exodus of people in the region. As soon as word came of the attack, Charlotte, the Grand Duchess of Luxembourg, assembled her leaders and headed a cortège of ducal cars that crossed the Belgian frontier early on the morning of May 10 on the way to Dunkirk and London. On the French side of the frontier, villages east of the Meuse were cleared and the inhabitants dispatched by train into the interior. On the night of May 10 the *maire* of Sedan received an order from the *préfet* of the Meuse department to evacuate the town. At four a.m. on May 11 the civilian population of Sedan gathered at rallying points and entrained. French railway officials expected the Germans to bomb the line. Stukas did strike in front of the last train, forcing the fugitives to continue their exodus on foot. Hospitals at Rethel to the south refused to take invalids of Sedan until President of the Republic Albert Lebrun himself intervened. The evacuations were complicated by the panicked flight of Belgians, who stirred French civilians to take to the roads.[1]

With the loss of Neufchâteau, there was no organized French resistance any closer than Bouillon, clustered around a peninsula formed by the Semois River, only 13 kilometers northeast of Sedan. The Germans had considered this town to be the main obstacle to a rapid advance on Sedan. Thus, when 1st Panzer Reg-

Heinz Guderian inspects a destroyed bridge in Bouillon, Belgium, May 12, 1940.

iment tanks burst through French delaying lines at the first rush, the commander, Colonel Johannes Nedtwig, decided to make an immediate push to seize the two bridges into the town.

Panzers punched right into the middle of enemy columns flooding to the bridges. A company commanded by Captain Matthias Graf von der Schulenburg made straight for the northern bridge at six thirty p.m. on May 11, but saw only its just-demolished remnants. Learning that the southern bridge was still intact, Schulenburg ordered fire on it to prevent demolition teams from approaching. But as the first panzer, manned by 1st Lieutenant Ernst Philipp, reached the southern bridge, it blew up with a tremendous roar. Immediately thereafter a French antitank gun hit Philipp's tank, killing the gunner and putting the vehicle out of action. Heavy fire from the panzers was able to keep down enemy gunners on the opposite bank, and at seven fifteen p.m. the company of Captain Friedrich Freiherr Kress von Kressenstein crossed the river at a ford 300 meters downstream.

The moment Kress's panzers reached the other bank, the town was bombed by twenty Stukas. All attempts to call off the dive-bombers failed. As soon as the aircraft pulled away, heavy French 155mm artillery guns began to pound Bouillon. The tanks could do nothing, and shortly after midnight on May 12 they returned across the same ford to the northern bank of the Semois.

The attack had failed. Both bridges were gone. But, unnoticed by the Germans, the French had evacuated Bouillon during the night, abandoning without a fight the last natural obstacle in front of Sedan.

While the struggle for Bouillon was going on, the 1st Motorcycle Battalion rushed into the village of Mouzaive a few kilometers to the northwest and seized intact the small bridge over the Semois there. The Germans were already on the south bank when a retreating cavalry troop of the 2nd Moroccan Spahi Regiment arrived on the north end and started across. The Germans beat

Tanks of the 1st Panzer Division cross a ford over the Semois River at Mouzaive, Belgium, on May 12 en route to Sedan.

back the Moroccans with heavy fire, and they faded away to cross the river at a ford elsewhere.

The Germans had made only one small penetration over the Semois, but it triggered abandonment by the French of their entire position along the river, although it was shielding Sedan. This decision resulted from the disastrous French fixation on a continuous front. If a line was breached in only a single place, so the doctrine went, then the flank of the line was exposed both left and right. Because the panzers were moving at such dizzying speed, the French commanders despaired of being able to seal a breach in their line. So their only option was to retreat, leaving the path wide open to Sedan.

The next morning, May 12, some 1st Panzer tanks and other vehicles moved up to Mouzaive, crossed over the bridge or a ford adjacent, and struck straight for Sedan. Meanwhile the division's 1st Infantry Regiment and other elements forded the river at Bouillon, and also struck straight for Sedan. During the day engineers completed a pontoon bridge over the Semois at Bouillon.

The tanks had little trouble, and pushed into that part of Sedan north of the Meuse River. The French had fully evacuated the right or northern bank of the Meuse at Sedan, and had blown the bridges. Night had fallen before first German patrols appeared near the Givonne ravine north of the town. The German infantry had a harder time advancing, being held up by a blockhouse for several hours, and reached open ground north of Sedan at seven p.m.[2]

The Germans hoped to keep secret as long as possible their massive thrust through the Ardennes. But hopes faded as thousands of vehicles bunched together along the narrow roads, and massive traffic jams developed. Yet no Allied bombs rained down on the stalled columns, and, though reconnaissance planes did fly over and take photographs, the French did not draw the proper conclusions.

The first day of the offensive, the Allies were totally fixed on northern Belgium and Holland. The penetration of Germans through the Ardennes was noted but raised no suspicions. On the night of May 10 and the morning of May 11, however, reconnaissance pilots observed numerous panzer and motorized columns in the Ardennes, but the chief of the French air forces in the northern zone, General François d'Astier de la Vigerie, suspected only a secondary German thrust toward the French border town of Givet. Still no suspicions were raised on the afternoon of May 11 when the French cavalry were exposed to such heavy panzer attacks that some withdrew in flight behind the Semois River.

French commanders discounted reconnaissance pilots who reported numerous miles-long convoys with their headlights blacked

The leading elements of the 1st Panzer Division as they move toward Sedan. German tanks generally advanced straight down the roads, ignoring enemy forces on either side. The effect was so shattering to the French that their defensive lines collapsed.

out on the night of May 11–12. They sent up another aircraft on the morning of May 12 to confirm the reports. The plane returned with its wings perforated and its fuel tank leaking. The pilot told of endless convoys and many panzers. The chief of intelligence of 9th Army refused to believe such an absurd message.

On May 12 reconnaissance pilots spotted columns carrying pontoons for building bridges, and reported that German formations reached the Meuse River in the afternoon. But again their reports were ignored.

Meanwhile Luftwaffe fighters pounced on every reconnaissance plane they saw, forcing the recce craft to fly mostly at night. These planes spotted columns of lights straight across the Ardennes. Roads were difficult and some vehicles needed lights to see the road. But the French command remained focused on northern Belgium and Holland.

The refusal of the French to see reality is quite baffling. The

A Panzer Mark III passes through a Belgian village.

first doubts should have arisen when no Luftwaffe bombers interfered with the Allied rush to the Dyle line. When a French officer wondered aloud why this was so, General Gamelin replied that the enemy planes were probably employed somewhere else! When it became impossible to deny that panzers were rushing through the Ardennes, commanders dismissed the evidence because it did not fit their preconceived ideas. When continued reports added up to certain knowledge, the French command decided the Germans would surely get bogged down along the Meuse.

If Gamelin had admitted his colossal error in time, it would still have been possible to withdraw the Allied armies threatened with encirclement behind the Somme. But he did not. The gullible commander walked willingly into the trap.[3]

The results of the first two days of the campaign were quite remarkable. The French and British had taken the bait of the noisy

German decoy attack into northern Belgium and Holland. They had rushed thirty of their most mobile divisions deep into Belgium, but—in the clash of armor in front of the Gembloux Gap—had used such poor tactics that they were now in full recoil westward to the line of the Schelde River. Meanwhile the bulk of the German panzers had penetrated the Ardennes and were threatening the main line of French resistance, the Meuse River.

Germans soldiers hurriedly board a rubber boat in preparation for a river crossing.

CHAPTER 4

CROSSING THE MEUSE AT SEDAN

The subordinate French commanders along the Meuse were no more ready to see what was happening than the supreme commander Gamelin. General Charles Huntziger, commander of 2nd Army defending Sedan and the region eastward to the Maginot Line, said on May 7: "I do not believe that the Germans will ever consider attacking in the region of Sedan." General Pierre-Paul-Charles Grandsard, commander of 10th Corps, the left wing of 2nd Army covering Sedan, noted that the terrain around the town rose south of the Meuse and favored defenders. He concluded that the Germans would make their main effort farther to the east. Accordingly, he stationed only the 55th Infantry Division under General Pierre Lafontaine at Sedan. This was a Category B outfit made up of older reservists. It had no tanks, and few antitank and antiaircraft guns.[1]

On May 12, with panzers driving into the northern parts of Sedan, General Guderian had to give final orders what to do next. He intended to strike across the Meuse the very next day, May 13.

This brought into play a decision that the group commander, General von Kleist, had made after a heated final planning session with Guderian on April 13. At this conference, Kleist insisted that the attack must be made 13 kilometers west of Sedan at the village of Flize. This would place the bridgehead over the Meuse beyond the north-flowing Bar River and the parallel Ardennes Canal that debouched into the Meuse seven kilometers west of Sedan.

If the assault was made at Flize, Kleist said, German troops would not be obliged to cross the canal and the Bar when they struck west. Guderian acknowledged this, but pointed out that the terrain north of Flize was wide open. German forces could not approach the river there under cover—which they could do at Sedan, since the town itself would mask their approach. Assaulting at Flize would also give French artillery at Charleville-Mézières, only seven kilometers northwest of Flize, superb targets of German tanks and vehicles approaching without cover. Finally, Guderian noted, the crossing at Sedan had been planned for months in map exercises, while a bombing assault there had long before been coordinated with the Luftwaffe. Air strikes were imperative, since the German heavy artillery was likely to be caught in traffic in the Ardennes. Shifting the attack to Flize would invalidate everything, Guderian insisted.[2]

After the conference Kleist dropped his requirement that the assault be made at Flize, but demanded that the attack still had to be made west of the Ardennes Canal and Bar River—thus not at Sedan.

But Guderian resolved privately that he was not going to follow Kleist's order, and he directed his corps to swing south out of the Ardennes and aim straight for Sedan. Thus, on May 12, Guderian presented Kleist with a fait accompli.

Meantime, Kleist made another decision to cast a monkey wrench into Guderian's plans. Kleist arranged with General Hugo Sperrle, commanding Luftflotte 3 (3rd Air Fleet), for a conventional bombing assault, a brief, concentrated mass bombing raid lasting twenty minutes, planned just prior to the scheduled crossing of the Meuse by infantry at four p.m. on May 13.

This was not at all what Guderian had worked out with the Luftwaffe staff before the campaign opened. Guderian planned to use bombers to take the place of heavy artillery. He developed the "rolling raid," in which Stukas would help his infantry get across the river in inflatable rubber boats. He wanted a few aircraft to remain over Sedan before and during the crossing to make both actual and fake bombing and strafing runs over the French positions. Guderian was less interested in destroying the enemy than in forcing defenders to keep their heads down so his infantry could rush across the stream and find lodgment on the far side. This is what he had worked out with the Luftwaffe staff.

A short raid, however intense, would end in a few minutes and would leave the infantry assaulting across the river unprotected. Guderian was livid when he heard of Kleist's decision, but there was nothing he could do.

The Luftwaffe bombing raid at Sedan on May 13 was the mightiest event of the campaign and one of the biggest tactical surprises of the war. It involved almost 1,500 aircraft—600 Heinkel 111, Dornier 17, and Junker 88 twin-engine bombers, 250 Stuka dive-bombers, 120 Messerschmitt 110 twin-engine destroyers, and 500 Messerschmitt 109 fighters. The shock effect was devastating.

Despite the agreement between Kleist and Sperrle, the aircraft did not make a single concerted assault and then depart. Instead, they performed precisely as Guderian had arranged with the air staff previously. Beginning at noon, Stukas began systematic attacks on specific targets. From three forty to four p.m. the Luftwaffe delivered a massive raid with the two-engine bombers against the sector around Gaulier just west of Sedan where Guderian planned to launch the main assault. From four to five thirty p.m., while the first infantry wave was crossing the Meuse, the Stukas both attacked and pretended to attack French gun positions, and infantry in trenches, pillboxes, and bunkers. The effect was to force gunners and infantry to seek cover and to stop firing while the infantry got across and seized a small bridgehead.

A lieutenant in the French 55th Infantry Division described

— BREAKTHROUGH AT SEDAN MAY 13, 1940 —

Monthermé
Semois R.

BELGIUM

Mouzaive

Meuse R.

Nouzonville

Bouillon

Semois R.

FRANCE

Charleville-Mézières

Vence R.

Bosseval

Fleigneux

Vrigne-aux-Bois
St. Menges
Illy
• La Chapelle

Vivier
St. Albert

Floing
• Givonne

1ST RIFLE REG., 1ST PANZER DIV.
Gaulier

Glaire
GROSSDEUTSCHLAND INF. REG.

Boulzicourt •
Flize •
Bellevue
Donchery
Sedan
86TH RIFLE REG., 10TH PANZER DIV.

Pont-a-Bar
Frénois
HILL 247
• Balan
Wadelincourt

Villers-sur-Bar •
HILL 301
La Boulette +
HILL 246 +
• Bazeilles

Hannogne •
Cheveuges •
Pont-Maugis

ARDENNES CANAL
Bar R.
Bois de la Marfée
• Noyers
Chiers R.

Sapogne •
St. Aignan
Remilly

• Singly
Omicourt •
Chéhéry •
Bulson Ridge

Connage •
Bulson •
+ HILL 322
• Haraucourt

Vendresse •
Malmy •
Chémery •
• Raucourt-et-Flaba

• Omont
Bar R.
Maisoncelle •

• Bouvellemont
Artaise-le-Vivier •
• Flaba

Bois de Mont-Dieu
La Besace •
• Yancq

Sauville •
• Stonne
Beaumont •

0 Miles   5
0 Kilometers 5
• Tannay
Bois de St. Pierremont

Le Chesne
• La Berlière

Jeffrey L. Ward

the attacks: "Explosions kept crashing all over the place. All you could feel was the nightmare noise of the bombs whose whistling became louder and louder the closer they got. You had the feeling that they were zeroed in precisely on you; you waited with tense muscles. The explosion came like relief. But then there was another one, then there were two more and ten more. The explosions blended in a ceaseless thunder. So here we were, motionless, silent, crouched, hunched over, mouths open so that our eardrums would not burst. The bunker trembled. Bombs of all caliber were being dropped. The noise from the sirens of the diving aircraft drilled into your ears and tore at your nerves. You wanted to scream and roar."[3]

When Guderian called Major General Bruno Loerzer, commanding the 2nd Fliegerkorps (2nd Air Corps) on the night of May 13 to thank him for following the previous plan, not Kleist's massive strike order, Loerzer replied slyly: "The order from Luftflotte 3, which turned everything upside down, came, well, let us say, too late. It would only have caused confusion among the air groups. That is why I didn't pass it on."[4]

Precisely at four p.m., infantry of the 1st Rifle Regiment, 1st Panzer Division, and of the attached Grossdeutschland Infantry Regiment started across the Meuse River, 70 meters wide, in rubber boats. They carried only their rifles, grenades, satchel explosives, and light machine guns. Everything heavy was left on the northern bank.

The 1st Rifle Regiment crossed at Gaulier, less than a kilometer west of Sedan. Soldiers rowed their boats over with no problems.

But nearby, just at the western edge of Sedan, the assault of the Grossdeutschland failed because none of the bunkers facing them on the south bank had been knocked out by the Luftwaffe. Fire from a reinforced concrete bunker on the southern shore defeated

German soldiers crossing the Meuse in their inflatable rubber boats. Note the smoke hanging in the background.

every attempt to launch the boats. The soldiers pulled up a short-barreled 75mm gun and fired at the bunker, but failed to silence it. Finally they pulled up an 88mm self-propelled gun. Its high-velocity shell penetrated the bunker at once. The Grossdeutschland soldiers once more launched their boats, but were stopped when three men were killed by a machine gun in a hidden bunker. After an intense search, the Germans located the bunker, and blasted it with the 88mm gun.

Now a company commanded by 1st Lieutenant Eberhard Wackernagel got across the river, stormed two strongpoints, and pushed along the western edge of the suburb of Torcy. They were aiming for Hill 247 (the number marked its height above sea level in meters), about 1,650 meters south of the river and just in front of the elevated height of the Bois de la Marfée. But they were stopped by fire from bunkers in front of the hill. Shortly afterward, a company under 1st Lieutenant René l'Homme de Courbière arrived, and the two lieutenants decided on a plan of attack. While Wackernagel placed heavy fire on the bunkers, Courbière mounted a surprise attack on them. There was a big pillbox 200 meters in front, and a smaller pillbox 250 meters on the right. Courbière's company launched a quick frontal assault on the closest bunker, but machine-gun fire forced the men to seek cover. Meantime a sergeant and two men swung around to the left, and, taking advantage of some bomb craters, rushed up on the bunker. The French were so surprised they at once surrendered. The three soldiers then stormed the other bunker and captured it as well.

Now a French antitank gun opened from the left flank, wounding several soldiers. At first Courbière could not locate the gun, but finally spotted it in another bunker concealed as an ordinary barn. The Germans rushed at this bunker and seized it quickly.

By now Wackernagel and a third company had come up, and the three companies charged at the field fortifications and bunkers guarding Hill 247, taking them by storm in hand-to-hand fighting at eight p.m. But the companies could not seize the Bois de la

Marfée directly ahead because there was too much open terrain in front of the wood, and the remainder of the regiment had been held up in house-to-house fighting in Torcy.

It had been a spectacular achievement, especially by Courbière's company. None of the infantry had any heavy weapons, but the men knew their mission was to capture Hill 247, and they used whatever means necessary to accomplish it.

The 1st Rifle Regiment had an easier time than the Grossdeutschland. There was no opposition, and many officers took the lead in the first boats. Guderian rode across in the first boat of the second wave. Waiting on the bank was Lieutenant Colonel Hermann Balck, commander of the regiment. As Guderian stepped ashore, Balck told his boss in mock-serious tones: "Joyriding in canoes on the Meuse River is forbidden." Earlier in the year some young, inexperienced officers had commented that they didn't think getting over a river was such a big deal. Guderian responded that crossing the Meuse under enemy fire could hardly be compared to a "canoe trip."

Once over the river the first infantry detachments pushed south 2,800 meters to a crossroads just south of Castle Bellevue. Here on September 2, 1870, the French emperor Napoleon III had capitulated to King Wilhelm of Prussia, sealing France's defeat in the Franco-Prussian War and guaranteeing Napoleon's removal from power.

This rapid advance stopped abruptly in front of an artillery casemate just southwest of the road junction that dominated all of the terrain in the sector. The casemate had already knocked out tanks of the 2nd Panzer Division on the opposite bank of the river. Just as the infantry were trying to figure what to do, an engineer demolition team commanded by 1st Lieutenant Günther Korthals arrived. The team specialized in attacking bunkers. Korthals used shaped charges that focus the power of a blast at a single point.[5] Engineers had employed the same method to seal off Fort Eben Emael.

Using smoke candles, Korthals blinded two bunkers along the

embankment of the Meuse that were firing on the 2nd Panzer's attempts to cross. The defenders were unable to see his team approach and fix shaped charges onto the bunkers. When the charges blew the bunkers apart, his team approached the artillery casemate. The occupants had seen what Korthals had done to the two bunkers. When his team threatened to circle around behind the casemate, the French immediately vacated it, as did the defenders of another nearby casemate.

Thus Korthals's team alone broke the line of bunkers and opened the way for 1st Rifle Regiment to penetrate deep into the French rear. It also eliminated the main barrier to 2nd Panzer Division. Though heavy French artillery fire from distant batteries continued to fall on this division and on 10th Panzer Division to the east of Sedan, both made lodgments on the farther shore before the end of the day.

Meanwhile, led by Korthals, whose team destroyed a number of fortifications along the way, elements of 1st Rifle Regiment advanced to Hill 301 (La Boulette) south of the village of Frénois. This was five kilometers south of the regiment's crossing point at Gaulier. The men were exhausted, but with Balck himself in the lead, they stormed Hill 301 shortly before midnight. As Balck told his men, "Something that is easy today can cost us rivers of blood tomorrow."

While fighting for Hill 301 was going on, recce units pushed on south and reached the northern edge of Chéhéry, four kilometers farther south. In eight hours 1st Rifle Regiment had punched nine kilometers through all the French lines of fortifications.

The 1st Rifle Regiment thus had achieved a total breakthrough of the French line. It had attained this feat entirely with handheld weapons and without vehicles of any sort. The tanks and the cannon of 1st Panzer were still waiting on the north side of the Meuse while engineers frantically were trying to complete a pontoon bridge at Gaulier.

*   *   *

Around six p.m., while Balck's infantry were advancing toward Hill 301 and Chéhéry, an astonishing development was taking place around Bulson, four kilometers southeast of Chéhéry. Here a captain, commanding two batteries of the French 169th Artillery Regiment, phoned the 10th Corps artillery commander that a violent fight was going on less than half a mile from his battle post. He said explosions had occurred, and he thought they might be hits of panzer shells. He added that he was about to be surrounded, and wondered whether he should withdraw. The corps artillery chief authorized the two batteries to pull back. The captain's fears were groundless, of course. There were no German tanks south of the Meuse and no German soldiers anywhere near Bulson. However, the captain's report spread like wildfire through the entire French defensive system. The explosions of panzer shells suddenly became muzzle flashes from panzer guns that were advancing directly on Bulson. Wild rumors of sightings of German tanks came from all over the place. Screams poured over the phones: "*Les Boches arrivent, on se replie, vite!* (The Boches [Germans] are coming, we are withdrawing, hurry up!)," and, "*Sauve qui peut!* (It's everybody for himself!)"

The commander of the corps artillery, urged on by panicked battalion commanders, gave the order for all of the artillery to withdraw at once. Entire battalions abandoned their guns and took to their heels. Within minutes the complete 55th Division and parts of the 71st Infantry Division on the east succumbed to mass hysteria and disintegrated. The road from Bulson to Maisoncelle, three kilometers south, was clogged with fleeing soldiers, horses, automobiles, and carts, but few weapons. The French soldiers had left their guns in place and were fleeing for their lives, though they were in no danger whatsoever. The entire defensive line along the Meuse at Sedan simply disappeared.

Around seven p.m. General Lafontaine, 55th Division commander, looked out of his command post bunker a couple kilometers south of Bulson and beheld the mass of stampeding soldiers, many of them shouting, "The panzers are in Bulson!" All of the men who could be grabbed and questioned asserted that they had seen panzers just ahead. Worst of all, officers of all ranks claimed they had received orders to withdraw, but they could not say from whom they had gotten those orders.

The panic infected the officers at the division command post. A rumor spread that the Germans were about to attack the command post. They directed signal men to smash the telephone exchange and burn the signal codes. In one act of lunacy, the division decapitated its command capability. The breakup of the division could not be stopped.[6]

Despite the collapse of the defensive line along the Meuse at Sedan, the French still could pinch off the bridgehead south of the river by a swift counterattack. The bridgehead was being held entirely by infantry with no heavy weapons whatsoever.

The success or failure of the entire campaign depended on the completion of the pontoon bridge at Gaulier. This bridge was the eye of the needle. Over it all of the tanks, artillery, heavy equipment, and supply trucks had to pass. The German engineers were fully aware that their work was imperative. But even working feverishly, it was not until ten minutes after midnight on May 14 that they finished the bridge. Very soon thereafter, Major General Rudolf Kirchner, commander of 1st Panzer, crossed the river in his armored command car, and headed straight for Hill 301. He was deeply worried about his exposed infantry there, and wanted to be on hand to do whatever necessary to save them.

Because of the chaos around the bridge, the first tanks did not cross until seven twenty a.m. But Guderian, anticipating that a counterattack could strike the exposed infantry at any time, gave absolute priority to tanks. The first on the south bank rushed at

A German crew mans a
20mm antiaircraft gun.

full speed to join the 1st Rifle Regiment nine kilometers south around Hill 301 and Chéhéry.

The Allies were as aware of the vital significance of the Gaulier bridge as the Germans. They mounted by far their most powerful aerial assault on May 14 to destroy this bridge. But the French air force was incredibly inefficient. Although it had 932 bombers in France and 242 ready at the front, it was able to employ only 43 bombers—mostly slow Amiot 143s and faster Potez 63-11s. The Royal Air Force did better. It gathered 73 single-engine Fairey Battles and 36 twin-engine Bristol Blenheims. To protect the bombers, the French and British sent out 250 fighter sorties. But the Luftwaffe flew 814 fighter sorties to intercept the Allied bombers en route to Sedan.

Despite the work of the Messerschmitt 109s, the main job of defending the bridge fell to the antiaircraft (AA or flak) battalions of the three panzer divisions firing 20mm AA guns, and an attached flak regiment (the 102nd) firing high-velocity 88mm AA guns. Guderian mounted 303 AA guns. They put up such a heavy curtain of fire that few Allied aircraft got through, and none hit the bridge.

The Allied air strikes commenced at five thirty a.m. on May 14 and were repeated throughout the day until midnight. But the Allies sent in 27 separate raids, mostly a few aircraft at a time. This permitted the flak batteries to concentrate on individual aircraft. The only massive strike was delivered by the RAF between four and five p.m. But this ended in disaster. Of 71 Fairey Battles and Bristol Blenheims, 40 were shot down. This was the highest loss ratio ever suffered by the RAF.

The culminating moment occurred when a bomber, already hit and burning, dived down at the bridge and unleashed its bombs. The bombs missed and so did the aircraft, which hit the ground and exploded. The pilot parachuted out at the last moment, and he floated down five meters above the bridge just as a tank was driv-

Crossing a pontoon bridge, this German follow-up artillery battery advances with the help of horses.

ing across. The pilot plunged into the Meuse and was never seen again.

Altogether the British lost 47 of their 109 bombers, and the French lost 5 of their 43 bombers. The French lost 30 fighters and the British 20 fighters. An additional 65 aircraft were heavily damaged.[7]

Guderian was extremely anxious about the bridge, and drove to it over and over. To make a statement to his soldiers about how vital it was, he positioned himself directly on the bridge. This was the single most dangerous place in all of western Europe at the moment, and when General von Rundstedt appeared around noon, Guderian made his report precisely in the middle of the bridge. Just at that moment, an aircraft attacked, so both generals had to duck for cover. "Is it always like this here?" Rundstedt asked. Guderian answered honestly that it was.[8]

Passage of tanks and vehicles continued unabated throughout the day, even during the height of the air raids. On May 14, Guderian got the main body of his corps, 60,000 men and 22,000 vehicles, including 850 tanks, across the Meuse. This meant that he now had a fully operational combat force south of the river.

A German soldier covers an
advance with a Karbiner-98 rifle.

CHAPTER 5

THE FRENCH TRY TO DESTROY THE BRIDGEHEAD

The French command had indeed set in motion a counteroffensive to snuff out the bridgehead across the river at Sedan. The 10th Corps commander, General Grandsard, had placed two infantry regiments and two tank battalions in reserve to make a counterattack if it became necessary. The 213th Regiment was at Artaisele-Vivier, 11 kilometers due south of Sedan; the 205th Regiment at La Besace, 14 kilometers south-southeast of Sedan; the 7th Tank Battalion near Le Chesne, 26 kilometers south-southwest of Sedan, and the 4th Tank Battalion at Beaumont, 20 kilometers southeast of Sedan.

The moment that Grandsard learned the Germans had crossed the river at Gaulier at four p.m. on May 13, he issued orders for the two infantry regiments and the two tank battalions to advance to their prearranged starting position at Bulson, eight kilometers south of Sedan. From Bulson, the counterattack was to drive all the way to the banks of the Meuse and destroy all German forces south of the river.

After Grandsard gave his command from his headquarters at La Berlière, twenty kilometers south of Sedan, an astonishing series of delays and failures engulfed the French forces. It took a motorcycle courier until five thirty p.m. to deliver the order to the 213th Regiment. That is, an hour and a half to go seven kilometers

(4.2 miles) to the regiment's command post (CP). It took the regimental commander, Lieutenant Colonel Pierre Labarthe, an hour to issue movement orders, and he designated eight p.m. as the departure time—or four hours after the Germans had crossed the river! The order to the 7th Tank Battalion arrived only at six p.m. and the commander, fearing a Luftwaffe attack, decided to wait until darkness at nine thirty p.m. to move out. Delivery of orders to the other regiment and tank battalion also took an inordinate amount of time.

Meantime the collapse of the 55th Division occurred, and the panic threatened to spread to the 213th Regiment. Labarthe delayed its departure. When the regiment finally advanced, it met a wave of fleeing soldiers, creating chaos. Likewise the 7th Tank Battalion met hordes of fleeing soldiers on its approach march, and moved forward only at a snail's pace. The 205th Regiment and the 4th Tank Battalion to the east were even slower, and got nowhere during the night of May 13–14.

At eight p.m. General Grandsard reached Lafontaine by phone and ordered him to take command of the counterattack. Lafontaine had abandoned his CP and the telephone exchange his officers had destroyed near Bulson, and had withdrawn to Chémery, four kilometers southwest of Bulson. There he had phone connections to the corps network. But Lafontaine made no effort to reach the outfits designated to carry out the attack, and learned only at ten p.m. from corps headquarters that Labarthe—because of the fleeing 55th Division soldiers—had decided to stop the 213th Regiment halfway to Bulson and go into a defensive position. Lafontaine did nothing to countermand the amazing dereliction of duty by Lieutenant Colonel Labarthe. Lafontaine himself waited until one a.m. on May 14 to make any effort to get the counterattack under way. But instead of going up to Bulson to determine whether any of the other units had arrived, he went in precisely the opposite direction to corps headquarters at La Berlière, a senseless move, since he had phone connections with 10th Corps and the time for mounting the counteroffensive was running out.

The reason for Lafontaine's bizarre action was that French procedures called for a written order to make attacks, and he didn't have one. But he couldn't get the order at La Berlière because the chief of staff had driven off to Chémery to deliver it to him, and they had missed each other.

Lafontaine arrived back at Chémery at four a.m., having wasted three hours on a wild-goose chase. Several officers were waiting impatiently for precise instructions, but Lafontaine—despite the fact that he knew exactly what was required—hesitated to give them because the chief of staff had still not arrived with written orders. The officer finally came in at four forty-five a.m. and at last delivered the coveted piece of paper.

At five a.m. on May 14, Lafontaine issued the attack order. During the night when France's fate was being decided, he had waited nine hours and had achieved nothing.

Lafontaine directed the counterattack to jump off at seven thirty a.m. Only the western group, the 213th Regiment and the 7th Tank Battalion, with forty FCM tanks armed with a 37mm gun and with 40mm of armor, was immediately available, because the 205th Regiment and 4th Tank Battalion had not come up on the east.

The three battalions of the 213th were to advance northward side by side, with one company of tanks to support each battalion. The left-hand battalion on the west was to move up along the Bar River valley, while the other two battalions on the east were to aim for Bulson. One battalion of artillery, twelve pieces, from the 8th Artillery Regiment was available to support the advance. Lieutenant Colonel Labarthe, the officer who had been so slow off the mark, said as he left the division CP: "This is a suicide mission for my regiment."

The French counterattack was little and it was late, but the 1st

Rifle Regiment of 1st Panzer was nevertheless in grave danger. It was deep into the French zone and it had only rifles, machine guns, and a few other handheld weapons to hold off enemy tanks and artillery. Indeed, the German soldiers were totally exhausted from the previous day's exertions, and, after finally seizing Hill 301, they had fallen into a leaden sleep. Reconnaissance patrols pushed forward only at dawn.

The French tanks moved up in step with the advancing infantry. They made no effort, as was the practice of Guderian's panzers, to advance in a probing attack ahead of the infantry to occupy the key elevation of Bulson Ridge (Hill 322) before the Germans could get there. Around eight fifteen a.m. the left and middle columns ran into German recce units and drove them back. But the advance continued at a walking pace, and it took until eight forty-five a.m. to go two kilometers.

General Kirchner was on top of Hill 301 in his command vehicle with excellent radios. The elevation gave him superb views over the whole terrain. This was the very hill where Helmuth von Moltke, the Prussian chief of staff, had directed the German armies against the French emperor at Sedan in 1870.

Aerial reconnaissance reported at seven a.m. that French tanks were advancing northward along the Bar River valley toward Chéhéry. Kirchner at once sent out two antitank platoons of the Grossdeutschland Regiment with two armored cars. At nine a.m. the left-hand French column ran into Grossdeutschland's antitank barrier a couple kilometers south of Chéhéry.

At seven fifty a.m. a Henschel reconnaissance aircraft radioed that French tanks and infantry were moving both along the Bar valley and toward Bulson Ridge south of the village of Bulson. At the moment only a single company of panzers had reached La Boulette pass next to Hill 301. Kirchner ordered the company to proceed immediately to Bulson and to tie down the enemy as far south as possible. The company moved off at eight a.m. While it had taken Grandsard and Lafontaine fifteen and a half hours to get the French counterattack started, it had taken Kirchner just ten minutes to launch a counteraction.

The panzer company had to go nine kilometers to reach Bulson Ridge (Hill 322). The French had just three kilometers to go. The Germans got there first. The tank company drove through Bulson and in single file approached Hill 322 southwest of town. The moment the panzers got on the hill, heavy fire erupted and the two lead panzers took several antitank gun hits and burned. The commander was able to get off only a radio message to Kirchner before his tank was also hit and he had to bail out. French antitank guns and artillery pieces firing point-blank over open sights overwhelmed the panzer company. Only one tank was left, but it moved back and forth on the ridge simulating a larger force and held the position until a second panzer company arrived thirty minutes later and stopped the French attack. When a third panzer company arrived, the Germans went on the offensive, aided by advance units of Grossdeutschland Regiment, which overpowered the line of French antitank guns.[1]

Meanwhile, four kilometers to the west, Grossdeutschland Regiment's antitank platoons with six 37mm AT guns had challenged thirteen French tanks advancing north down the Bar valley. But the AT gunners were dismayed to find that their rounds could not penetrate the 40mm armor of the French FCM tanks. It took numerous hits before a vulnerable spot could be found. Nevertheless the AT guns stopped the French tanks long enough for a fourth panzer company to arrive at nine forty-five a.m. and it beat back the French tanks. Meanwhile an engineer outfit took on the French infantry and drove them back.

Although only four companies of German panzers had come up, Lafontaine decided to order retreat at ten forty-five a.m. About this time other German units arrived, including some heavy artillery and an 88mm antiaircraft gun, whose high-velocity shells

Heinz Guderian gives orders to a German soldier.

were proving to be the best tank-killer in the German arsenal. By afternoon the 7th Tank Battalion's forty tanks had been almost wiped out. The 213th Regiment also had suffered heavy losses.

At the same time the 205th Infantry Regiment and the 4th Tank Battalion to the east had performed abysmally. They had advanced only a single kilometer northward by seven fifteen a.m. on May 14. Ordered by Lafontaine to attack, the units got into a firefight with a scattered French unit that they mistook for German paratroops. As a result of this fiasco, the two units had moved only a short distance north by the time Lafontaine ordered a general retreat.

At noon General Kirchner called a commanders' conference at the square in front of the church at Chémery, five kilometers south of Chéhéry. Just as the officers assembled, Stukas attacked the village and hit the vehicles parked in the square. The strike killed four officers and wounded a number of other officers and men. Guderian had been trying since ten a.m. to get the Stuka mission scrubbed, but the tanks had advanced too fast for the Luftwaffe.[2]

At twelve thirty p.m. Guderian received a message that a unit of 1st Panzer had seized undamaged the bridge over the Ardennes Canal and the parallel Bar River at Malmy, a kilometer west of Chémery, and was continuing to push on west. The unexpectedly easy crossing of this barrier led Guderian to immediate action. He hurried to the 1st Panzer CP at Chémery to make a decision upon which the entire fate of the campaign in the West in 1940 would hinge. Meeting with the division commander, General Kirchner, and other officers, Guderian posed a fundamental question: Should he secure the still-unstable bridgehead against another anticipated French counterattack, or should he exploit the enemy's confusion and the opportunity of an easy passage over the canal and strike west at once?

Orthodox doctrine on this point was clear. Securing a bridgehead took precedence over any offensive action. Besides, the matter had already been decided by the high command before the campaign had opened. The panzers were to be held back until infantry divisions could come forward and secure the bridgehead. Only then, so Chief of Staff Franz Halder had ordained, could a plan for the panzers to strike for the English Channel be considered.

But this was entirely at odds with Guderian's thinking. He believed in uninterrupted attack. He believed the panzers should push immediately deep into enemy territory before the French could organize a defense.

However, Guderian could not ignore the possibility of a renewed French counterattack, and, with the infantry divisions still far behind, only his panzer corps was available to stop one if it came.

As the German officers were discussing what should be done, Major Walther Wenck, 1st Panzer's operations officer, reminded Guderian of his favorite saying: *Klotzen nicht kleckern!* Hit with the fist, don't feel with the fingers—or in military terms, strike concentrated, not dispersed.

"That really answered my question," Guderian wrote.[3]

At two p.m. on May 14 he ordered 1st and 2nd Panzer (commander Rudolf Veiel) to wheel immediately southwestward "toward Rethel," 50 kilometers (30 miles) away on the Aisne River. The strike for the English Channel had begun.

Before hurrying after the panzers, Guderian held a conference with General Gustav von Wietersheim. Guderian left the 10th Panzer Division (commander Ferdinand Schaal) and the Grossdeutschland Infantry Regiment with him to seize the elevated heights of Stonne as an anchor to the south, and to secure the bridgehead until Wietersheim's 14th Motorized Corps of two divisions could come up.

Guderian figured that the bridgehead would be safe, despite being so weakly defended. The French command system was so methodical and slow, he believed, that any strike could be contained until more German forces could arrive.[4]

While Guderian's corps was making spectacular advances at Sedan, Hans Reinhardt's 41st Panzer Corps was running into one difficulty after another in trying to seize Monthermé, fifteen miles northwest.

The corps was made up of the 6th and 8th Panzer Divisions and the 2nd Motorized Division. But in the tremendous traffic jam in the Ardennes, only a part of the 6th Panzer had reached the Meuse on May 13, when the corps was supposed to cross the river at the same moment that Guderian was crossing at Sedan.

But Reinhardt had just one infantry battalion, one panzer battalion, and one artillery battalion in place opposite Monthermé, located in a precipitous, canyonlike gorge through which the Meuse meanders. Even so, this small force was able to cross the Meuse, take the town, and form a bridgehead by the evening of May 13.

Nothing had been decided, however. Monthermé lies at the northern end of a steep and narrow spit or peninsula nearly

Guderian stands on the side of the road, waving to panzer forces as they advance through France.

surrounded by the river. Although the Germans seized the lowest, northernmost part of the town, the defending French force, a battalion of the 42nd Colonial Infantry Regiment, fought tenaciously and well, in contrast to the 55th Division at Sedan. The French pulled back to a previously prepared line of concrete pillboxes and armored bunkers down the peninsula and held on grimly.

The next day the Germans still were unable to break through. This brought on a command crisis in Army Group A. General von Kleist had demanded and gotten operational independence for his panzer group, but the commanders of the field armies in the Army Group were extremely unhappy, and had complained to General von Rundstedt.

He had agreed to a disastrous compromise. If the panzer group managed to cross the Meuse on the first attempt, then Kleist's group would retain its independence. But otherwise, it would be placed under one of the field armies, taken from the fighting line, and moved back into operational reserve, leaving to the infantry divisions the main effort of building bridgeheads and then breaking out of them. This decision was based on the conservative, orthodox thinking of the senior German generals, who thought—much like their French and British counterparts—that tanks should be used to support infantry, and who never had been convinced that the panzers could operate alone.

Therefore, despite the fact that Guderian had achieved brilliant success at Sedan, the field army commanders used the failure of Reinhardt to break through at Monthermé as reason to dissolve Panzer Group Kleist and throw its elements into reserve.

Accordingly Army Group A issued an order on May 14 that, effective at noon on May 15, the panzer group was to be placed under command of 12th Army. The panzer group war diary on May 14 stated the problem succinctly: "Everything depends on whether we are now able to get across the Meuse where we are temporarily stopped [at Monthermé], on our own strength so that we may thus retain operational freedom of action. Otherwise there is reason to fear that the fast-moving formations will be employed to stick closely to the infantry corps with a correspondingly shorter-range objective. That would practically signify the end of the von Kleist Group as an independent operational formation."

The very first orders from 12th Army confirmed the panzer group's worst dread. At four a.m. on May 15 the army ruled that Reinhardt's corps was to be taken out of the front line and placed in the reserve. Only 6th Panzer was to be left in the front, but was to be placed under 3rd Corps, and this infantry organization was to seize the bridgehead at Monthermé.

The order incensed Kleist. He decided to ignore it, and sent directives to all of his corps to continue the attack. Reinhardt urged 6th Panzer to achieve a breakthrough at all costs. The division needed no motivation. When the troops learned that an ordinary infantry division was to replace them, they returned to the attack with a will. A pontoon bridge the division had been able to build

across the river at night had helped to bring forward more powerful weapons. The French were holding a wooded sector with many
rock outcrops that restricted tanks. The job thus was left to the
infantry and combat engineers, who attacked at five a.m. on May
15, assaulting pillboxes with flamethrowers and explosives. This
violent onslaught succeeded, and the Germans got through the
French position by nine thirty a.m., allowing 6th Panzer tanks to
cross the river and move on.

But 3rd Corps, though impressed with the victory, ordered
Reinhardt to pivot 6th Panzer south to come up behind French
defenders who had been keeping the 3rd Infantry Division from
getting across the Meuse at Nouzonville, a few kilometers up-
stream, a process that would have tied the panzers to the pedes-
trian pace of the infantry, and a fate that the *Schnell Truppen,* or
fast troops, of the German army wished to avoid at all costs.

Reinhardt rose in rebellion. This was not the proper role of the
panzer division. Its job was to thrust as deep as possible into enemy
positions, not help an infantry division to cross a river. Reinhardt
and Brigadier General Werner Kempf, commander of 6th Panzer,
came up with a radical solution that threw the doctrine of military
subordination and obeying orders to the winds. They devised a
totally unauthorized way to get out of the military straitjacket that
Army Group A and the field armies were trying to place on the
panzers: *Die Flucht nach vorn,* or escape to the front.

Reinhardt and Kempf, in short, decided to confront their superiors with an accomplishment that they could not ignore. Kempf
found Colonel Hans-Karl Freiherr von Esebeck, and told him to
assemble an ad hoc *Kampfgruppe,* or battle group, with whatever
forces were immediately available for a very special mission. Esebeck
located a panzer battalion, a motorcycle rifle battalion, a company
of engineers, two batteries of light artillery, an antitank battalion, a
recce detachment, and one antiaircraft or flak battery. It was only a
small part of 6th Panzer, but it was on hand, and at three p.m. on
May 15 Kempf told Esebeck to go for broke—to turn his back on

the Meuse River and push as fast as he could possibly push and get as far west as he could possibly get.

The so-called Pursuit Detachment von Esebeck launched itself west at lightning speed. The Germans simply rolled over the retreating French columns they encountered on the road. There was no organized resistance. The French did not expect any enemy formations that far in the rear, and were stunned when they appeared. They thought on many occasions that the dust-covered Germans were British columns and greeted them with friendly waves before they realized their mistake.

The detachment stopped for nothing, yet still collected (though they left in place) 2,000 French prisoners of war.

At eight p.m. on May 15 the detachment rolled into the undefended town of Montcornet, 55 kilometers (33 miles) southwest of Monthermé and the Meuse River.

Esebeck's advance was a stunning surprise to the French command. It had concentrated its attention on Guderian's breakthrough at Sedan, and had virtually ignored Reinhardt's attack at Monthermé. The result was that Esebeck broke entirely through the French front, and his tanks and vehicles were able to push into a total power vacuum.

The French front and all of the command's planning collapsed within hours after Esebeck reached Montcornet. It was now useless for the newly created 6th Army to form a defense line west of the Bar River and the Ardennes Canal to block Guderian, since 6th Panzer was already far to the rear of that line. With no anchors on which to hook a new defense line, the entire French defense in the central sector of the Meuse evaporated.[5]

This is precisely what Guderian and the other panzer leaders had expected to happen. The revolution that they were bringing about signified a radical shift away from the linear or static form of warfare with a continuous front or main line of resistance that the French and the British were still trying to conduct. In its place the panzer commanders had created a nonlinear form of combat that used tanks to strike deep into enemy territory like the thrusts of rapiers, and that did not bother with defense of flanks, since the panzer movements were so fast and so shattering that the enemy did not have time to make any strike behind the points of the rapiers before they had moved entirely out of range.

But most of the German general officers were as much traditionalists as their counterparts in the French and British armies, and they were still trapped in linear thinking. As Colonel Karl-Heinz Frieser writes in the official German army history of the 1940 campaign, "Their instinctive fear of gaps and exposed flanks came from a time when there were as yet no panzers. The advance of the completely isolated panzer divisions through the enemy's rear areas was a dizzying proposition to them. On top of that came the breathtaking tempo of that attack. This is why they repeatedly demanded the slowing of the advance of the panzers so that the infantry divisions assigned to provide flank protection could close up."[6]

Guderian had spent the years before the war instilling his diametrically opposite doctrine in panzer commanders. He believed that confusing the enemy was the best flank protection. "So long as you yourself stay in motion, so long will you also keep the enemy in motion and prevent him from getting a strong foothold," he wrote.

Colonel von Esebeck's spectacular strike into the depths of the French rear did not transform the thinking of the senior German generals, but it did have the immediate effect that Generals Reinhardt and Kempf were seeking. Army Group A returned Panzer Corps Reinhardt to the command of Panzer Group Kleist, and gave Kleist permission, once again, to attack far ahead of 12th Army's infantry divisions.

A German crew fires a 100mm flat-trajectory gun in France.

CHAPTER 6

THE INCREDIBLE FIGHT FOR THE STONNE HEIGHTS

When Guderian turned over to General Gustav von Wietersheim on May 14 the task of holding the Stonne heights 17 kilometers (10 miles) south of the Meuse, he figured the job would be relatively easy. The 1st Panzer Division had just turned back the inadequate and tardy counterattack by General Lafontaine, and Guderian assumed that the French wouldn't try another strike anytime soon. Consequently Guderian left Wietersheim only the 10th Panzer Division and the Grossdeutschland Infantry Regiment until Wietersheim's own 14th Motorized Corps could come up and take over the defense of the bridgehead. Guderian then switched west with his 1st and 2nd Panzer Divisions with the English Channel as his goal.

But this in fact was not the situation on the Stonne heights. The French 2nd Army commander, General Charles Huntziger, was preparing an immense counteroffensive to deprive the Germans of Stonne and drive them back across the Meuse. If Guderian had guessed such an attack was in the works, he would never have broken out of the bridgehead and left only one panzer division and one infantry regiment behind.

Stonne was a formidable massif that towered over the landscape and offered both the best shield to the Germans to protect the bridgehead and the best jump-off point for the French to attack the Germans. Its dominating terrain had been exploited by the Romans.

The Germans had marched on Stonne only because Guderian insisted. General von Kleist thought a bridgehead six to eight kilometers deep was big enough, and denied Guderian's plan to seize it. Guderian simply disobeyed orders and sent his forces to it anyway. Guderian subscribed to the doctrine of Erich von Manstein that the bridgehead had to be secured by an "offensive defense," that is, by a protective zone deep enough that a solid base could be set up to break up any counteroffensive by the French, and also to strike out to the south if necessary.

General Huntziger had not been discouraged by Lafontaine's failed counterattack, and was concentrating a mighty force to overwhelm the Sedan bridgehead. He assembled a complete armored division (the 3rd), four infantry divisions, a cavalry brigade, two tank battalions, and various other outfits under General Jean-Adolphe-Louis-Robert Flavigny. Altogether Flavigny had 300 tanks, and numerous armored reconnaissance vehicles in the cavalry units.

The 3rd Armored Division alone was far superior to the 10th Panzer Division. It had 138 battle tanks, half of them Hotchkiss 39s, with 45mm of armor and 37mm guns, and half Char Bs, with 60mm of armor and both 47mm and 75mm guns. In comparison, 10th Panzer had only 30 Panzer IIIs with 37mm guns and 30 Panzer IVs with short-barreled 75mm guns. Two-thirds of the division's armor were Panzer Is and IIs, far too thin-skinned and poorly armed to challenge French tanks.

Moreover, there was not the slightest chance that the Germans could have stopped the French tanks on May 14. Much of the 10th Panzer Division and the Grossdeutschland Regiment were still north of the Meuse, and neither was in a position to seize Stonne that day.

Huntziger had demanded an immediate attack by Flavigny. But the unbelievably long time that the French needed to move their forces worked once more in the Germans' favor. The 3rd Armored Division was near Reims when Guderian's forces reached Sedan on May 12. At four p.m. that day, the division was ordered to move to a standby position at Le Chesne, 60 kilometers (37 miles) north. At Le Chesne the division would be 23 kilometers (14 miles) southwest of Sedan and 13 kilometers (8 miles) southwest of Stonne.

But the fuel tanks on all French tanks were tiny, since armor's mission under French doctrine was to work with the infantry. So the distances that infantry could walk in World War I governed the size of French fuel tanks in 1940. The 32-ton Char B, for example, could move only about as fast as a rifleman could walk, and it could operate for only two hours before it had to be refueled. And since the French had an inconceivably inefficient system of refueling, by which tanker trucks had to replenish one vehicle at a time, like a one-pump ambulatory filling station, it took inordinately long to refuel the division, during which time it sat immobile and useless.

Accordingly, the 3rd Armored required until six a.m. on May 14 to travel the 37 miles to Le Chesne. This, of course, was the very moment that General Lafontaine's counterattack was under way against 1st Panzer Division. General Huntziger was well aware of this and had ordered the 3rd Armored, commanded by General Antoine Brocard, to attack the same morning. Brocard replied that he couldn't obey, because it would take five to six hours to refuel, and another two to three hours to move to the assigned starting position for the attack, the northern edge of the Bois du Mont-Dieu, 14 kilometers (8.5 miles) northeast and directly north of the Stonne heights.

General Flavigny thought Brocard's time demands were excessive, but, being lenient, he set the jump-off from the Bois du Mont-Dieu at two p.m. However, it took motorcycle couriers until nine a.m. to carry the written order to General Brocard, and it took Brocard until eleven to complete orders for the units, and until one p.m. to get these orders to the units. Brocard was finally in position at the Bois du Mont-Dieu and ready to launch his attack at five thirty p.m. Meantime, large elements of the supporting infantry had moved into position east of Stonne.

But now the French forces waited. They got no order to commence the offensive. The reason was that General Flavigny, on the way to the front, kept running into frightened soldiers who told him disaster stories. Some officers of the 213th Infantry Regiment gave emotional accounts of how their units had been smashed by the 1st Panzer earlier in the day. Flavigny also was shaken by the enormous delays of Brocard's division in getting to the start line.

With a huge force poised to strike for the Meuse River against what amounted to no opposition, General Flavigny now made an unbelievably wrong decision: He called off the attack and went over to the defense! Not only that, Flavigny ordered 3rd Armored Division and the two tank battalions to dissolve and to disperse over an 18-kilometer front from Omont, west of the Bar River and Ardennes Canal, to La Besace, a few kilometers northeast of Stonne.

He directed that, on all roads and passes across this span, one heavy and two light tanks were to be posted as *bouchons,* or corks, that theoretically would keep German panzers from breaking out. He had totally missed the fact that—as had been proved in numerous places in the campaign already—German tanks attacked in masses, not in penny packets. Three tanks would have no chance of stopping a panzer assault down any road the Germans selected. This was refusal to look at the facts carried to a ridiculous level.

General Flavigny in one overwhelming act of stupidity had eliminated the only French force, 3rd Armored, that was capable of carrying out an offensive against the Germans.

There was a bizarre logic to Flavigny's action, however. The French had become so obsessed with sealing off (*colmater*) penetrations during World War I that defense was far more important to them than offense. For the French, defending meant spreading out their units in a linear fashion along a front line. Such a decision was wholly inappropriate for the situation Flavigny faced on May 14, but for a man such as Flavigny, with no imagination whatsoever, it was a reasonable decision.

Thus on this day of absolute failure by the French, 10th Panzer and Grossdeutschland Regiment moved up to seize the heights of Stonne. This little village of a dozen farmsteads was on the northeastern edge of the heavily wooded Mont-Dieu (God's Mountain), which rises steep and isolated above the surrounding countryside. The Bois du Mont-Dieu forest spread out north and northeast of Stonne, and the Bois de St. Pierremont forest extended for several kilometers southeast of Stonne. The massif of Stonne blocked access from the south like a natural fortress. Just on the eastern edge of the village a conical mountain, Pain de Sucre (*Zuckerhut* in German, Sugarloaf in English), offered the best observation post over many miles of terrain in all directions.

The battle for Stonne commenced at dawn on May 15, when elements of Grossdeutschland Regiment, supported by a battalion of 10th Panzer's tanks, moved cautiously up the steep hairpin turns of the mountain road leading to the village. The French were defending Stonne with Char B tanks from the 49th Tank Battalion, with FCM tanks from the 4th Tank Battalion, and with a reinforced battalion of the 67th Infantry Regiment. Here, at least, Flavigny's *bouchons* order to disperse the armor had not been obeyed.

The panzers were sitting ducks for the French tanks. They knocked out seven panzers before the remainder, along with Grossdeutschland, pushed into the village, and by eight a.m. drove the French down the only road leading from Stonne to the south. The French regrouped almost at once and counterattacked, driving the Germans out of the village. The Germans now struck back. Stonne had changed hands four times by ten forty-five a.m.

Each time French tanks penetrated into the village and forced the Germans to retreat. German shells bounced off the thick hides of the Char Bs, while their 47mm and 75mm guns did great execution to any Germans that appeared. However, the French tanks did not coordinate their advances with the French infantry, and, when they arrived in the village with no infantry to support them, they withdrew. Because of this unbelievably flawed tactical practice, the Germans were able to reoccupy the village as soon as the tanks departed.

The critical action took place at eleven a.m. The French were preparing for a new attack. They concentrated a company of Char Bs, a company of FCMs, and the 67th Infantry Regiment. Once again, the infantry were slow in getting ready, and the Char Bs mounted a probing attack all on their own. At the moment Stonne was being held by a battalion of Grossdeutschland, plus nine of the regiment's 12 AT guns. There was a sudden cry of "panzer" as the French heavies appeared. On his own volition, Sergeant Hans Hindelang rode into the village with the three AT guns being held in reserve. He was barely able to get into position when the Char Bs came at him. Every round of the 37mm guns bounced off the tanks. The Char Bs crunched through orchards coming at the guns. One tank knocked out the right-hand AT gun at a range of 100 meters. The wounded gun commander dragged his also-wounded gunner behind a house.

Panic began to grip the German soldiers. They felt powerless against the enormous tanks, and were terrified of being crushed under their tracks. Some soldiers bolted, but the AT crews held their position and kept on firing. Hindelang had only two guns, but he saw that one of the Char Bs had turned sideways. A gun commander spotted a small ribbed surface on the tank's right side. It might be a radiator. He aimed right at it. A jet of flames shot out. With a shout of joy, the Germans realized the Char Bs were not totally invulnerable, and they directed their shots at these little squares that they saw were on both sides of the tank. Hindelang lost his second AT gun shortly afterward, but his guns knocked out three Char Bs.

At that moment everything turned around. Up to this point the Char B tankers had felt safe, but now they saw three Char Bs burning. Suddenly the crews of the other tanks panicked and drove away south off the mountain.

Around noon the French infantry managed to take the village in a massive assault without the help of tanks. But Hindelang's success had ended the myth of invincibility that the Char B was beginning to enjoy. Although the Germans had been pushed out of the village, they prepared for a counterattack. The task was made easier for them in the afternoon, because the French tanks withdrew after General Flavigny, in the face of intense pressure from northeast front commander Alphonse-Joseph Georges, and the 2nd Army commander, General Huntziger, ordered a major counteroffensive.

The Germans exploited the advantage. The 10th Panzer sent in a battalion of its own infantry to support Grossdeutschland. Together, they were able to take the village around five thirty p.m.

The withdrawal of the French tanks from Stonne was the consequence of a peremptory command by General Georges. He was furious with General Huntziger for failing to launch a counterstrike. He pointed out to Huntziger that he had been given the 3rd Armored Division just for that purpose, but he had done nothing. Huntziger had an excuse of sorts. He had spent the night of May 14–15 moving his 2nd Army headquarters 50 kilometers south from Senuc to Verdun, and was mostly out of touch with what was happening.

Georges got Huntziger on the phone at seven fifteen a.m. on May 15 and told him to make haste. This at last got Huntziger in motion. He phoned Flavigny at eight a.m. and gave him an express command to counterattack with tanks, using the 3rd Armored, the independent tank battalions, and the 3rd Motorized Division. But once again the French comedy of delays began to play out. The official directive to Flavigny took a half hour to reach him. He didn't bring together the commanders of the 3rd Armored and the 3rd Motorized until ten a.m. He set the deadline for attack at two p.m. But because Flavigny had ordered the tanks to disperse, some of the commanders didn't know where their armored vehicles were. The tanks also had to be refueled. Most of the radios weren't working because there had been no time to recharge the batteries.

Once more Flavigny postponed the attack, this time to four p.m. Then he postponed it again to six thirty p.m. But now Flavigny belatedly realized that Germans were about to storm Stonne again with every chance of success. Holding Stonne, they would be in the rear of the French attack and could sever the supply line. On the other hand, the Germans could also be attacked from the north and the south at Stonne, pushed into a pocket, and forced to surrender. But this possibility didn't occur to Flavigny, and— seeing only what the Germans might do to him, not what he could do to the isolated Germans—he canceled the attack order.

Two companies of the 49th Tank Battalion had not been informed. They attacked all alone with their Char B tanks from the northern edge of the Bois du Mont-Dieu toward Chémery, six kilometers northwest, without infantry or artillery support. After two kilometers they ran into German AT guns in blocking positions. But the 37mm projectiles mostly bounced off the French behemoths. The Germans were able to put only two Char Bs out of action. When the French commanders realized they were all alone, however, they retreated. This separate thrust shows what might have happened if the French had mounted a true counteroffensive. But thanks to incredibly poor French leadership and to their hopelessly slow response, it did not happen.

The French high command had been baffled by the German strike at Sedan, and this confusion affected their response. From this town the Germans could push southwest toward Paris, southeast into the rear of the Maginot Line, or west toward the English Channel. It was characteristic of the traditional thinking of the top French leadership that their first suspicion was that the Germans were aiming straight at Paris.

A German crew fires a 37mm antitank gun.

General Huntziger and some of his senior generals thought the Germans might instead be trying to get behind the Maginot Line. The aggressive manner in which they seized Stonne played directly into this fear. This may have been a factor in Flavigny's abrupt turn from the offensive to the defensive on May 14.

The move to the south bore Manstein's signature. From the beginning he had called for a thrust south at the same time as the thrust west, a proposal ignored by the German high command. But Guderian followed Manstein's concept. Though he did not have the forces to make a strong move south, he bluffed by making the strike at Stonne. The French were taken in by the bluff. As Colonel Karl-Heinz Frieser, the official German historian of the 1940 campaign, writes, "it must be kept in mind here that the German generals also did not know what to do with the brilliant chess move that Manstein had suggested. It was solely due to Guderian's disobedience [to Kleist] that the chess move was successfully made."[1]

It did not occur to any of the French leaders that the Germans in fact would strike straight west for the English Channel. This was so bold an idea that, when it did happen, the French were unprepared to challenge it. Even after it commenced, the supreme commander, General Maurice Gamelin, was slow to realize that it was the main thrust and that the armies in Belgium were in grave peril. This is shown by the fact that the government leaders, Gamelin included, seemed relieved when they learned that the Germans were heading west, and that their target was not Paris, as they had first thought.

After Flavigny canceled the last counterattack on May 15, the French continued to try to capture and hold Stonne. Early on May 16, after a heavy artillery barrage, two French tank battalions and an infantry battalion attacked Stonne. But a single Char B took the village all by itself. Captain Pierre-Gaston Billotte pushed into Stonne. A German panzer company of 13 tanks on both sides of the village's single street opened fire. But the Char B drove right through the column, destroying or disabling all of the panzers and also wiping out two antitank guns. The Char B received 140 hits, but not a single one penetrated its armor. The next afternoon another Char B driven by a lieutenant attacked toward Stonne. About 800 meters northwest of the village he ran into a column of German infantry seeking cover in a ditch. When the infantry opened fire with their small arms, the Char B simply rolled over the entire column. The tank pushed on into Stonne. The men of the 64th Rifle Regiment panicked when they saw the still-bloody tracks of the monster, and fled from the village.

These episodes illustrate both the power of the Char B tank and the inadequacy of French armored tactics. The basic problem was that, unlike the case with the Germans, few French tanks had radios, and the few radios they did have frequently failed. French commanders were thus unable to concentrate tanks and supervise massed attacks, and, being unable to communicate with the infantry, could not coordinate joint assaults. When communications failed, French doctrine did not call for commanders to take charge and carry out a mission on their own. This was in direct contrast to the German doctrine of *Auftragstaktik*, by which commanders of even the smallest units were given a mission to perform, and they had the authority to carry it out in their own way, even if they had to improvise or do something unorthodox.

On the night of May 16–17, the German 6th Corps, an infantry outfit, replaced 10th Panzer and Grossdeutschland at Stonne, and also released Wietersheim's 14th Motorized Corps to press on after the panzers rolling westward. Grossdeutschland had suffered 570 casualties, and received a short break. It took the 6th Corps until May 25 before they seized the plateau of Stonne for keeps. But it was an anticlimax. The real war had moved far to the west.[2]

Hitler meets with Rommel in the field, May 1940.

CHAPTER 7

ROMMEL OPENS THE FLOODGATES

Erwin Rommel had been a famous *Stosstrupp*, or storm troop, commander in World War I. He acted intuitively, and exploited every opportunity quickly and resolutely. As a young first lieutenant in October 1917 he captured 1,400 Italians, seized 81 cannon, and stormed the summit of Mount Matajur in the Italian Alps. He was promoted to captain and decorated with the coveted Pour le Mérite for this exploit.

Unlike Manstein, Rommel was not part of the Junker aristocracy that dominated the Prussian army and the German army after unification in 1871. The son of a rural schoolmaster who lived near Ulm in southwest Germany, he joined the local 124th Württemberg Infantry Regiment in 1912, at the age of 19. Between the wars he was an infantry unit commander and instructor. He gained new renown in 1937 when he published *Infantry Attacks*, a highly successful account of his combat actions in the First World War. The book led Hitler to place him in charge of his personal guard in the Polish campaign. At Rommel's request, Hitler gave him command of the new 7th Panzer Division in February 1940.

Rommel still continued to act as if he were leading a small *Stosstrupp* in person, however.

As part of Hermann Hoth's 15th Panzer Corps, Rommel's

division pushed through the Ardennes parallel to but 35 kilometers north of Panzer Group Kleist on May 10. Meanwhile, the French 9th Army wheeled northward to occupy positions along the Meuse River directly in front of Hoth's corps.

Advance elements of Rommel's division and a detachment of 5th Panzer Division under Colonel Hermann Werner came up on the Meuse at Dinant, Belgium, on the afternoon of May 12. Rommel intended to rush a crossing if possible on the heels of the retreating French 1st and 4th Light Cavalry Divisions and gain a bridgehead on the west bank. But the bridges at Dinant and nearby Houx were blown up by the French, and Rommel was compelled to mount a river crossing early on May 13 with rubber boats.

During the afternoon of May 12, however, a reconnaissance aircraft reported to Colonel Werner that the bridge at Yvoir, seven kilometers north of Dinant, was still intact. The Belgians were waiting for the last French cavalry, who had just finished crossing, before blowing this final span. Werner ordered 2nd Lieutenant Heinz Zobel's armored assault team to race for the bridge and get over it before the Belgians could blow it.

The Belgian engineers were in no hurry because they thought the Germans were still far away. Then a sudden cry went up: *"Ils sont là!* (They are here!)"* Two of Zobel's armored scout cars were charging along a road next to the east bank of the river. They opened fire on the Belgians guarding the bridge. The Belgian engineer pushed the electrical ignition, but there was no explosion.

Meantime the first scout car drove onto the bridge, but stopped when it was hit by an antitank gun. A soldier jumped out with wire cutters to sever the ignition wire he had spotted. He was laid low by machine-gun fire. But other Germans were approaching under the covering fire of Zobel's three panzers. The Belgian engineer left his shelter and pushed the manual ignition device. As he was trying to get back to his bunker, he was mortally wounded by a machine gun. At the same moment the explosives went off. When the gigantic smoke cloud cleared, only remnants of the bridge pillars could be seen. Bridge and car had sunk into the water.

Some of Werner's men had better luck three kilometers south of the broken bridge. A weir and a lock connected an island at the village of Houx to both banks. The weir was a low dam that raised the level of the river water. The lock allowed boats to move between the two water levels. To avoid lowering the water level of the river, the Belgians had kept the weir and lock intact. German volunteers waited until dark to tiptoe over the slippery weir to the island and to reach the other bank by a catwalk on the lock. By eleven p.m. May 12, they had secured a lodgment on the west bank. A battalion of the French 39th Infantry Regiment guarding this section remained on the rocky bluffs behind the river, instead of moving directly to the riverbank as ordered. When they spotted the German soldiers, they fired at them, but made no attempt to oust them.

This failure to engage the Germans was fatal to holding their position. Early on the morning of May 13 under the shield of fog, three infantry battalions of the 5th Panzer crossed single file over weir and lock and joined the men on the other side. Although French artillery caused a number of casualties, the infantry knocked the French battalion aside, and pushed four kilometers west to the village of Haut-le-Wastia on high ground.

Meanwhile Rommel designated two sites for his infantry to cross the 120-yard-wide river on May 13. The first one was immediately south of the island at Houx by the 6th Rifle Regiment, and the second 2,500 meters farther south at Leffe, on the northern edge of Dinant, by the 7th Rifle Regiment.

When Rommel arrived at the 6th Rifle Regiment crossing site, he discovered that French shells were dropping all around, and there were a number of knocked-out tanks in the streets. The infantry were about to cross in rubber boats, but were being held up by artillery fire and by small-arms fire of French troops of the 18th Infantry Division installed among the rocks on the west bank.

Rommel passes in his staff car in the advance through Belgium.

"The situation when I arrived was none too pleasant," Rommel wrote. "Our boats were being destroyed one after the other by the French flanking fire, and the crossing eventually came to a standstill. The enemy infantry were so well concealed that they were impossible to locate even after a long search through glasses."[1]

Rommel rode down to the 7th Regiment at Leffe. He found that a company had gotten across under the cover of morning fog, but when the fog lifted enemy fire became so heavy that the crossing had to be halted. Rommel realized there was no hope of gaining a bridgehead until the French fire was silenced. He called up several tanks and a battery of artillery and brought under fire all places likely to hold enemy soldiers.

Under protection of this fire, the crossings got under way again. The men set up a cable ferry using several large pontoons to speed the process.

When Rommel arrived back at the 6th Regiment's site, the

crossings had resumed, primarily because the antitank battalion commander had posted twenty 37mm AT guns, and they were firing at anything that looked suspicious on the western bank. Rommel ordered the engineers to build 16-ton pontoons, so tanks could be ferried across the river one at a time. Rommel rode across on the first trip of the cable ferry in his eight-wheeled signals vehicle. Leaving the vehicle on the west bank, Rommel rode back on the ferry. At Leffe, he ordered the engineers to build a pontoon bridge as soon as possible to serve as the main supply line for the panzer corps. Meanwhile, every tank possible was to be ferried over during the night. By the morning of May 14 thirty panzers had been pulled across.

The French response to the German attacks was astonishing. The two 7th Panzer bridgeheads around Dinant were weak because Rommel was able to ferry over only a few panzers on the afternoon of May 13. The 5th Panzer bridgehead across from Houx was even weaker. There were no panzers or heavy weapons there. The French, on the other hand, had ample mobile forces in two light cavalry divisions, the 18th Infantry Division around Dinant, and the 5th Motorized Infantry Division around Houx, plus the 6th Tank Battalion. They could have mounted a powerful counterattack.

But the French were so lackadaisical and slow to move that they seemed to be indifferent. Though infantry of 5th Panzer got across at Houx before midnight on May 12, it was five a.m. on May 13 before the French 11th Corps commander, General Julien-François-René Martin, received the news, and it was noon before he informed the 9th Army commander, General André-Georg Corap. None of this impressed the French high command. General Alphonse-Joseph Georges, commander of the northeastern front, merely reported that "a battalion has gotten into trouble" at Houx.

On the critical day of May 13, the 18th Division made no serious attempt to drive the Germans back. Division headquarters did not even inform General Martin, the corps commander, that the Germans had been attacking across the river since four thirty a.m. and had formed two bridgeheads. Martin learned of this only when he visited the division CP at noon.

Martin now ordered the 39th Infantry Regiment, 6th Tank Battalion, and some cavalry armored cars to attack the northerly 6th Rifle Regiment bridgehead. He made no effort to strike the 7th Rifle Regiment bridgehead. He set the jump-off time at an extraordinarily distant eight p.m., found that even this could not be met, and postponed it to nine p.m. on May 13. Just before H-hour the colonel in command phoned and said the infantry was still not ready. So Martin ordered the thirty-five Renault R35 tanks of the Tank Battalion and the armored cars to attack alone. They advanced almost to the Meuse, but encountered no Germans. As darkness fell and the infantry still had not arrived, they withdrew, having accomplished nothing.

The efforts of 2nd Corps were not any better. The corps' 5th Motorized Division was holding the Meuse from Houx northward. The commander, General G. F. Boucher, had known since two a.m. on May 13 that German infantry had crossed at the Houx weir and lock, but he did not react until seven thirty a.m. At that time he sent elements of his reconnaissance battalion to restore contact with 18th Division. Only then did he learn that the Germans had expanded their bridgehead into his sector. He ordered a battalion of the 129th Infantry Regiment to counterattack, but he postponed the start time to three p.m. During the approach, the battalion was caught in a Stuka attack, and it retreated in haste.

Boucher's planning and the unit's performance were so comically inadequate that his superiors rained down scorn. Boucher now decided to launch a massive counterattack. For the assault he designated the same 129th Regiment battalion, his reconnaissance battalion, a squadron of infantry from the 4th Light Cavalry Division, and a company of Hotchkiss 39 tanks. The attack was to be made from several directions on the 5th Panzer spear point at Haut-le-Wastia. At first the attack was to start at eight fifteen p.m. But the infantry were slow in approaching. So Boucher postponed the attack to nine p.m., then to ten p.m. But now the commanders of the artillery supporting the attack objected because it was dark. So Boucher called off the attack until the next morning, May 14.

That was all that two French corps did on the crucial day of May 13.

In complete contrast to the French, Rommel did not wait until he got enough men and matériel across the Meuse on the night of May 13–14. He ordered the 7th Rifle Regiment commander Colonel Georg von Bismarck to take what troops he had and mount a probing attack against Onhaye, three miles west of Dinant, during the early morning hours of May 14. At daybreak Rommel heard from Bismarck that he was closing in on the village, and was engaged with a powerful force of the 1st Light Cavalry Division.

Then at eight a.m. Rommel received an alarming message. It read: "*Bismarck bei Onhaye eingeschlossen* (Bismarck encircled at Onhaye)." Radio contact was lost immediately thereafter. All attempts to reach Bismarck were in vain. Rommel ordered the panzers already across the river to push immediately for Onhaye to rescue the trapped infantry. All at once the situation returned to normal. Radio contact was reestablished. The message was in error. The actual text was, "*Bismarck bei Onhaye eingetroffen* (Bismarck arrived in Onhaye)." But someone misheard *eingetroffen*, or arrived, as *eingeschlossen*, or encircled.

Meanwhile Rommel was on the way to Onhaye. He was in a Panzer III right behind the spearhead of the column. At the edge of a wood near the village, several French AT guns opened fire, along with two 75mm artillery batteries. Rommel's tank took two

A German crew prepares a 20mm antiaircraft gun, mounted on a half-track carrier, for action.

quick hits. The driver throttled straight for the nearest bushes, but they concealed a steep slope. The tank slid down it and stopped, canted over on its side. Enemy guns 500 meters away had a perfect shot. Rommel and the crew bailed out, but the French didn't fire at the stalled tank.

The rest of the German tanks advanced on Onhaye, shielded from the heavy French fire by a screen from smoke candles on the tank of Colonel Karl Rothenburg, commander of 25th Panzer Regiment of Rommel's division. They had been set alight by an enemy shell. The tanks, contrary to a rule that Rommel had set in place, did not spray with machine-gun and cannon fire the wood where the enemy was located.

"Experience in this early fighting showed that in tank attacks especially," Rommel wrote, "the action of opening fire immediately into the area which the enemy is believed to be holding, instead of waiting until several of one's own tanks have been hit, usually decides the issue. Even indiscriminate machine-gun fire and

20mm antiaircraft fire into a wood in which enemy antitank guns have installed themselves is so effective that in most cases the enemy is completely unable to get into action or else gives up his position."[2]

The Germans seized Onhaye after a stiff fight. Afterward, 7th Panzer pushed all the way to Morville, 14 kilometers west of the Meuse. This pierced the second and last French line of resistance.

Meanwhile Boucher's 5th Motorized Division finally launched its counterattack against the 5th Panzer bridgehead at Haut-le-Wastia. The French soldiers made a courageous effort, but it was too late. The Germans had ferried enough panzers across during the night to stop the attack, and even to drive on south for 6,000 meters to capture Sommières. Thus, the two panzer divisions had blown a hole eight kilometers wide at Dinant, and Rommel at Morville was already deep into the French rear.

At eight p.m. on May 14 engineers completed the military bridge at Dinant so vehicles could exploit the breakthrough. Construction of this pontoon bridge had spawned a huge feud between Rommel and Brigadier General Max von Hartlieb Walsporn, commander of 5th Panzer. Bridge-building materials sufficed for only a single bridge, and Rommel, in tough bargaining with corps commander Hoth, got all of it. Hartlieb now had to ask permission to route his panzers across Rommel's bridge. Rommel was not impressed with Hartlieb's protests, and complained rather about the alleged passive attitude of 5th Panzer, which was always caught somewhere back. The 7th Panzer, he told Hoth, "could not be expected to fight the war all by itself."

Hoth could not argue with Rommel's success. He had crossed the Meuse faster at Dinant than Guderian at Sedan, although he had no support from the Luftwaffe. Besides, he faced more difficult terrain, since rocks rose like a wall on the west bank of the river, making the French defense easier. There was also the irony that panzer expert Guderian waited until the military bridge had been built before he sent the first tanks across. But Rommel put

A Panzer Mark IV leads a German column in Belgium.

some panzers over by ferries at the first possible moment. There-fore, he broke out from the bridgehead even before the bridge was finished.[3]

The total failure of 11th and 5th Corps to stop or even slow the advance of Panzer Corps Hoth forced the French supreme com-mand to call on the 1st Armored Division to restore the situation along the Meuse. This powerful force had moved to Charleroi im-mediately after the German offensive opened on May 10, but it remained there, only 40 kilometers (24 miles) away from the river, all day on May 13. The French command still believed the main German effort was coming in northern Belgium, and still thought the attacks at Dinant and at Sedan were only diversions.

But shortly before midnight on May 13, the supreme com-mand released the division to General Corap's 9th Army, and he alerted it to be prepared to mount a counterattack toward Dinant. But in typical French fashion, Corap did not commit the division in a timely manner, and it spent the entire morning of May 14 on standby, doing nothing. During this time Rommel's 7th Panzer was overwhelming French resistance at Onhaye and was moving on to Morville, and 5th Panzer was shattering the 5th Motorized Division's counterattack at Haut-le-Wastia.

The 1st Armored Division got an execution order only at two p.m., and its first elements did not start moving until four p.m. It took the division five hours to cover 35 kilometers (21 miles) to the area north of Flavion, where it stopped for the night—only four kilometers northwest of Morville, which Rommel had already reached, and where his division had gone into a bivouac for the night. Neither knew of the presence of the other.

The extreme slowness of approach of 1st Armored was due to the fact that the roads were jammed with fleeing soldiers and civilians, and to the slow speed of French tanks. But the reason the division commander, General Marie-Germain-Christian Bruneau, called a halt north of Flavion was because his heavy Char B tanks had run out of gas. Once again, short cruise ranges would pose a crippling limitation on tanks obliged to make long approach marches to engage enemy armor—much less fight protracted battles with enemy tanks.

Bruneau had made a colossal error in planning his movement from Charleroi. He had placed his fuel vehicles near the end of the convoy, and now no one knew where they were. The division had to move into a standby area to wait for the fuel trucks to be found and then to come forward.

The Germans solved the problem of refueling vehicles on the run by requiring all drivers to load full 20-liter "jerrycans" of fuel in any empty spot they could find on their trucks, and to dump the cans at designated stations along the route of advance. Crews of panzers and other vehicles filled their tanks at these stations, left the empty cans on the ground, and moved on. Any truck heading back was obligated to pick up the empties and return them to tank stations in the rear. There they were refilled and picked up by the next trucks heading to the front.

The French method of refueling vehicles, on the other hand, was so manifestly inefficient that it almost defies belief. All refueling was done by special fuel trucks, whose cross-country capability was very restricted, thus causing many problems of access to armor off the roads. These trucks had to refuel each tank in succession. It took a very long time. And while the tanks were immobile, they were extremely vulnerable to attack.

On the morning of May 15, Rommel pushed into the French standby area, catching the 28th Tank Battalion with Char B tanks and the 25th Tank Battalion with Hotchkiss 39 tanks in the act of refueling. There was a short collision, but Rommel intended to move west far and fast. When he learned that the 31st Panzer Regiment of 5th Panzer under Colonel Hermann Werner was coming up on the north of Flavion, Rommel left disposition of the French tanks to him. He circled around to the south of the French

1st Armored, and pushed on toward Philippeville, 13 kilometers southwest of Flavion.

Werner's panzer regiment was quite inferior to the 1st Armored Division. He had two tank battalions; Bruneau had four. Werner had only 30 Panzer IIIs and 30 Panzer IVs. With 30mm of armor and 37mm and 75mm guns respectively, they were capable of challenging French battle tanks. His remaining 90 tanks were all lightweight Panzer Is and IIs, incapable of standing up to any French battle tank. Bruneau, on the other hand, had 170 battle tanks: 90 Hotchkiss 39s and 15 Renault R35s, both with 37mm guns and 45mm of armor, and 65 Char Bs with 60mm of armor and both 75mm and 47mm guns.

Werner had three great advantages, however. Many if not most of the French tanks were out of fuel, Werner used his artillery while Bruneau fought only with his tanks, and the Germans had excellent radios, whereas few French tanks had radios and most of these had broken down because of weak batteries.

Werner could coordinate the actions of his units by radio. Again and again, the panzers formed "wolf packs" that surrounded small groups of often-immobile French tanks and fired at them from all sides. Whenever they encountered a moving Char B, whose armor none of the German tanks could penetrate, the German gunners concentrated on smashing the tracks, to immobilize it. Werner held back at a respectful distance his vulnerable Panzer Is and IIs, but he used them to make fake attacks on the flanks of the French, to hold them in place so his battle tanks could tackle them.

To trap the French tanks that could move, Werner sometimes had his tanks withdraw to coax the French to chase after them in a "cavalry charge." The retreating panzers drew the French tanks in front of artillery and flak pieces that Werner had pulled up to point-blank range. Some of the artillery projectiles, and especially the shells from the high-velocity 88mm antiaircraft guns, could pierce the Char B.

German soldiers on a motorcycle advance through a burned-out French town.

Finally Stuka dive-bombers went into action, pounced on tanks, and hit several of them.

A number of the Char B tanks were destroyed, but others never got refueled and stood immobile on the battlefield, while some ran out of fuel after being engaged for a couple hours. The crews of the stalled monsters set them on fire and abandoned them.

Bruneau finally gave the order to retreat. By the evening, out of 170 battle tanks, he had only 36 left. They disengaged toward the French border. Next morning their number had dwindled to 16, mostly because they ran out of fuel.

Totally inadequate French response had allowed Panzer Corps Hoth to open an enormous hole at Dinant. By the end of the day on May 15 Rommel's 7th Panzer Division was beyond Philippeville at Cerfontaine, 36 kilometers (22 miles) west of Dinant, and was poised to keep going against no organized French opposition.

German panzers roll through France.

CHAPTER 8

THE STRIKE FOR THE
ENGLISH CHANNEL

The spectacular events in northern Belgium and Holland had absorbed the attention of the government in Paris during the first days of the invasion. Although French prime minister Paul Reynaud was uneasy about events in general, and spoke of his disquiet to Minister of Defense Édouard Daladier, it was midday on May 14 before he received notice of the German attack at Sedan, and he got no details. At that moment, Allied bombers were trying in vain to destroy the pontoon bridge over the Meuse at Sedan, while Guderian's panzers were crossing the bridge even as bombs were raining down.

It was not until early on May 15 that Reynaud got confirmation of German passage of the Meuse there, and perceived the danger. At seven thirty a.m. Reynaud phoned Winston Churchill in London. He was obviously under stress and spoke in English. He blurted out that the French had been defeated. Churchill thought the alarm was exaggerated, but said he'd come to Paris the next day to talk things over.

Reynaud sent a message to Daladier asking what reaction the supreme commander, General Maurice Gamelin, had to the news about Sedan. Daladier replied: "General Gamelin has no reaction." Reynaud was furious, and decided that he should be minister of defense. That evening he sent a messenger to Madrid to fetch

French minister of defense
Édouard Daladier.

Marshal Henri-Philippe Pétain, the war hero and French ambassador to Spain.

That same evening of May 15, William Bullitt, the United States ambassador to France, was talking with Daladier in his quarters on the rue St. Dominique when the phone rang. General Gamelin was on the line. Bullitt heard one end of the conversation. Daladier was stupefied, and said to Gamelin: "But that means the destruction of our army." Gamelin hung up and told Bullitt that Gamelin had said German tanks were at Laon, 75 miles northeast of Paris, and there was nothing to stop them from striking straight for the capital. "Between Laon and Paris not a single body of troops can be concentrated," Daladier said. "Then the French army is doomed?" Bullitt asked. "Yes," he answered.

Later that night Roger Langeron, *préfet* of police, called the minister of interior, Henri Roy, who summoned Reynaud and all the defense ministers to his ministry at Place Beauvau. A discussion went on for most of the night. General Pierre Héring, military governor of Paris, advised the ministries to quit the capital at once. A call at three a.m. on May 16 from General Alphonse-Joseph Georges's northeastern front headquarters at La Ferté that things were not so bad brought a bit of calm. Reynaud decided to keep the capital in Paris for the time being.

Even so panic swept the city. On the Quai d'Orsay, Foreign Minister Alexis Léger ordered immediate destruction of the most secret files and documents. Pyres rose on the lawn next to the Foreign Ministry building. Clerks staggered down with arms full of papers, and threw them onto the bonfires.[1]

It was this scene that struck Churchill when he reached Paris in the middle of the afternoon on May 16, accompanied by General John Greer Dill, assistant chief of the Imperial General Staff, and a few other military advisers. They stood in one of the gorgeous salons of the Foreign Ministry. In front of General Gamelin on a student's easel was a map, about two yards square, with a black ink line purporting to show the Allied front. In this line there was drawn a small but sinister bulge at Sedan.

Churchill described the events: "The Commander in Chief briefly explained what had happened. North and south of Sedan, on a front of fifty or sixty miles, the Germans had broken through. The French army in front of them was destroyed or scattered. A heavy onrush of armored vehicles was advancing with unheard-of speed toward Amiens and Arras, with the intention, apparently, of reaching the coast at Abbeville or thereabouts. Alternatively they might make for Paris. Behind the armor, he said, eight or ten German divisions, all motorized, were driving onwards, making flanks for themselves as they advanced against the two disconnected French armies on either side.

"The general talked perhaps five minutes without anyone saying a word. When he stopped there was a considerable silence. Then I asked, 'Where is the strategic reserve?' and breaking into French which I used indifferently (in every sense), '*Où est la masse de manoeuvre?'* General Gamelin turned to me and with a shake of the head and a shrug said: *'Aucune'* [none]. I was dumbfounded. Presently I asked where he proposed to attack the flanks of the [German] bulge. His reply: 'Inferiority of numbers, inferiority of equipment, inferiority of method'—and then a hopeless shrug of the shoulders. There was no argument; there was no need of argument. This was the last I saw of General Gamelin."[2]

After the war, Churchill wrote that "by the 14th [of May] at the latest the French high command should have given imperative orders to these armies [in Belgium] to make a general retreat at full speed, accepting not only the risks but heavy losses of material."[3] This, of course, was true. And a wise general would have seen this and acted. But it was not perceived by the Allied military and political leaders at the time. Indeed, Churchill and his cabinet pushed Lord Gort to send the BEF in an attack southward as late as May 20.

There was little that the British could do to help at the moment. But General Gamelin had told Churchill that he needed more fighter aircraft to cleanse the skies (*nettoyer le ciel*) over the battlefields. He did not mention the damning fact that the French could not do this themselves, because they had kept most of their airpower far from the front. Churchill, trying to boost French resolve in any way he could, decided to send ten fighter squadrons (about 160 Hurricane fighters) to France, leaving only 25 squadrons to defend English skies. This, he told his cabinet by phone, would permit "French and British aviation to dominate the air above the bulge [at Sedan] for the next two or three days to give the last chance to the French army to rally its bravery and strength."[4]

It was well-meant, but all that fighters could possibly do would be to challenge German Messerschmitts. Even if French bombers might have gained clear skies to fly, they could only bomb areas, not strike at individual tanks, as the Stuka dive-bombers could do. Stopping Guderian and company would require French artillery and tanks. And there were few enough of these in front of the advancing panzers.

The next day, May 17, it became clear that the German tanks were not descending on Paris. The advance was directed at the English Channel. Gamelin and the other senior commanders were relieved. They had thought the Germans would aim right at the capital. But they realized belatedly that they had no forces between the Germans and the channel. There was nothing to stop the *boches*.

After General Guderian told 1st and 2nd Panzer Divisions to strike westward on the afternoon of May 14, the two outfits rushed forward with a will. Elements of 1st Panzer had already crossed the Ardennes Canal and Bar River at Malmy just west of Chémery, and by the end of the day reached Vendresse, another four kilometers on. Other elements of 1st Panzer crossed the canal and river a couple kilometers north at Omicourt, and reached Singly, nine kilometers west. Meanwhile, 2nd Panzer breached the barrier at Pont-à-Bar where the canal and Bar entered the Meuse seven kilometers west of Sedan, and got both to Flize, four kilometers downstream, and to Sepogne, five kilometers southwest. At all three places the bridges were intact.

Only isolated detachments of French forces opposed the advances, mainly fragments of infantry divisions and elements of the French cavalry divisions that had gone into the Ardennes on May 10. All were now in a state of imminent dissolution.

The resulting chaos sent the French command in search of a scapegoat. General Gaston Billotte, commander of the 1st Army Group, wrote northeastern front commander Georges on the night of May 14 that General André-Georg Corap, commander of 9th Army, should be the sacrificial victim. This army was covering the Meuse from just west of Sedan to a point below Namur in Belgium, and its line had been blown apart in three places, Dinant, Monthermé, and Sedan.

Billotte wrote: "The 9th Army is in a critical state; its whole front is giving way. It is absolutely necessary to put some spirit back into this dissolving army. General [Henri] Giraud, whose energy we all recognize, seems to me just the man to take up this heavy task and administer the indispensable psychological shock."[5]

General Georges told General Gamelin that he agreed with Billotte. Corap was an easy choice. Not only had he failed demonstrably in command, but he came from a poor family, had been a scholarship student at Saint-Cyr military academy, and was not part of the social elite that made up most of the French command. He also was a protégé of General Maxime Weygand, who was the principal rival of General Gamelin.[6] Gamelin therefore agreed, and command was handed over to General Giraud, whose 7th Army had rushed to Breda. By the time Giraud arrived on the scene, 9th Army had been thoroughly broken up by the Germans. In the chaos that followed, Giraud told his staff to fend for themselves. He was wandering alone in the countryside near Le Catelet, between Cambrai and St. Quentin, when he was captured by a patrol of three German tanks on May 18.[7]

Georges told Gamelin that he thought 2nd Army commander Huntziger also should be removed. Huntziger, he said, had shown neither energy nor capacity and had failed to use the 3rd Armored Division to counterattack. But Huntziger, small, trim, precise, and self-controlled, was part of the inner circle of French military leadership, and, despite his poor performance, Gamelin refused to relieve him.

Guderian's decision to strike for the English Channel without delay was his alone. Manstein and Guderian had assumed that, once the panzers got across the Meuse at Sedan, they would push at once for the channel. Otherwise, they feared the Germans would lose the race against the Allies. But this was not the view of the German high command. In orthodox fashion, they intended to hold the panzers back until infantry divisions had secured the bridgehead. Hitler was afraid of the threat of exposed flanks, and placed his own reservation on any further measures after forcing the Meuse.[8]

In the euphoria after the successful creation of a bridgehead, however, Guderian's boss, General von Kleist, mellowed and approved Guderian's order to strike for Rethel on the Aisne River 50 kilometers (30 miles) away. But on the night of May 15 Kleist began to worry about his left or southern flank, and canceled the advance. This aroused the ire of Guderian, who called Kleist to get the orders reversed.

"I neither would nor could agree to these orders, which involved the sacrifice of the element of surprise we had gained and of the whole initial success that we had achieved," Guderian wrote.

The discussion with Kleist got very heated, during which Guderian implied that Kleist's stop order compared to one of the most disastrous command decisions in German history. It had occurred on September 9, 1914, in the early days of World War I. A gap had opened between the German 1st Army and the adjacent 2nd Army along the Marne River near Paris. Fearing that the British Expeditionary Force would move into this gap, Lieutenant Colonel Richard Hentsch, sent by the German chief of staff, Helmuth von Moltke the Younger, ordered a German retreat. This withdrawal was not necessary and it created the "miracle of the Marne" for the Allies, ending any chance for a German victory.

"That was no doubt not very well received by the Panzer Group," Guderian wrote.[9]

Kleist finally gave in and authorized the advance to continue to Rethel.

Guderian, delighted, drove early on May 16 to the 1st Panzer CP at Omont, four kilometers west of Vendresse. All anybody knew was that there had been heavy fighting in the neighborhood of Bouvellemont, another six kilometers on. Guderian drove into

German infantry crouch in a defensive holding position.

the main street of this village, which was still in flames. He found Lieutenant Colonel Hermann Balck, commander of the 1st Rifle Regiment.[10]

Balck described what had happened. The men were totally exhausted, having had no real sleep since May 9. Ammunition was running low. Rations had run out. There was nothing to drink. It was very hot. The men were falling asleep in their slit trenches. Balck called the officers together, and said the village had to be captured. "We cannot go on," the officers complained. "We need one night's sleep. Tomorrow we can go on." Balck cut them short. "Gentlemen," he said, "we are attacking or we are simply giving victory away." "The men will not follow you," the officers responded. "If you do not want to go on, I will take the village myself," Balck said. With that he marched off toward the village across an open field. He went for 50 meters and there was no response. At 100 meters, the officers and the men got up and followed Balck. A few seconds earlier they had been at the end of their tether. Now they passed Balck by. No one thought of taking cover. With wild cheering, the exhausted riflemen pushed into the village. The French, a group of cavalry Spahis and a battalion of the 152nd Infantry Regiment from Normandy, withdrew in haste. Bouvellemont was in German hands.[11] For this feat Balck received the Knight's Cross.

Bouvellemont was the last point of organized French resistance. The path to the channel lay open.

Guderian had captured a French order from General Gamelin that contained this admonition: "The torrent of German tanks must finally be stopped!" Guderian, delighted, read the French order to the German troops by companies. "I thanked them for their achievements to date, and told them that they must now strike with all their power to complete our victory," Guderian wrote.[12]

Panzer Corps Guderian was in the open, and both 1st and 2nd Panzer struck out at full speed on roads leading west. There was virtually no opposition. Although the target had been Rethel, both divisions turned away to the northwest and both reached Montcornet, 50 kilometers (30 miles) from Bouvellemont, on the evening of May 16, and kept on going. Montcornet was the same place that Colonel von Esebeck's pursuit detachment from 6th Panzer had reached from Monthermé the evening before. In the marketplace, Guderian found General Kempf, commander of 6th Panzer, and they congratulated each other on their success. Then they set about disentangling their commands—which were pouring through the town—allotting specific roads to specific outfits.

"We ordered the advance to go on until the last drop of petrol was used up," Guderian wrote. "My foremost units reached Marle and Dercy, 64 kilometers [40 miles] from that morning's starting point, and 88 kilometers [55 miles] from Sedan."[13] That same evening, recce units of 1st Panzer and 6th Panzer got all the way to the south-flowing Oise River, nearly 50 kilometers (30 miles) west of Montcornet.

While most of the forces had moved on, Guderian told his small security force to go through the houses on the marketplace at Montcornet. Within a few minutes they had collected several hundred prisoners from various units. Guderian set up his headquarters in the village of Soize, just east of Montcornet. He informed Panzer Group Kleist by wireless of the day's events, and he announced his intention of continuing the pursuit the next day, May 17.

"After our splendid success on the 16th of May and the simultaneous victory won by 41st Corps [General Reinhardt], it did not occur to me that my superiors could possibly still hold the same views as before, nor that they would now be satisfied with simply holding the bridgehead we had established across the Meuse," Guderian wrote.

Guderian was astonished to get a message from Panzer Group Kleist early on May 17. Guderian tells the story: "The advance was to be halted at once and I was personally to report to General von

Kleist, who would come to see me at my airstrip [the field at Montcornet] at 0700 hours. He was there punctually and, without even wishing me a good morning, began in very violent terms to berate me for having disobeyed orders. He did not see fit to waste a word of praise on the performance of the troops. When the first storm was passed, and he had stopped to draw breath, I asked that I might be relieved of my command. General von Kleist was momentarily taken aback, but then he nodded and ordered me to hand over my command to the most senior general of my corps [Major General Rudolf Veiel]. And that was the end of our conversation. I returned to my corps headquarters and asked General Veiel to come to see me, that I might hand over to him.

"I then sent a message to Army Group von Rundstedt by wireless in which I said that I had handed over my command and at noon I would be flying to the Army Group headquarters to make a report. I received an answer almost at once: I was to remain at my headquarters and wait the arrival of Colonel General [Wilhelm] List, who was in command of 12th Army and who had been instructed to clear this matter up."[14]

The mix-up had occurred because General von Rundstedt, commander of Army Group A, got cold feet early on May 16. He decided to stop the panzers temporarily to enable infantry divisions to close up. He directed that only advance detachments were to go beyond a north–south line drawn through Montcornet. Kleist accordingly sent out an order late on May 16 that named a stop line east of this town, which Guderian's and Reinhardt's corps had already passed well beyond. Guderian had assumed the order was out-of-date, and therefore had radioed Kleist that he would continue the attack. Hence Kleist's anger.

"The Montcornet command crisis" caused tremendous consternation in the high command. When General List turned up in the afternoon, he did everything to calm things down. By direction of Rundstedt, he restored Guderian to his command. At the same time he managed a compromise. With the approval of Rundstedt, he allowed Guderian to push "strong reconnaissance forces" ahead on the condition that Guderian not move his corps CP forward. This was a marvelous job of papering over the problem. Kleist's face was saved, and Guderian got what he wanted. Of course, he did not stay back at his corps CP. He routed his orders through the CP by field telephone, not by wireless, so his whereabouts couldn't be monitored by wireless intercept units of the OKH or army high command.[15]

The stop order of May 16 came from Rundstedt, but he may have been responding to a fear of flank attacks that Adolf Hitler was already expressing, and that he put into a directive on May 17. Lieutenant Colonel Adolf Heusinger, an operations officer at OKH, conveyed this order by phone to Lieutenant Colonel Henning von Tresckow, operations officer at Army Group A.

Heusinger told Tresckow: "The führer has ordered: 'The bulk of the panzer formations will not cross the line Le Cateau–Laon to the west.'"

This north–south line was more or less equivalent to the line of the south-flowing Oise River. It was some 30 kilometers (18 miles) west of Montcornet. Reinhardt's and Guderian's recce groups had already passed that line on May 17.

Tresckow exploded in anger. "But that is sheer madness," he shouted. "We have got the whole thing rolling now. We have to get to the coast as quickly as possible. And we are supposed to stop now?"

Hitler provided his justification when he came to Rundstedt's headquarters at Bastogne in the Ardennes on May 17. Army Group A's war diary stated explicitly that Hitler was concerned about the security of the southern flank, and did not want any setback there that might give a boost to the enemy. This order demonstrated the extreme anxiety of Hitler. His fears grew more and more as the offensive succeeded beyond his wildest expectations. He was horrified at maps showing the advances of the panzers without any units along their flanks. He didn't understand

Hitler is greeted by German troops on a visit to Belgium.

Guderian's and Manstein's assurances that the French were far too slow to mount a successful counterstrike against the flanks.

Army chief of staff Franz Halder noted in his diary on May 17: "An unpleasant day. The Führer is terribly nervous. Frightened by his own success, he is afraid to take any chances and so he would rather pull the reins on us. Puts forward the excuse that it is all because of his concern for the left flank." Likewise Halder's entry on May 18: "Highly unpleasant dispute" at the führer's headquarters. "The Führer unaccountably keeps worrying about the south flank. He rages and screams that we are on the best way to ruin the whole campaign and that we are leading up to a defeat."

Halder had become a convert to the Manstein plan, and tried to circumvent Hitler's order. He loosened up the restrictions to allow "strong advance detachments" to proceed beyond the stop line. But when Hitler figured out what Halder was doing, he flew into a rage. Only at six p.m. on May 18 was Halder able to get Hitler to cancel the stop order beginning the next day.[16]

But Hitler's anxieties had caused all Guderian's and Reinhardt's panzers to halt for two full days.

Although the German high command and Adolf Hitler continually feared a French counteroffensive on the panzers' ever-lengthening flanks as they raced westward, there was never any chance of this happening. The French failure to concentrate their armor and their fatal inability to move with any speed spelled the doom of any effective counterstrike. The experiences of the last two French armored divisions (the 2nd and 4th) show why this was so.

The story of the 2nd Armored Division is the saddest of all. On May 13, the high command directed the division to assemble at Charleroi, Belgium, to join the 1st Armored Division, ordered to go there on May 10. The 2nd Armored, under the command of General A. C. Bruché, was stationed at Haut-Moivre, a few miles east of Châlons-sur-Marne. The division was ordered to move its wheeled vehicles by road, and its tracked engines, tanks, artillery, and infantry by rail from sidings near the camp. When they arrived, they found that the flatbed transporters had not yet returned from carrying 1st Armored. The rail component didn't leave until the morning of May 14. Meanwhile the wheeled echelon of noncombatant elements, 1,200 vehicles, was well on the road to Charleroi.

After Guderian's crossing at Sedan, the northeastern front commander, Georges, decided to send 2nd Armored Division to form a blocking force with other French troops north and south of Signy-l'Abbaye, 20 miles west of Sedan, in hopes of stopping Guderian's advance.

When the change in orders came, the 2nd Armored's noncombatant wheeled column had nearly reached Vervins, 15 miles north of Montcornet. It turned about and headed southeast toward Signy. Meanwhile the army's Movement Control ordered the trains to halt in the neighborhood of Hirson, since there were no means of unloading railcars at Signy. Infantry, artillery, tanks and other tracked vehicles then were to move the 20 miles southeast to Signy by road.

While this was happening, the wheeled column was bowling along on the road to Signy. When it reached six miles from the town, the officer in charge of the column noticed growing confusion on the road. He learned from the stream of fugitives that the *boches* were coming—in fact, Guderian's panzer corps. The officer at once turned his column south to Rethel and rushed to shelter across the Aisne River.

The rail authorities actually detrained 2nd Armored infantry, artillery, and tracked vehicles at Hirson and at three other localities some distances away. Communication between units collapsed. On the morning of May 16, General Bruché could locate only seven of his 12 tank companies. And these seven were scattered over a region 80 kilometers wide and 60 kilometers deep.

The division's fuel trucks were with the wheeled convoy south of the Aisne, its tanks, artillery, and infantry scattered in the path

Charles de Gaulle, commander of the newly formed French 4th Armored Division.

of the onrushing Germans. Most of the armor ran out of fuel and, like the infantry and artillery, was simply bypassed by the Germans. Some of the tanks were snatched up to guard the bridges over the Oise River. Here they were picked off group by group by advanced guards of Guderian's Panzer Corps and Wietersheim's following 14th Motorized Corps.

Without having struck a single blow, the 2nd Armored Division disappeared in chaos.[17]

The 4th Armored Division had a different story. It was formed only on May 11, 1940, the day after the Germans attacked, and it was thrown into battle before it became fully organized or equipped. Command went to Colonel Charles de Gaulle, who had been pushing hard for a stronger armored force. When General

Georges handed command over to him, he said: "There, de Gaulle! For you who have for so long held the ideas which the enemy is putting into practice, here is the chance to act."

De Gaulle arrived at 4th Armored's station at Bruyères, a few kilometers south of Laon, on May 16. He found two understrength armored brigades, the 6th, with two companies totaling 20 Char B heavy tanks and one of 15 D.2 tanks, and the 8th, with 50 Renault R35 tanks. The D.2s had 40mm of armor and carried the formidable French 47mm high-velocity gun. The Renaults had 45mm of armor but were armed with the weaker 37mm gun. In all, de Gaulle had 93 tanks, including command vehicles, instead of the 166 at full strength. He had no signaling equipment, no radios. All messages had to be carried by dispatch riders.

De Gaulle decided to attack at once. He wanted to thrust into the flank of the German advance, and he concluded that the Montcornet highway junction was the best place to interrupt German communications. He struck on the morning of May 17, just while Guderian was having his confrontation with Kleist in the same town. The thrust was aimed at a crucial point. The road through Montcornet was the main supply line of the corps. Guderian's headquarters were just out of town. And the rear service areas of 1st Panzer Division were there.

On the approach from Bruyères, the column ran through some marshes near the Serre River, and six Char Bs slid off the road. The French reached the village of Lislet, just across Serre, but did not penetrate into Montcornet.

The Germans did not expect such a bold attack, and had only a few isolated units to protect the southern flank. The French tanks ran into a few German vehicles as they approached the town, and shot them up. The first officer to notice their approach was Captain Johann Adolf Graf von Kielmansegg, supply officer for 1st Panzer. Several German engineers ran toward him, saying French tanks were coming after them.

Kielmansegg ordered the engineers immediately to put up a

mine barrier, and he improvised a defensive position with some randomly collected troops. He was lucky to find some AT and flak guns. He put a battery of 88mm flak guns on a hill above Lislet, and it knocked out several French light tanks. The shelling set the village on fire. When an 88mm shell blew up the Char B of a squadron commander, the remaining Char Bs and the lighter tanks retreated at once. Kielmansegg was able to throw in some panzers that had just come back from the repair shops. Hastily called-in Stuka dive-bombers pounced on the French tanks in the afternoon, and 10th Panzer Division, just arriving at Montcornet, was moving to demolish the French tank force quickly. De Gaulle later wrote that his division was "lost children thirty kilometers in advance of the Aisne. We had to put an end to a situation that was risky, to say the least."[18]

The French retired into the Forêt de Samoussy between Sissonne and Bruyères, where they spent a disturbed night. De Gaulle had lost 23 of his 93 tanks. Five of the six tanks that slid off the road were recovered. Meantime the 19th Panzer Corps continued its untroubled advance north of the Serre.

De Gaulle attacked again two days later, against Crécy-sur-Serre, 30 kilometers farther west. He now had 150 tanks. When they advanced on the bridges over the Serre at Crécy, they were met by heavy antitank fire, then were set upon by Stukas. The entire force drew off to the south, having accomplished nothing.

The attack by the 4th Armored was too little and too late. De Gaulle did not have the power to break the German line of communications. All he could do was make pinprick attacks on the flanks that had no effect on the German advance.[19]

In the spectacular course of events from the morning of May 10, when the Germans crossed the Belgian and Luxembourg frontiers, to May 18, the panzer divisions had cracked gaping holes in the French line at Sedan, Monthermé, and Dinant, and were now

rushing across the plains of northern France with no other restrictions on their advance than the unfounded paranoia of Adolf
Hitler and Gerd von Rundstedt. They continued to fear that the
French, somehow, somewhere, would destroy everything by a massive counteroffensive against the southern flank. This was not
going to happen, as Guderian well knew. But he and the other
panzer leaders, in spite of all their successes, had not fully convinced the high command. So the *Sichelschnitt*, or sickle-cut, advance to the English Channel and the destruction of the Allied
armies in Belgium depended not on what the enemy might do, but
on whether the German führer, disbelieving his own success, and
Rundstedt, cautious in the extreme, would frantically apply the
brakes. The only persons who could prevent complete victory now
were Hitler and Rundstedt.

A German tanker, dressed in his black panzer uniform, leans against his vehicle in France.

CHAPTER 9

THE GHOST DIVISION

'Ihere was one exception to the halting of panzer forces by Hitler and Rundstedt, and it was carried out by Erwin Rommel, who flagrantly violated orders. But he was so fantastically successful that, instead of court-martialing him, Hitler had no choice but to award him his highest decoration, the Knight's Cross.

By the end of the day on May 15, 1940, Rommel's 7th Panzer Division had created a breach that had momentous consequences for the entire campaign in the West. His division had made the first significant passage of the Meuse River at Dinant on May 13. After Guderian crossed at Sedan and General Reinhardt's 41st Panzer Corps got a foothold at Monthermé later the same day, the commander of the French 9th Army, General André-Georg Corap, made a fatal decision. With wild reports of "thousands" of German panzers pouring through the breach at Dinant, Corap ordered his army to abandon defense of the Meuse and to move back to a more westerly line.

On Rommel's front, Corap's intended stop line ran along a railway east of Philippeville and 15 miles (24 kilometers) west of the Meuse. But Rommel penetrated this line before it could be occupied. And under this deep-thrusting advance, the pandemonium of the French withdrawal quickly turned into a general collapse of the 9th Army.

Rommel was at Morville, 14 kilometers west of the Meuse, on the morning of May 15. His goals for the day were Philippeville, 15 kilometers farther west, and Cerfontaine, another ten kilometers on. As the advance got under way, 7th Panzer pushed into the standby area of the French 1st Armored Division at Flavion. It had come up the night before. After a brief clash with this force, Rommel left its disposition to the 5th Panzer Division coming behind, and struck out straight down the main road to Philippeville (see chapter 7).[1]

As his panzers were starting to move, a Luftwaffe major appeared and told Rommel that Stuka dive-bombers would be made available. Rommel called for them immediately to go into action ahead of the advance. Rommel then climbed into the tank of the 25th Panzer Regiment commander Colonel Karl Rothenburg, and instructed his *Gefechtsstaffel,* or his small headquarters group of signals troops and combat team, to follow up the tank attack from cover to cover with their armored cars and signal vehicle.

As the tank column proceeded, numerous individuals and vehicles of French units tumbled into the adjacent woods. The French had already been hit by the dive-bombers, and were unwilling to challenge the panzers. Rommel bypassed Philippeville to avoid getting into a street-by-street fight with the French. There was a brief exchange with French troops occupying the hills and woods to the south. The panzers fought this action on the move, their turrets traversed left. The French fire soon ceased, and the panzers reached Cerfontaine without stopping.

Once there, Rommel took a panzer company back to establish contact with infantry coming up in the rear. On the way he discovered two tanks that had fallen out due to mechanical trouble. Their crews had collected a few French prisoners. When Rommel came up, hundreds of French motorcycle troops, along with their officers, emerged from the woods and surrendered, although some made a quick getaway down a road leading south.

Crew members of a Panzer III tank watch shell fire against French targets ahead.

At Neuville, a couple miles south of Philippeville, Rommel found his leading panzers getting into a fight with French infantry trying to escape the town. He had no interest in pursuing fleeing soldiers, and quickly broke off the clash. A little farther east Rommel collided with fifteen French tanks. But they ceased fire quickly, and the Germans fetched the crews out of their tanks. The quickness of the French to surrender was a measure of the breakdown of order and cohesion in the French army.

Continuing on, Rommel found the advance elements of his Rifle Brigade, which had been far too slow in following the panzers. He took several commanding officers into his armored car and berated them for their tardiness. "All units had known the start time of the attack," he recounted, "and they should have formed up at that time." Officers had to think for themselves, and not wait to receive orders. With the whole column behind him—

including the motorized infantry—Rommel drove at top speed back to Cerfontaine, where the infantry deployed quickly into a defensive hedgehog for the night.[2]

Rommel intended to strike out farther west first thing the next morning. A few miles ahead was the so-called "extended" Maginot Line along the Belgian frontier. This line of fortifications was much less massive than the true Maginot Line farther east, and contained fewer reinforced concrete gun emplacements and other defenses. Even so, it represented a formidable challenge. But this was the challenge that Rommel wanted to tackle.

Early on the morning of May 16, however, Rommel got orders to remain in his headquarters until nine thirty a.m. He didn't know the reason, but it was due to the fact that at seven fifty a.m. that day 4th Army received an order from Army Group A that its lead elements were not to cross the extended Maginot Line. This was part of the general anxiety being felt at Army Group A about the unprotected flanks of the panzer thrusts, the same anxiety that was going to get Guderian in trouble with his boss Kleist at Montcornet the next morning (see chapter 8).

On the night of May 15, Major General Georg von Sodenstern, chief of staff of Army Group A, had ruled that a swift move against the Maginot Line was impractical. Instead, the panzers were to be spared for "subsequent missions." Accordingly, the chief of staff of 4th Army decided that, if the extended Maginot Line turned out to be heavily occupied, the 5th Corps was to make the breakthrough with two infantry divisions. This was the same issue that had been raised earlier about Sedan: Should panzers be up front or should the infantry lead?[3]

General Hans Günther von Kluge, commander of the 4th Army, arrived at Rommel's headquarters on the morning of May 16. After hearing Rommel explain his plans, Kluge deviated from Army Group A's orders and authorized a limited push west with the panzers. Panzer corps commander Hermann Hoth immediately radioed Rommel a preliminary order to punch through the Maginot Line and attack toward Avesnes, 15 kilometers west of the line.[4] The written order restricted the advance just to these two places. But it did not arrive at the CP of 7th Panzer until later. By this time Rommel and his panzers had disappeared. And, most curiously, Rommel seemed to have lost radio contact with his superiors for a very long time thereafter.

It's most probable that Kluge conveyed to Rommel the extreme reticence of Army Group A to the unfettered advances that he, Guderian, and Reinhardt were carrying out. Rommel had no intention whatsoever of being relegated to the role of assisting infantry divisions, however. Therefore, he seized on the small opening that Kluge offered him, and closed himself off from any further orders until he had reached his goal.

And what Rommel achieved was one of the most astonishing and decisive advances in military history. It was this accomplishment of turning up at wholly unexpected places that earned for the 7th Panzer the French sobriquet *la division fantôme*, the ghost division, by which name it has gone down in history.

Rommel immediately set 7th Panzer in motion. It crossed the French border at Clairfayts at six p.m. on May 16. Soon Rommel saw the sharp contours of the extended Maginot Line with concrete bunkers, armored cupolas, minefields, and barbed wire. Any other general would probably have hesitated. But this would have meant forgoing surprise. Rommel had won fame in World War I by surprise raids. He decided to do the same against the Maginot Line. It was a perfectly unheard-of idea, a massive panzer attack at twilight against a well-fortified position. Rommel made no preparation whatsoever. The attack went in straight from the move. Surprise was total.[5]

Rommel was riding in Rothenburg's command tank, one of

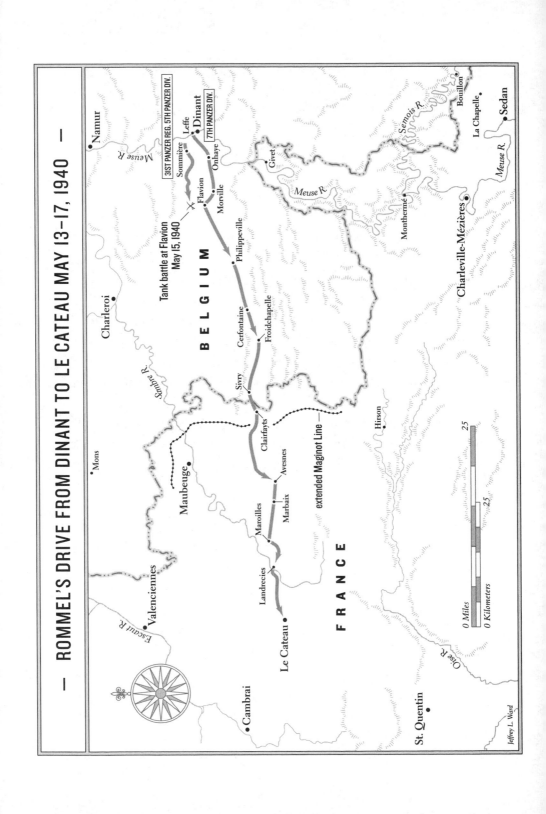

— ROMMEL'S DRIVE FROM DINANT TO LE CATEAU MAY 13–17, 1940 —

31ST PANZER REG, 5TH PANZER DIV

7TH PANZER DIV

Tank battle at Flavion
May 15, 1940

extended Maginot Line

BELGIUM

FRANCE

Namur

Meuse R.

Leffe
Dinant
Sommière
Onhaye
Flavion
Morville

Givet

Meuse R.

Semois R.

Bouillon

La Chapelle

Sedan

Meuse R.

Philippeville

Monthermé

Charleville-Mézières

Charleroi

Cerfontaine
Froidchapelle

Sambre R.

Sivry

Clairfayts

Hirson

Oise R.

Mons

Maubeuge

Avesnes

Marbaix

Maroilles

Landrecies

Le Cateau

Valenciennes

Escaut R.

Cambrai

St. Quentin

0 Miles   25

0 Kilometers   25

Jeffrey L. Ward

the leading vehicles in the column. "Suddenly we saw the angular outlines of a French fortification about 100 meters ahead," Rommel said. "Close beside it were a number of fully armed French troops, who, at the first sight of our tanks, made as if to surrender." But sudden fire from another panzer elsewhere caused the garrison to vanish into their concrete pillbox. The leading tanks now came under heavy antitank and machine-gun fire. Two panzers were knocked out. Fire soon quieted down, and recce groups discovered a deep antitank ditch near a French fort. The length of this barrier was unknown. Its existence meant that the best way forward was straight down the road to Avesnes. But the road was blocked with antitank steel hedgehogs.

Enemy artillery began to bombard the area. On Rommel's orders, his artillery laid down smoke over this section of the line to hide tanks and engineers from the French. Under covering fire of tanks and artillery, engineers pushed into the fortified zone. One team demolished the hedgehogs blocking the road. Another team crawled up to the embrasure of the pillbox, where the French had withdrawn shortly before, and threw a six-pound charge through the firing slit. When the garrison refused to give up, the engineers threw in another charge. An officer and 35 men surrendered, but shortly afterward they overcame the assault team and escaped when machine guns opened fire from a nearby pillbox. Meanwhile, violent firing broke out from antitank guns and a few cannon at a cluster of houses 1,000 meters west of Clairfayts. The French fired over open sights at German tanks and infantry. But rounds from a Panzer IV silenced the fire.

It was getting dark, but the engineers had opened a narrow passage by demolishing the steel hedgehogs in the road. Rommel ordered an immediate advance along this road, with the thrust to go as far as Avesnes.

"The way to the west was now open," Rommel narrated. "The moon was up and for the time being we could expect no real darkness."

A French crew mans a .50-caliber machine gun.

The tanks rolled single file in a long column through the line of fortifications. Once in a while an enemy machine gun or AT gun would fire, but no shots were aimed at the column. German artillery kept dropping harassing fire on the road ahead of the advancing panzers.

"Gradually the speed increased," Rommel said. "Before long we were 500-1,000-2,000-3,000 meters into the fortified zone. Engines roared, tank tracks clanked and clattered. Whether or not the enemy was firing was impossible to tell in the ear-splitting noise."

The column swung along the main road toward Avesnes. People in houses were awakened by the din of the tanks. French troops lay bivouacked beside the roads; vehicles were parked in farmyards or alongside the road itself. Civilians and French troops lay huddled in ditches as the tanks passed. Refugees abandoned their carts and fled into the fields.

"Every so often a quick glance at the map by a shaded light

and a short wireless message to divisional HQ to report the position and thus the success of 25th Panzer Regiment," Rommel recounted. "Every so often a look out of the hatch to assure myself that there was still no resistance, and that contact was being maintained with the rear. The flat countryside spread out around us under the cold light of the moon. We were through the Maginot Line! It was hardly conceivable."

Suddenly there was a flash of fire from a pillbox 300 meters away. More flashes came from other points. This was the second line of fortifications. Rommel gave orders for the panzers to keep on going, but to fire broadsides left and right as they went. Rommel said later that the method of "driving into the enemy with all guns firing worked magnificently. It costs us a lot of ammunition, but it saves tanks and lives. The enemy have not found any answer to this method yet. When we come up on them like this, their nerves fail."

Much of the German ammunition was tracer, and the regiment drove through the second defense line spraying a rain of fire far into the country on either side. Soon the tanks were past the danger zone, without serious casualties. But it was hard to get the firing stopped, and the panzers rolled through the next couple of villages with guns blazing. All around French soldiers were lying flat on the ground. Farms everywhere were jammed with guns, tanks, and other military vehicles. At last Rommel succeeded in silencing the guns.

The column kept on going. At a fork, one road led northwest to Maubeuge, only about ten miles away; the other led southwest down into a valley toward Avesnes. The column took the Avesnes road. It was thick with carts and people, who moved off to the side as the tanks passed, or had to be directed off by the Germans. The nearer the column came to Avesnes, the greater was the crush of vehicles. In Avesnes itself, the whole population was on the move.

Rommel drove on to high ground west of Avesnes, where the

panzers made a halt around midnight. But it turned out that only the leading battalion of the panzer regiment had arrived. The 2nd Battalion of the panzer regiment had been held up by the crush of people and traffic in Avesnes, and had been pounced on by the last 16 tanks of the 1st Armored Division that had been shattered at Flavion. These tanks were Hotchkiss 39s, with 45mm of armor and 37mm guns, and were less formidable to the German Panzer IIIs and IVs than the more heavily armored and armed Char Bs. They got into a huge firefight with the 2nd Battalion in the streets of Avesnes. It finally ended around four a.m. on May 17, when the last three French tanks made their escape.

Rommel recorded carefully in his report on the campaign that he sent repeated signals to Panzer Corps Hoth asking to continue his advance to secure the bridge over the north-flowing Sambre River at Landrecies, 18 kilometers (11 miles) farther on. His report said that he received no reply, so he decided on his own to continue the attack at dawn. It is evident that whether the breakdown of radio contact was real or contrived, Rommel was delighted not to be obliged to obey orders from the higher commands, for they most certainly would have been horrified—and would have told Rommel not to go forward one more inch.

So the advance that he now ordered on Landrecies not only was entirely unauthorized and entirely contrary to orders from Adolf Hitler on down, but it also was one of the boldest, most daring, and most consequential strikes in history. For it was a penetration right into the heart of enemy country, without any flank protection whatsoever, but also so deep, sudden, and unexpected that it bewildered the French. This strike was an extreme example of the theory propounded by Heinz Guderian—that a drive straight into the vitals of the enemy was like a blow of a boxer into an opponent's solar plexus, leaving him utterly incapable of response. There had never been anything like this before in warfare.

Even Guderian's advances were not as overwhelming and as spectacular as this plunge by Rommel.

At Avesnes, Rommel's division was already strung out on a single road deep in the enemy rear surrounded by many thousands more French soldiers and more weapons than he possessed. There was absolutely nothing protecting the 7th Panzer—except shock, incredulity, and consternation at the sheer audacity of this unsupported attack. The concept of a panzer strike being like a narrow rapier thrust was being carried by Erwin Rommel to its ultimate extent.

To continue this advance even deeper into the enemy rear—and on the same terms of a single column rushing down a single road—was taking the concept of an unsupported offensive to an entirely new level. This is precisely what Rommel ordered.

"At about 4.00 hours [on May 17] I moved off toward Landrecies with the leading battalion of Rothenburg's panzer regiment," Rommel reported. "The 7th Motorcycle Battalion, which had now closed up, followed behind, and I was firmly convinced that behind them again the remaining units of the division would take part in the attack."

It turned out that Rommel's faith in the ability of his rear detachments to keep up was greatly misplaced. No supplies had come up. The leading forces had little ammunition left, so Rommel ordered the guns to keep silent. The advance quickly ran into refugee columns and detachments of French troops. Guns, tanks, soldiers, and vehicles were entangled with horse-drawn refugee carts, goods-filled baby carriages, and fleeing civilians. By keeping the guns quiet and occasionally driving their vehicles off the road, the Germans were able to get by the constricted columns. Nowhere did the French soldiers offer any resistance. Hundreds and hundreds of soldiers, with their officers, surrendered. But there was no possibility of taking them along, so they were left just where they were, while the German column continued on westward.

At length the column arrived at Landrecies. The town was a

Rommel stops briefly to confer with his staff while on the march. Note his panzers waiting in the field behind him.

vast crush of vehicles and French troops in every lane and alley, but no opposition.

"We rolled across the Sambre bridge," Rommel recounted, "on the other side of which we found a French barracks full of troops. As the tank column clattered past, Lieutenant Karl Hanke drove into the courtyard and instructed the French officers to have their troops paraded and marched off to the east."

Having met no opposition, Rommel resolved to keep on going. He ordered the column on to Le Cateau, 13 kilometers (eight miles) farther west. On the way the column captured an ammunition dump and accepted the surrender of numbers of soldiers, but had no way of rounding them up.

"I kept the advance going until the hill just east of Le Cateau, where we finally halted," Rommel said. "It was six fifteen a.m."

Rommel's division had advanced nearly 80 kilometers (50 miles) since the previous morning, creating absolute bedlam in the French rear and destroying any possibility of the French forming a defensive line.

Ammunition and fuel were nearly gone. There was little food. Only now did it dawn on Rommel that he was in a very precarious situation. He discovered that just two panzer battalions and a few motorcycle platoons had followed him. The third panzer battalion and the main body of the recce battalion were stuck on the way. Rommel realized that he had conducted the entire push from the Maginot Line, almost 50 kilometers, with the advance detachment only. The main body, including the two rifle regiments and the artillery, were still in front of the extended Maginot Line in Belgian territory, and had settled down for the night![6]

Anxiety was great at the division CP, which had been left behind at Froidchapelle, 16 kilometers southwest of Philippeville. The operations officer, Major Otto Heidkämper, was the only person left in charge, and he was unable to answer nervous inquiries from corps as to where the commander and his panzers had van-

A column of French prisoners of war marches to the rear.

ished. At four twenty a.m. Heidkämper received an urgent order from corps: "Do not advance beyond Avesnes."

Heidkämper had no contact with Rommel, so he stuck strictly to the corps order and allowed the division to move on toward Avesnes only around eight a.m. A traffic jam occurred on the single road where Rommel had pushed through the Maginot Line.

A report of the 6th Rifle Regiment was graphic: "On reaching the Maginot Line, we saw the following picture: a lane ran through the line of pillboxes with their dense barrier belt. The pillboxes on both sides of the route of advance had been knocked out by the panzers, but we found that the pillboxes farther south were completely untouched. A lane had been blasted or cut through the thick and deep wire entanglement, just about the width of the road, and our battalion now pushed through that opening. We thought we would at any moment get a sudden and devastating barrage from the bunkers. Nothing of the sort! Not a round was fired! We could not believe that we were sending an entire division through such a narrow lane."[7]

Rommel was getting increasingly anxious about the rest of his division. He closed up the panzers and the motorcycle troops into a hedgehog (all-around) defense under command of Colonel Rothenburg, and started back with his armored signals vehicle and a Panzer III as escort. This was an astonishing decision. Here was the division commander going back over the route of advance with only a tiny defensive shield, while thousands of French soldiers and their guns were still on the road he was traveling. Rommel's confidence was remarkable. But he had concluded that the French had lost all stomach for fighting, and that he was safe.

When Rommel got to Maroilles, 14 kilometers west of Avesnes, the Panzer III dropped out with mechanical trouble, so he continued on with only his signals vehicle. East of the village, Rommel found a Panzer IV that had been stranded with mechanical trouble. He told the tank commander to hold his position and to tell any prisoners who came by to continue on east.

A column of German vehicles, overseen by soldiers directing traffic, advances in France.

A short distance farther east, a French car came out of a side road and crossed in front of Rommel's signals vehicle. At Rommel's shouts, the car stopped and a French officer got out and surrendered. Behind the car was a whole convoy of trucks approaching in a cloud of dust. At once Rommel had the convoy turned off toward Avesnes. Lieutenant Hanke swung onto the first truck while Rommel stayed at the crossroads signaling the trucks behind to follow the lead vehicle. After about 15 vehicles had passed, Rommel put his signals vehicle at the head of the column and they drove to Avesnes.

At the edge of Avesnes, Rommel found a battalion of his infantry installed next to the road. Hanke directed the French trucks to stop here. There were 40 vehicles, many carrying troops and machine guns.

Unit after unit of the division arrived at Avesnes, and Rommel sent them toward Le Cateau. It had been a spectacular march. The 7th Panzer captured 10,000 prisoners, 100 tanks, 30 armored cars, and 27 guns. But many uncounted thousands of other Frenchmen had laid down their arms and were taken as prisoners by German forces that came behind. The division's losses were only 35 killed and 59 wounded.

German soldiers pose above the tally on the hood of an artillery vehicle showing *Abschüsse* (number of firings) in the west (France) and the east (Poland).

CHAPTER 10

THE BRITISH ATTACK
ROMMEL AT ARRAS

At daybreak on May 18, 1940, Guderian, Rommel, and the other panzer leaders resumed their drive toward the channel. They advanced against virtually no opposition across the open plains of France north of the Somme River. Guderian's 2nd Panzer captured St. Quentin, while 1st Panzer advanced on Péronne and seized a bridgehead over the Somme River there. Meanwhile Rommel captured Cambrai, 25 kilometers west of Le Cateau. But here he paused briefly to reorganize, bring up supplies, and give his troops a much-needed rest.[1]

Guderian did not pause for an instant. On May 20, he at last received his freedom of movement. He entrusted the 10th Panzer Division to defense of his left flank, relieving 1st Panzer to move on Amiens on the Somme, 60 kilometers from the English Channel, and 2nd Panzer to drive through Albert to Abbeville, only 25 kilometers from the channel, there to seize another bridgehead across the Somme.

Winston Churchill described the process: "These hideous, fatal scythes encountered little or no resistance once the front had been broken. The German tanks—the dreaded *chars allemands*—ranged freely through the open country, and aided and supplied by mechanized transport, advanced thirty or forty miles a day. They had passed through scores of towns and hundreds of villages without the slightest opposition, their officers looking out of the open cupolas and waving jauntily to the inhabitants. Eyewitnesses spoke of crowds of French prisoners marching along with them, many still carrying their rifles, which were from time to time collected and broken under the tanks. I was shocked by the utter failure to grapple with the German armor, which, with a few thousand vehicles, was compassing the entire destruction of mighty armies, and by the swift collapse of all French resistance once the fighting front had been pierced. The whole German movement was proceeding along the main roads, at no point on which did they seem to be blocked."[2]

On the way to Amiens on the morning of May 20, Guderian visited the Péronne bridgehead to make sure 10th Panzer was in position. The units of 1st Panzer holding the bridgehead had not waited for 10th Panzer to arrive before pulling out. Lieutenant Colonel Hermann Balck, the officer in charge, feared that otherwise he'd be late for the attack on Amiens. His successor was angry at such cavalier behavior, and even more infuriated by Balck's answer to his complaints: "If we lose it you can always take it again. I had to capture it in the first place, didn't I?" Luckily the French did not move and 10th Panzer reoccupied the site without incident.

After watching 1st Panzer capture Amiens easily and build a bridgehead across the Somme there, Guderian hurried back to Albert, 30 kilometers northeast of Amiens, where 2nd Panzer had advanced so fast that it captured a British artillery battery drawn up in a barrack square equipped only with training ammunition. British and French prisoners filled the market square. Division officers told Guderian they were almost out of fuel, and proposed a stop at Albert.

"One must always distrust the report of troop commanders:

'We have no fuel,'" Guderian wrote. "Generally they have. But if they become tired they lack fuel."

Guderian ordered 2nd Panzer to advance at once, and it arrived, not out of fuel, at Abbeville at seven p.m. on May 20.[3] Meanwhile Guderian made his way to Querrieu, northeast of Amiens, the new location of his corps headquarters. There his CP was attacked by German aircraft.

"It was perhaps an unfriendly action on our part," Guderian wrote, "but our flak opened fire and brought down one of the careless machines. The crew of two floated down by parachute and were unpleasantly surprised to find me waiting for them on the ground. When the more disagreeable part of our conversation was over, I fortified the two young men with a glass of champagne."

During the night of May 20 a battalion of 2nd Panzer passed through Noyelle-sur-Mer, becoming the first German unit to reach the Atlantic coast. In just ten days, the panzers had encircled the entire northern wing of the Allied armies. A gigantic pocket, 200 kilometers long and up to 140 kilometers wide, contained the Belgian army, 1st Army Group with the BEF, 1st and 7th Armies, and scattered elements of 9th Army.

At the end of this astonishing day, Guderian and the other panzer leaders did not know which direction their advance would go. The obvious path was straight up the coast to cut off all the ports of the channel from the Allied troops. But Panzer Group Kleist had received no instructions. So the panzers stopped on May 21 and waited for orders. For Guderian it was precious time wasted.[4]

Adolf Hitler and Gerd von Rundstedt, Army Group A commander, were more anxious than any other senior German leaders about the fact that the farther the panzers pushed to the channel, the longer their exposed flanks spread out. The Allied forces had formed a line along the Schelde River with their southern flank resting on Arras, only 25 miles from Péronne on the Somme. Thus the Germans had only this narrow gap through which to nourish their panzers and their offensive.

The movement west was actually a series of isolated panzer wedges by the individual panzer divisions that created this corridor. Behind these wedges virtually a vacuum was left. A few motorized divisions were coming along, but there were not nearly enough to secure the flanks, while the infantry were several days' march even farther behind.

This corridor, with its largely unprotected flanks, presented a tremendous weakness, provided it could be exploited. Winston Churchill recognized the opportunity. He told General Gamelin on May 19: "The tortoise has protruded its head very far from its shell. Some days must elapse before their main body can reach our lines of communication. It would appear that powerful blows struck from north and south of this drawn-out pocket could yield surprising results."[5]

General Gamelin actually produced a proposal, Directive No. 12, observing that mobile forces could be pushed into the rear of the panzer divisions and prevent encirclement of the armies in Belgium. But his directive was only a vaguely worded memorandum, and General Georges, the northeastern front commander, and other senior French officers did not move fast enough to implement it.

Meanwhile, the unfortunate Gamelin was ousted from his command. On May 19, Marshal Henri-Philippe Pétain arrived in Paris from his post as ambassador to Spain, and sat down with the French premier, Paul Reynaud, and the French president, Albert Lebrun, to draft an order to remove General Gamelin, and replace him with General Maxime Weygand. Weygand arrived in Paris on the same evening from Beirut, where he was military commander in the French colony of Syria.

General Maxime Weygand, who replaced Gamelin as supreme French commander on May 19.

Reynaud also expelled Daladier from the War Office and the Ministry of Defense, and took the job himself. And he named Marshal Pétain as deputy premier. He also promoted Charles de Gaulle to brigadier general, and made him state undersecretary beginning June 6.

Weygand was 73 years old. He had retired in 1935 but was recalled just before the war broke out to command French armed forces in Syria. Weygand had been a protégé of Marshal Ferdinand Foch, who became supreme Allied commander in World War I. Weygand emerged from the war as a major general, and was named army chief of staff in 1931. He was unable to prevent his rival Gamelin from succeeding him, but he left Gamelin surrounded by a coterie of his own supporters. Like Weygand, they were more politically and professionally conservative than Gamelin, and more resistant to modernizing the army. For example, one of his backers, General Marie-Robert Altmayer, cavalry chief, insisted that tanks could not take the place of horses. And another, General Julien Dufieux, infantry chief, opposed allowing infantry to travel in trucks, instead of on foot.[6] Gamelin nevertheless introduced a large number of tank battalions, a few mechanized divisions, some motorized infantry, and modern aircraft, but he did not alter traditional methods of conducting war.

Weygand could be expected to be little interested in new ideas in this moment of impending collapse of the French army and state. In fact, Weygand was as hopelessly ineffective as Gamelin had been. He did not understand that the slow tempo of World War I no longer was possible. While the panzers were advancing farther by the minute, Weygand wasted a day in courtesy calls on political dignitaries in Paris, then flew into the northern cauldron to talk with the commanders at Ypres. There he canceled Gamelin's proposed strike at the German flanks, but produced no immediate alternative. And he lost three days.

While the change in supreme command was being played out in Paris, the British in the cauldron were getting more and more anxious. General John Standish, Lord Gort, commander of the BEF, was dismayed at the inability of the French leadership to take any meaningful action.

Acuteness of the crisis was sharpened by the abrupt withdrawal of the Royal Air Force's Advanced Air Striking Force of

General John Standish, Lord Gort, commander of the BEF in France and Belgium.

three bomber wings from east of Reims back to England. The force had suffered heavy casualties. Its strength had fallen from ten to six squadrons. The RAF fighter squadrons in France were also pulled back to England.

On the night of May 18–19, Lord Gort told General Gaston Billotte, commander of the French 1st Army Group, that he didn't see any other choice except retreat toward the channel ports, and there to form a bridgehead and possibly withdraw the BEF from the Continent. He told his chief of staff, Lieutenant General Sir Henry Pownall, to phone the War Office in London and discuss the options.

Unless the yawning gap between the northern armies and the

Somme could be closed, the Allied armies in the north were doomed. But action had to be fast and decisive. Lord Gort did not believe the French would be either fast or decisive.[7]

Gort felt most profoundly that his primary job was to extract the only army Britain possessed as soon as possible. A British garrison at Arras was in immediate danger. It was more than half surrounded by the Germans. To relieve pressure on this force, Gort on May 20 instructed Major General Harold E. Franklyn to form the 5th and 50th Infantry Divisions and the 1st Army Tank Brigade of heavily armored Matilda tanks into "Frankforce" and cut off German access to the city.

The same day he issued the order, General Sir Edmund Ironside, chief of the Imperial General Staff, arrived at Gort's CP. The visit stemmed from General Pownall's phoned comments to the War Office. Pownall said the French were unable to close the gap, and Lord Gort was considering withdrawing to the coast.

This dire prognosis led Churchill to order the admiralty to assemble a large number of small vessels in readiness to proceed to the French coast at a moment's notice. Admiral Bertram H. Ramsay, commander at Dover, summoned an emergency conference to plan for the evacuation of the BEF and French armies with all available vessels, labeled Operation Dynamo. Thirty ferries, twelve drifters, and six coasters were provided immediately. And from Harwich around to Weymouth, sea-transport officers listed all suitable ships up to a thousand tons.[8]

The British cabinet was not as pessimistic as Gort, however, and Ironside carried with him the cabinet's order for the BEF to move southward upon Amiens, on the other side of the gap, and attack all enemy forces it encountered. It was an astonishingly quixotic command, given the situation on the ground.

Lord Gort convinced Ironside that the BEF could not close this gap alone, and doing so must depend on the French. He pointed out that most of the BEF was helping to hold off the German 6th Army on the east, and his only two available divisions had already been ordered to operate south of Arras on May 21.

In this mounting emergency, Ironside and Pownall went to see General Billotte, and urged immediate action to close the gap. They told Billotte of the British action planned the next day at Arras. Billotte ruled that the French would attack with two divisions toward Cambrai the same day, and would coordinate their plans with General Franklyn.

But French and British command inefficiency now began to dictate events. Although Franklyn's operation had become part of a larger effort to close the gap, Lord Gort sent Franklyn no fresh orders. Meanwhile the French were characteristically slow, and before the day was out, they announced that they could not launch their attack until May 22.

So the move at Arras on May 21 remained as it had originally been conceived, a mopping-up operation to clear out any Germans south of the city and to block German moves to the east. It never had any greater aspiration. But the Germans saw a far vaster motive than the British intended—and this was going to have world-shaking consequences in just a few days.

Franklyn used most of his force to defend the Scarpe River to the east of Arras, and sent only a minor part to evict the Germans south of the city. He grossly underestimated the strength of the German forces, and he completely misunderstood what the Germans were doing. This is all the more remarkable since his intelligence reports coming in on May 21 were quite accurate. The reports said that German tanks had been seen west of Arras, and later in the day that enemy tanks and trucks were on the road to St. Pol *northwest* of Arras. The report also stated that "strong columns of infantry with tanks" had been seen leaving Cambrai on the road west to Arras on the evening of May 20. These reports indicated a powerful German move to swing around Arras on the south and west, and then strike northward against the Allied armies in Belgium.

Franklyn's operation order on May 21 ignored the danger of tanks to the northwest of Arras, and designated merely the 151st Brigade of infantry with the 1st Army Tank Brigade to carry out mopping-up operations to the south and southwest of the city. The order said that enemy numbers in those areas were not believed to be great.

Only two of the infantry brigade's three battalions were used, the other being kept back in reserve. Of a total of 88 tanks, including light vehicles, that the tank brigade could muster, 58 were Mark I and 16 Mark II Matildas. Both were extremely slow infantry tanks with 80mm of armor. But the Mark I was armed merely with a 7.9mm machine gun, and was useful only against enemy infantry in the open. The Mark II was armed with a two-pounder (40mm) gun and a 7.9mm machine gun. The Matilda armor was virtually impossible for the German tank guns to penetrate, but only the 16 Matildas with 40mm guns had a weapon big enough to damage German battle tanks.[9]

Erwin Rommel intended to wheel 7th Panzer around Arras on the south and west and seize crossings over the Scarpe River at Acq, ten kilometers northwest of the city, and then strike for the French industrial city of Lille, 40 kilometers north. This plan posed considerable risk, since throughout the wheeling movement his right flank would be open toward Arras and the garrison known to be there. To the right or north of Rommel the 5th Panzer Division was to attack to relieve the pressure on the flank of 7th Panzer. However, its advance was delayed, so it was unable to accomplish its mission.

Rommel was not worried about the risk. He led off, as usual, with the 25th Panzer Regiment, and ordered his infantry and artillery to follow close behind. But the infantry regiments and artillery were so slow in coming up that Rommel drove back to chase the laggards forward.

Thus the tanks were well separated from the infantry and artillery. In this situation, with his panzers far away, Rommel ran into the most dangerous encounter in the entire campaign. The British tank attack was mounted without prior reconnaissance, and it hit at the worst moment and in the worst spot. It punched full force into the unprotected flank of the German infantry.

Around four p.m. near Ficheux, a few kilometers southwest of Arras, Rommel came across part of the infantry. He turned with this force toward Wailly, a couple kilometers on, and came under fire from the north. He found one of his howitzer batteries already in position at the northern edge of the village, firing rapidly at enemy tanks attacking southward.

"As we were now coming under machine-gun fire and the infantry had already taken cover, I ran on in front of the armored cars toward the battery position," Rommel recounted. "The gunners were calmly hurling round after round into the tanks in complete disregard of the return fire."

The British fire had created chaos among the German infantry, and they were jamming the roads and the yards of houses with their vehicles, instead of going into action against the oncoming enemy. Rommel notified the divisional staff by radio of the critical situation—so it could recall the panzers and ask for Luftwaffe help. He drove to a hill a thousand meters west of Wailly. There he found a light (20mm) antiaircraft artillery troop and a number of 37mm antitank guns, most of them under cover. Several enemy tanks were advancing down a road toward Wailly from the northwest, and other enemy tanks were advancing from the north. Being "infantry" tanks, they were slow-moving, and were still some distance away, but the peril was great. The crew of a howitzer battery abandoned their guns, swept along by the retreating infantry.

Seeing disintegration spreading, Rommel, along with his aide, rushed back to the hill and brought every available gun into action at top speed. Rommel formed an advanced line of 37mm antitank

Soldiers fire an 88mm antiaircraft gun, which turned out to be the best tank-killer in the German arsenal.

guns and light 20mm AA pieces that did not stop the Matildas. Indeed, the AT shells bounced off the tanks, and the monsters simply rolled over the AT guns and their crews. But these light weapons did slow the few lighter tanks.

The real barrier that finally stopped the tanks was a second "gun line" of field artillery pieces and 88mm high-velocity flak or AAA guns that Rommel set up farther to the rear and whose fire he directed personally. These "88s" had already emerged as the real tank-killers in the war. Mainly because of the 88s, the British lost two dozen tanks in a few minutes. About six p.m. the first Stuka dive-bombers arrived, and they pounced on the British tanks that were now retreating.

The Germans were greatly helped by the uncoordinated nature of the British attack. The Matildas advanced bravely toward the Germans, but they had poor radio contact and no cooperation with the infantry, or even between tanks. Officers were forced to dismount or open their hatches and direct tank movements by hand signals. This cost the lives of Lieutenant Colonel H. M. Heyland and an aide in the attack on Wailly. The tanks charged ahead at random. None of their actions were coordinated. The isolated commitment of a single tank brigade at Arras was the exact opposite of massed attacks with all arms that Guderian had been teaching.[10]

The English strategist and tank pioneer Basil H. Liddell Hart wrote: "The British tank advance had been handicapped by having little infantry support, less artillery support, and no air support."[11]

As the day was waning, the 25th Panzer Regiment rushed back on Rommel's orders. It was instructed to cut off the retreat of the withdrawing British. On the way, however, it bumped into a column of French tanks from the Cavalry Corps that was screening the right flank of the British. The French tanks were Hotchkiss 39s mounting 37mm guns and Somuas carrying 47mm guns. Both were more heavily armored than the panzers. The Germans were able to prevail only after bitter fighting, with losses of three Panzer IVs, six Panzer IIIs, and a number of light tanks. The battle of Arras had been decided well before the panzers arrived on the battlefield. The British had already left in the darkness.

The fight at Arras was by far the costliest for the 7th Panzer, and was one of the most brutal actions in the entire campaign. The division lost about 180 killed and 116 wounded.[12] Only 28 out of 88 British tanks returned.

It had been a tactical defeat for the British, but the attack had stunned the German high command, most especially Adolf Hitler, because it played directly into his fear of a flank attack. This was going to have enormous repercussions.

*   *   *

The new French supreme commander, General Weygand, came up with a plan for a pincer attack against the Arras corridor on May 22, the day after the fight between the British and 7th Panzer at Arras. The 1st Army Group would strike from the north and the newly formed 3rd Army Group under General Antoine-Marie-Benoît Besson from the south. The situation required fast action with as many troops as possible. But preparations were slow and nothing was done.

The last chance for a counteroffensive was May 23. Having seen no action by the French by that evening, Lord Gort decided to retreat to the coast, and ordered the British still at Arras to fall back to join the rest of the BEF. The French command had already suffered a setback because General Billotte had died from a traffic accident the evening of May 21 returning from his meeting with Weygand in Ypres. Weygand took his time to name General Georges Blanchard, 1st Army commander, as his successor three days later. General Alan Brooke, a corps commander in the BEF, saw Blanchard at this time. "He was standing studying the map as I looked at him carefully," Brooke wrote in his diary. "And I gathered the impression that he might as well have been staring at a blank wall. He gave me the impression of a man whose brain had ceased to function; he was merely existing and hardly aware of what was going on around him."[13] In a typical process of delays, the French counteroffensive was postponed to May 24, then to May 26 or 27, and finally canceled entirely. The French command had missed its chance to avert catastrophe.[14]

The situation had become an extreme emergency for the Allies. Over half a million troops were cut off in the giant cauldron in Belgium and northern France. French responses were so slow that no meaningful move had been made to break through the 25-mile-wide German panzer corridor to the south. The French government had responded to the crisis by changing commanders, but the new chief was no better than the old one, and days were lost in the transition. There was now no other choice but to retreat to the English Channel, form a defensive perimeter, and use British sea power to evacuate as many of the trapped Allied soldiers as possible. But this, too, seemed to be out of the question, because Heinz Guderian's panzers were on the coast and faced little opposition in rushing for the channel ports.[15]

British soldiers line up in long columns on the beach at Dunkirk, awaiting evacuation back to England.

CHAPTER 11

THE MIRACLE OF DUNKIRK

The attack by the British at Arras on May 21 created a sensation in the German high command. Hitler thought it confirmed his fears of a massive offensive on the flank. He sent urgent inquiries to Army Group A on May 22. General von Rundstedt decided to straighten out the situation around Arras, and only then push Guderian's panzers toward the closest channel ports of Calais and Boulogne.[1]

Army chief of staff Franz Halder and Guderian drew an entirely different conclusion. Both felt that the Allies were now bound to withdraw to the coast. The principal danger was that they might go too fast to be cut off and captured. For them the problem was to beat the Allied armies to Dunkirk, the last and most probable Allied escape port.

Guderian's panzers around Abbeville on the Somme, and the Allied armies in Belgium and northern France, were both about 100 kilometers from Dunkirk. But Guderian faced comparatively little opposition, whereas the Allied armies were still locked in a battle embrace with Army Group B, and would find it difficult to disengage. There was nothing to stop the panzers from getting to Dunkirk—as well as Boulogne and Calais along the way—well before the Allies could build a defensive arc around it.

On May 21 Guderian set out to do just that. He had received orders to advance northward to capture Boulogne, Calais, and Dunkirk. He planned to send 10th Panzer Division straight to Dunkirk, 1st Panzer to Calais, and 2nd Panzer to Boulogne. But early on May 22, as a result of the anxiety caused by the attack at Arras, Army Group A held back 10th Panzer in reserve, and allowed only 1st and 2nd Panzer to advance on Calais and Boulogne. Thus Guderian's planned quick strike on Dunkirk, which was virtually unoccupied, was not carried out.

The 2nd Panzer had to fight fierce clashes with mostly French forces on the approach to Boulogne, but got into the city on the twenty-second. The next day the division confronted the old town walls, which neither the tank guns nor the field artillery could penetrate. At last, the commander brought up an 88mm flak gun—the same weapon that had stopped the Matilda tanks at Arras—and blew a hole in the wall. Using a ladder from the kitchen of a nearby house, the German infantry climbed through the breach and forced their way into the old town itself.

Army Group released 10th Panzer to Guderian on May 23. He decided to redirect 1st Panzer, which was already close to Calais, on to Dunkirk at once, and ordered 10th Panzer to move up and seize Calais. The division got into a fierce battle with the Allied forces defending the port. When the Germans sent in a demand to surrender, British Brigadier C. N. Nicholson, commander of the 30th Infantry Brigade, responded: "The answer is no, as it is the British Army's duty to fight as well as it is the German's." So the Germans had to gain the port by assault. It took them until May 26 to overwhelm the mostly British defenders. Although the Germans captured 3,000 British prisoners, they also gained 17,000 French, Belgian, and Dutch soldiers as prisoners, the majority of whom did not want to fight in the first place, and whom the British therefore had locked up in cellars.[2]

The 1st Panzer struck for Gravelines, near the coast on the Aa

Canal, on May 23, meeting strong resistance. But on May 24, the division reached the canal, and seized bridgeheads across it at two places a few kilometers south of Gravelines, while the SS Division Leibstandarte Adolf Hitler, attached to Guderian's corps, seized another bridgehead a little farther inland. Meanwhile Reinhardt's 41st Panzer Corps secured a bridgehead over the Aa Canal at Saint-Omer, 30 kilometers inland. Guderian's forces were now just ten miles from Dunkirk. The port had very few Allied troops holding it. The great bulk of the Allied armies were nearly 100 kilometers away, still defending against Army Group B, although they were trying desperately to withdraw.

On this day, May 24, the world turned upside down. The 4th Army ordered the left wing of the army to stop on the Aa Canal. The troops were forbidden to cross the stream. The panzer divisions were instructed to hold the line of the canal and "make use of the period of rest for general recuperation." The order went on to say that Dunkirk was to be left to the Luftwaffe, whose bombers would prevent the Allies from embarking from the port.

Guderian was stunned. He thought Hitler had ordered the halt. Although Hitler was ultimately responsible, the original stop order stemmed from Gerd von Rundstedt. His decision came after a day of heated argument within the army command. The panzer divisional and corps commanders wanted to attack as soon as possible, and army chief of staff Halder and army commander Walther von Brauchitsch agreed with them. Rundstedt and Hans Günther von Kluge, commander of the 4th Army, on the other hand, wanted the panzers to stop long enough for the infantry divisions to catch up. Hitler, his paranoia about a flank attack inflamed by the British attack at Arras, supported them.

Rundstedt later explained his reasoning to General Fedor von Bock, commander of Army Group B: "I was worried that Kleist's weak forces would be overrun by the fleeing English." Bock had a more realistic estimate. He thought the British would be happy to escape with their lives.

It was General von Kleist, chief of the panzer group, who inadvertently pushed over the first domino that set a row of dominoes to falling. The result was to transform a total victory into a partial victory and to send Adolf Hitler and Nazi Germany down the road to total defeat and *die Stunde Null,* or the zero hour, only five years hence. The famous military parable that, for want of a nail, a war was lost, was reflected here in a real sequence of events and a real chain of unintended consequences.

Everything started on the morning of May 23. Army Group A was still reeling from shock after the Arras attack, and ordered Kleist to provide flank protection along the Somme in case the French attacked there. Kleist complained that he couldn't both provide protection on the south and also mount an attack toward Dunkirk against strong enemy forces. He asserted that his panzers had lost 50 percent of their strength over the past fourteen days. "If the enemy attacks in major strength [along the Somme]," he informed Army Group, "then I would like to note for the record that the panzer divisions are little suited for defense."

Halder ridiculed Kleist's complaints, downplayed the risks, and refused to believe Kleist's claim that he had lost half of his tanks. This, in fact, was not true. But Kleist's worries nevertheless had an effect on 4th Army commander Kluge, who told Rundstedt that he thought the panzers should be halted long enough for the remainder of the army to "close up" (*aufschliessen*). Rundstedt agreed fully, and he authorized 4th Army to issue a "close-up" order effective May 24, with infantry corps on the east to keep moving toward Arras, while the panzers on the west were to interrupt their advance.

This action by Rundstedt triggered a wild controversy. The decision was a direct contradiction of the entire sickle-cut concept.

Brauchitsch and Halder had already concluded during the campaign that Rundstedt and his extremely conservative chief of staff, Georg von Sodenstern, were typical of the old school and were actively sabotaging the war of movement.

At midnight on May 23–24, Brauchitsch intervened directly. To unleash the panzers, Brauchitsch ordered 4th Army to be removed from command of Army Group A and placed under command of Army Group B (General von Bock) as of eight p.m. on May 24. Bock would order the panzers to move at once, and Army Group B would finish up the destruction of the Allied armies in the north. Rundstedt was to lose all of his panzers, and was to concern himself solely with protection of the Somme River line to the south.

On the morning of May 24, Hitler visited Rundstedt's headquarters, now at Charleville, France, and was astonished to learn of Brauchitsch's order. The decision had been made without Hitler's knowledge or approval. He immediately declared it null and void. At the same time he agreed with Rundstedt's pessimistic estimate of the situation.

Thus at twelve forty-five p.m. on May 24, headquarters of Army Group A issued the famous halt order that confirmed Rundstedt's earlier "close-up" order and changed the history of the world. It required a stop on "the general line Lens-Bethune-Aire-Saint-Omer-Gravelines" [the line of the Aa Canal].

Hitler thus endorsed Rundstedt's order, and did not originate it. Later Rundstedt tried to put all the blame on Hitler, as if the order had been forced on him. "After all, in the end, I had to obey Hitler's order which he kept repeating over and over again," Rundstedt said after the war.[3] He also told Basil H. Liddell Hart that the order came directly from Hitler, a view spread by Günther Blumentritt, Rundstedt's operations officer.[4]

Hitler actually gave Rundstedt freedom of action as to the use of the panzers. Alfred Jodl, chief of operations of the armed forces command (*Oberkommando der Wehrmacht* or OKW), wrote in his

Alfred Jodl, chief of operations of the OKW.

diary: "Führer leaves decision to Army Group A." And the Army Group A war diary stated that Hitler "expressly left the manner of the fighting by the 4th Army" to Rundstedt.[5]

The halt order raised enormous protests from the divisional and corps commanders, especially Guderian. Army chief of staff Halder was livid. In his diary, Halder wrote that he and Brauchitsch had planned for Army Group B to hold the Allied armies by frontal attacks, while the panzers cut into the enemy rear and delivered the decisive blow—by cutting off all means of retreat at Dunkirk. But with the halt order, he fumed, this movement no longer could be carried out.

General von Bock was likewise unable to understand why his army group was ordered to push with his infantry directly on Dunkirk, now 75 kilometers away, while the panzers were standing around the enemy rear and doing nothing. Kluge and Kleist also had a change of heart and pleaded with Rundstedt for a continu-ation of the attack. Kluge got on the phone and reproached Soden-stern directly about the order. Guderian was speechless, and wrote that the supreme command's intervention was "to have a most disastrous influence on the whole future course of the war."[6]

Now the German army's panzers were lined up neatly along the Aa Canal from the channel to near Arras, and had to watch helplessly as the Allied armies marched unopposed right past them and set up powerful defenses around Dunkirk.

On May 24 Army Group B broke the Belgian Army's line at Courtrai (Kortrijk), only 30 miles from Ostend and Dunkirk, leaving a gaping hole in the Allied front. King Leopold of Bel-gium considered his situation hopeless, and surrendered four days later. Despite the Belgian defection, the BEF—primarily due to the skillful extraction of units by 2nd Corps commander Alan Brooke—withdrew by stages and closed in on Dunkirk. The French 16th Corps was holding the line at Gravelines and shield-ing Dunkirk. The rest of the French armies in the north, eleven divisions, were being squeezed into a small area north and east of Douai. Most of them withdrew through a narrow corridor at Lille, but the Germans cut off five divisions in that city and forced their surrender.

Brauchitsch and Halder tried to do everything in their power to get the halt order lifted. Brauchitsch had an opportunity on May 24, when he was summoned to Hitler. He tried to convince Hitler of the irrationality of the decision. But Brauchitsch reported that the interview was "very unpleasant." Hitler, instead of looking at the problem objectively, berated Brauchitsch for having taken an action (removal of 4th Army from Army Group A) without autho-rization. Hitler had a very offhand view of the situation, and told Brauchitsch that Hermann Göring's Luftwaffe would foil any at-tempt by the British to embark from Dunkirk, and would sink any boat that managed to reach the open sea.

This demonstrates that Hitler saw the matter as a purely tacti-

Surrendered French soldiers are paraded past a German honor guard in Lille, France.

cal battlefield problem, and had no concept whatsoever of the worldwide, potentially war-winning strategic implications of what could be achieved by capturing the entire British army.

Hitler's inability to see the obvious at Dunkirk demonstrated his blindness to strategic possibilities in general. He could never see how to achieve his goals by indirect means, and always opted for headlong attacks.[7] This blindness led to one disastrous military decision after another in the months and years ahead. It was the cardinal reason for his destruction.

Lieutenant Colonel Bernhard von Lossberg, on the operations staff at OKW, protested the decision directly to General Jodl. To him, it was all the more unbelievable, since it was doubtful whether Göring could accomplish the task.

"I pointed out," he wrote, "that by doing this we were unconcernedly throwing away the chance of capturing the entire BEF. But Jodl simply answered that the war was already won, that it was merely a question of bringing it to a close, and that it was useless to sacrifice a single tank in achieving what the Luftwaffe could do much more economically."[8]

In this emergency, Halder figured a way out. He sent the following radio message to both Army Groups A and B: "The go-ahead is hereby given for the continuation of the attack up to the line Dunkirk-Cassel-Estaires-Armentières-Ypres-Ostende." The key words were "go-ahead given" while the term "is ordered" was avoided on purpose. Halder guessed that the vaguely worded directive would be forwarded through normal command channels to the panzer generals. And they would seize the opportunity and move out at once.

But when the message arrived at Army Group A, Rundstedt refused to pass it down the line. He gave his excuse in the war diary: The directive was not forwarded because Hitler had expressly left operations of 4th Army to him.[9]

Thus the querulous and peevish Rundstedt deprived Germany of final victory. In the end, he turned away from the brilliant vision of Erich von Manstein. He was unwilling to allow the panzers to strike while there remained the slightest danger of an attack on the army's flanks. It was irrational and unwarranted. More, it was painfully similar to the reactionary way of thinking of the Allied generals who opposed him. One wonders what would have happened in the campaign in the West in 1940 if Erich von Manstein had not pushed his singular solution so hard and so successfully. With generals like Rundstedt on one side and Gamelin and Weygand on the other, the war could have turned quickly into a bloody stalemate.

The halt order was finally lifted on May 26. But now it was too late. A solid defense had been thrown up around Dunkirk, and the British and French resisted every effort to break through.

While these dramatic events were being played out in the northern cauldron, relations between Britain and France were deteriorating rapidly. The French high command had not been informed at once about British intentions of evacuating the BEF. Accordingly, it was impossible to disguise the deepening French-British differences at a meeting of the Supreme War Council (Inter-Allied Council) in Premier Reynaud's office in Paris on May 25. Major General Edward Spears, an old friend of Churchill, fluent in French, but on cool terms with Weygand, represented the prime minister.

Almost at once Major Joseph Fauvelle, head of the operations bureau of the French 1st Army Group, was brought in. He told the council that in his opinion the battle for France was as good as over. He said the French troops were exhausted, all heavy artillery had been lost, all the horse-drawn artillery was immobilized because the horses had been killed by aircraft, and gun ammunition was down to one unit of fire. Moreover, he said, the French 1st Army had no more bread, though it did have plenty of meat and wine. (The BEF meanwhile had been on half rations for some days.) The

Major General Edward Spears, seen here in plain clothes, was a close friend of Churchill and fluent in French.

British, he said, were preoccupied with reembarkation. Spears commented: "He was the very embodiment of catastrophe."

General Weygand likewise described a hopeless military situation. He told the council that he and northeastern front commander General Georges had examined the possibilities of shortening the line, but retreat south of the Seine River would mean abandonment of the troops on the Maginot Line and abandonment of Paris. Weygand said that, while an agreement with Britain had been signed March 28, 1940, forbidding a separate peace, this agreement should be examined if Germany offered terms. Marshal Pétain reinforced this view. He claimed—because of the small British assistance in the war—the right of France to question the alliance in general.

Reynaud said he was going to London the following day and would put the question of destruction of the French army and its consequences to Churchill. The French officials agreed that, if the government was driven from Paris, it should retire to Bordeaux. In London, Reynaud met with Churchill and the senior members of the government, and he got nowhere with his idea of a separate French peace. The British held to the March 28 agreement.[10]

On the evening of May 26 a British admiralty signal put into play Operation Dynamo, or the evacuation from the northern cauldron. The first troops were brought home that night. At this time the British thought they could rescue only about 45,000 men in two days. Early on May 27 emergency measures were taken to find additional small craft. The government now resolved for no less than the full evacuation of the BEF. Admiralty officers searched boatyards and found forty motorboats and launches. Lifeboats on liners in the London docks, tugs from the Thames, yachts, fishing craft, lighters, barges, and pleasure boats—anything that could be of use along the beaches—were called into service. By the night of May 27 a great tide of small vessels began to flow toward the sea and Dunkirk.

Churchill described how a spontaneous movement swept the seafaring population of the south and southeastern coasts of England. "Everyone who had a boat of any kind, steam or sail, put out for Dunkirk, and the preparations, fortunately begun a week earlier, were now aided by the brilliant improvisations of volunteers on an amazing scale."[11] Nearly 400 small craft played a vital part in ferrying from the beaches to the off-lying ships almost 100,000 men.

Churchill noted that he missed several faces in the admiralty map room in these days. The men had gotten hold of a small Dutch *schuit*, or boat, which in four days brought off 800 soldiers. Altogether 861 vessels came to the rescue of the army.

On the beaches the troops were placed in order along the defenses. Those in the best shape formed a defensive line. Divisions that had suffered most were embarked early. Hard fighting was

A Royal Navy destroyer crew mans a five-inch gun as British soldiers approach on the beach at Dunkirk.

incessant. As the evacuation went on, the steady decrease in the number of troops, British and French, was accompanied by a corresponding contraction of the defense. On the beaches among the sand dunes scores of thousands of men remained under continuous air attack for three, four, or five days.

The German bombs mostly plunged into the soft sand, which muffled the explosions. In the early stages, after a crashing air raid, the troops were astonished to find that hardly anybody had been killed or wounded. The soldiers now, as Churchill remarked, "crouched in the sand dunes with composure and growing hope. Before them lay the grey but not unfriendly sea. Beyond, the rescuing ships and— Home."[12]

For the French, the crisis of Dunkirk aroused different memories and different emotions.

Captain Marc Bloch, a fuel-supply officer for the French 1st Army and a history professor at the Sorbonne in Paris in civilian life, described the frantic efforts of French soldiers to escape from the chaos. On May 26, 1st Army moved into its last headquarters, at Steenwerck, a few miles northwest of Lille. The army was now commanded by General René Prioux, who had led the Cavalry Corps in the armored clash at Hannut. On May 28 Prioux announced that he was unable to extract several divisions from a cauldron around Lille, and that he had decided to remain at Steen-werck and await the arrival of the Germans. He kept only a few officers with him.

"The rest of us, he said, had better make for the coast under cover of darkness and get on board what ships we could find," Bloch wrote. "We left that night: a long, slow column of cars moving across the Belgian countryside, for the French roads were already cut. By first light we had covered barely ten kilometers."

They arrived at Hondschoote, ten miles southeast of Dunkirk, around noon. Here they were stopped by broken bridges and "by an incredible jam of lorries which were halted head to tail and three deep.

"We set out again at nightfall," Bloch wrote, "this time on foot. We had to make our way through an extraordinary confusion of motor traffic in a darkness that every minute was becoming more dense. A sort of escape hysteria had got hold of this mob of men. They were to all intents and purposes unarmed, and, from where they stood packed together on the beaches, they could watch the English ahead of them already putting out to sea."

On May 31 Bloch and two friends got an official movement order from the Cavalry Corps. That night they and other French soldiers boarded a British vessel, *Royal Daffodil.* "All things, as we slipped away, seemed to be in a conspiracy to accentuate the over-whelming and purely selfish feelings of relief which filled my mind as I thought of the prisoners' fate which I had so narrowly es-caped," Bloch wrote.

"We landed at Dover. Then came a whole day spent in travel-ing by train across southern England. That journey has left in my mind the memory of a sort of drugged exhaustion broken by cha-otic sensations and images: the pleasure of devouring ham and cheese sandwiches handed through the windows by girls in multi-colored dresses; the sweet smell of cigarettes showered on us with the same generous profusion; the cozy green of lawns; a landscape made up of parks, cathedral spires, hedges, and Devonshire cliffs; groups of cheering children at level crossings. But what struck us more than anything else was the warmth of our reception. 'How genuinely kind they are!' said my companions. Toward evening we re-embarked at Plymouth and dropped anchor at dawn off Cherbourg. We had to wait a long time in the harbor. 'You see,' said the ship's officers (French this time), 'the dock officials don't get to their offices until nine.' No more cheering crowds, no more sandwiches and cigarettes. We were given on landing a formal, dry, rather suspicious welcome."[13]

A factor that Hitler had not anticipated at Dunkirk was the slaughter of his airmen. By intense effort RAF Fighter Command maintained successive patrols over the port, and, being close to their bases, fought the enemy under good competitive conditions. They bit into the German fighter and bomber squadrons, taking a heavy toll. Day after day this went on, until the RAF gained air superiority. The whole Metropolitan Air Force, the last reserve of Britain, was thrown into the fight. Some pilots flew four sorties a day. This was a decisive clash, though the troops on the ground at Dunkirk saw little of it. It was fought often miles away or above the clouds.

The idea that the Luftwaffe would make it unnecessary to use the panzers had no support among Luftwaffe officers. The Luftwaffe was extremely worn down after supporting the advance to the channel. Most of the bombers had to take off from fields in Germany because few air stations had yet been set up in Belgium. Often aircraft had to refuel in Germany before reaching Dunkirk. Pilots not only were overtaxed and overloaded, but they ran into a fresh, rested opponent, the British home defense fighters. Churchill had kept most of the British fighters back on the island. The clash with a new British fighter plane, the Spitfire, was a bad surprise. It

A British Supermarine Spitfire over England in the summer of 1940. The Royal Air Force Fighter Command committed its entire strength, the last reserve of Britain, to protecting the evacuation of British and French soldiers from Dunkirk in late May and early June 1940.

was the first time that pilots had to cope with an aircraft that was equivalent and in some respects superior to the Messerschmitt 109. Dunkirk was right at the front door of the British squadrons. They flew 2,739 sorties during the evacuation. For the German fighters Dunkirk was at the outermost limit of their range. They could stay over the area only a short time. As a result, the Germans suffered painful losses.

Weather also became a decisive ally to the British. For the first two weeks of the campaign, the weather had been excellent. Now rain clouds spread over western Europe. Sometimes the cloud cover was as low as 100 meters. Bomber and fighter sorties thus had to be aborted time and again. During the nine-day evacuation, the Luftwaffe was available only for the first seven days. And it was able to go in strong only on two and a half days.

In the evacuation itself, discipline prevailed ashore and afloat. The sea was calm. To and fro between the shore and the ships little boats plied, gathering the men from the beaches as they waded out or picking them from the water. Their numbers defied air attack. The "Mosquito Armada" as a whole was unsinkable. Notwithstanding, the heaviest burden fell on the ships plying from Dunkirk harbor, where two-thirds of the men were embarked. Navy destroyers played the predominant part. Of the 39 employed, six were sunk by German bombers. In all, 243 of the 861 craft used in the evacuation were sunk.

From May 26 to June 4 the Allies transported 338,682 men to England. Together with 27,936 evacuated earlier from various ports, plus 4,000 British rescued in other French ports, a total of 370,000 were taken back to England. Of that number, 247,000 were British and 123,000 French. Most of the French were immediately transshipped back to unoccupied France. But 80,000 French soldiers were left behind around Dunkirk and wound up as captives. Just a few days earlier, 35,000 had capitulated in the "witch's cauldron" of Lille. Including the Belgians, about 500,000 men laid down their arms and surrendered in the northern pocket.

French and British prisoners walk away from the beach at Dunkirk after its final occupation by the Germans in early June 1940.

The RAF lost 177 aircraft, the Luftwaffe about twice as many. The BEF left almost all its equipment behind—63,000 vehicles, 20,000 motorcycles, 475 tanks, 2,400 artillery pieces, vast quantities of handguns, ammunition, and gear. The British army got back to England. But it had virtually no weapons, and was not going to have any new weapons for some time. Britain's only defense now was the Royal Navy, the RAF, and 21 miles of sea separating it from the Continent.

Why did Hitler insist on stopping the panzers before they got to Dunkirk? Many explanations and myths have been offered, but none has ever satisfactorily answered the question—except the simplest and most probable answer that Hitler just did not see the importance of capturing the BEF. Because of this almost inconceivable lack of foresight and comprehension, exhibited at Dunkirk and in nearly all of his future military decisions, the world was saved from Nazi dictatorship.

The three principal reasons given for stopping the panzers are that Hitler feared his tanks would get bogged down in the soft ground of Flanders, he didn't want to destroy the BEF because he hoped to come to an accommodation with Britain, and he figured the Luftwaffe would prevent any escape from Dunkirk anyway.

Lieutenant Colonel von Lossberg presented the soft-Flanders-earth theory. After General Jodl had dismissed his reasons for releasing the panzers, Lossberg took the issue directly to General Wilhelm Keitel, chief of OKW.

"He answered that he could not but approve of Hitler's decision as the ground in Flanders was too marshy for the panzers and that Göring would be able to finish the job by himself."[14] Winston Churchill reinforced this idea by quoting Halder: "It is most likely that Keitel, who was for a considerable time in Flanders in the First World War, had originated these ideas by his tales."[15] There was little reality to the fears. Panzer leaders on the spot rejected

Wilhelm Keitel, chief of staff of the OKW. Keitel, a toady of Hitler's who blindly carried out all of the führer's orders, endorsed halting the German assault based on the false idea that panzers would sink into the soft earth of Flanders.

this as a reason. They knew how to avoid wet spots. And the tanks mostly ran right down the all-weather roads anyway.

The idea that Hitler wanted to save the BEF was floated by a number of postwar writers, notably by Günther Blumentritt to Basil H. Liddell Hart. The concept was that Britain would be so grateful that it would agree to a peace with Germany. Blumentritt described a conversation with Hitler, Rundstedt, Sodenstern, and himself at Army Group A on May 24. Hitler said he wished to conclude a reasonable peace with France, and then the way would be free for an agreement with Britain. He expressed admiration for Britain. "He said that all he wanted from Britain was that she should acknowledge Germany's position on the Continent," Blumentritt told Liddell Hart.[16]

If indeed saving the BEF was in Hitler's mind—and there is immense doubt whether he ever truly entertained this thought—allowing the British army to escape was precisely the opposite way of getting peace. It would encourage the British in their resistance. Churchill and the other British leaders were well aware that, if Britain signed a peace with Hitler, it would become nothing more than a junior partner in a vast new demarcation of spheres of influence. This would spell the end of Britain and its empire as an independent entity, and would never be entered into willingly. The only way Hitler could get British acquiescence would be by extreme force.

On June 4, Winston Churchill rose to speak in the House of Commons. He closed his address with these words that inspired the world:

> We shall go on to the end, we shall fight in France, we shall fight in the seas and oceans, we shall fight with growing confidence and growing strength in the air; we shall defend our island, whatever the cost may be, we shall fight on the beaches, we shall fight on the landing-grounds, we shall fight in the

Hitler examines a damaged enemy tank in France.

fields and in the streets, we shall fight in the hills; we shall *never* surrender, and even if, which I do not for a moment believe, this island or a large part of it were subjugated and starving, then our empire beyond the seas, armed and guarded by the British fleet, would carry on the struggle, until, in God's good time, the New World, with all its power and might, steps forth to the rescue and the liberation of the Old.

In the United States, strong emotions were stirring. As early as June 1, 1940, President Roosevelt sent out queries as to what weapons the military could spare for Britain. General George C. Marshall, army chief of staff, brought back an answer in forty-eight hours—half a million .30-caliber rifles, 250 cartridges for each rifle, 900 75mm field guns with a million rounds, 80,000 machine guns, and various other items. On June 3, army depots and arsenals started packing the matériel for shipment. By the end of the week, 600 heavily loaded freight cars were rolling toward the army docks at Raritan, New Jersey. On June 11, a dozen British merchant ships began loading the war matériel.

"It was a supreme act of faith and leadership for the United States to deprive itself of this very considerable mass of arms for the sake of a country which many deemed already beaten," Churchill wrote. "It never had need to repent of it."[17]

With victory over France nearly complete, a German soldier inspects a plundered portable record player and a bottle of champagne.

CHAPTER 12

THE FALL OF FRANCE

The end in France came swiftly. In three weeks, the Germans had captured a million prisoners, while suffering 60,000 casualties. The Belgian and Dutch armies had been eliminated, and the French had lost 30 divisions, nearly a third of their total strength, and this the best and most mobile part. They had also lost the assistance of nine British divisions, now back in Britain, with nearly all of their equipment lost. Only one British infantry division, a third of an armored division, and rear-echelon troops remained in France south of the Somme.

General Weygand was left with 66 divisions, most of them understrength, to hold a front along the Somme, the Aisne, and a Maginot Line that was longer than the original. He committed 49 divisions to defend the rivers, leaving 17 to shield the Maginot Line. Most of the mechanized divisions had been lost or badly shattered. On the other hand, the Germans quickly brought their ten panzer divisions back to strength and deployed 130 infantry divisions, only a few of which had been engaged.

The German high command reorganized the *Schnell Truppen*, or fast troops, combining armored divisions and motorized divisions in a new type of panzer corps, with one motorized and two armored divisions to each corps.[1]

OKH promoted Guderian to command a new panzer group

of two panzer corps, and ordered him to drive from Rethel on the Aisne to the Swiss frontier. Kleist kept two panzer corps to strike south from bridgeheads over the Somme at Amiens and Péronne, but these later shifted eastward to reinforce Guderian's drive. The remaining armored corps, under Hermann Hoth, was to advance between Amiens and the sea.

Weygand had been able to use the short pause while the German army shifted south to strengthen the line of the Somme and the Aisne (the Weygand Line). Once this line was breached, however, there was nothing behind it that could be held and no reserves to close any breaches. Weygand told the French premier Paul Reynaud that a retreat from the Somme and Aisne and total defeat of the French army were more or less the same.

Weygand was proposing only the standard French solution: a continuous front, the same system that had failed so signally already. He made just one tactical change. Instead of a continuous line, he set up a system of small defensive circles or "hedgehogs" of strongpoints in natural obstacles, mainly villages and forests along the Somme and Aisne and south of both rivers. These hedgehogs, armed with 75mm guns as antitank protection, would be capable of being defended on all sides even when they were surrounded or bypassed.

Unfortunately, the spaces between the hedgehogs were neither effectively covered by artillery fire nor blocked by mines. They were generally too far from one another to be mutually supportive. They were provided with insufficient armor or none at all to sweep the gaps. It was impossible to supply them. Thus, they could be quickly surrounded, and would be likely to fall to the enemy one after another. This type of defense could be effective only for a short period.

Newly minted brigadier general Charles de Gaulle, the undersecretary of state for war in Reynaud's government, protested Weygand's plan vehemently: "We should not be content with organizing a single line of defense on the Somme, another linear

A column of German infantry passes through a French town under the gaze of civilians.

battle, in the 1918 style. We should give up the idea of a continuous line and use maneuver, and only maneuver."

De Gaulle proposed that Weygand take the 1,200 tanks France still possessed, and divide them into two groups, with two or three infantry divisions and powerful artillery in each. One group, de Gaulle said, should be placed north of Paris and the other south of Reims in order to operate against the flanks of the German armored corps when they broke through the French positions. Even if the Germans could defeat these armored forces, it would be a battle instead of a collapse.

Weygand ignored de Gaulle's proposals. Neither he nor any of his senior generals were capable of conducting a war of maneuver. In any case, de Gaulle's plan could be only a stopgap solution. The only effective antitank ditch left to France was the Mediterranean Sea.

Evacuations could have been started on May 25 to take troops to North Africa, and continue the war from there. Such evacuations, if done swiftly while the Germans were finishing up destruction of the northern cauldron, would have transformed the whole outlook of the war. Without this strategic withdrawal, France would have to accept an armistice soon after the front along the Somme and Aisne was breached.

The ousted supreme commander, General Gamelin, wrote: "We could not expect to hold central France for any length of time. Two solutions were therefore open to us: giving up the struggle, i.e., an armistice, or a withdrawal to our empire. The second alternative was the only one worthy of France, but we had to prepare for it at once, to prepare bridgeheads and strongpoints covering our ports, and to start evacuating."[2]

But this was not done, and it was never seriously considered by the French government or the military.

As the German forces were concentrating for the final campaign (designated *Fall Rot,* or Case Red), General Weygand informed the government that the army could only fight for its honor, and it was the job of the politicians to find a way to end the war. Both Weygand and Marshal Pétain maintained that the entry of France into the war had been an irresponsible and frivolous political decision. The army, they said, should be spared from being the last sacrifice, since it was the guarantor of the inner order of the state and thus was indispensable.

Reynaud worked against the pessimism of the military, and had an ally in Churchill. He came to Paris on May 31 and emphasized Britain's readiness to continue the war, even if the Germans were able to make a successful landing in England.

Churchill pressed Reynaud's government to resolve that, whatever happened to metropolitan France, its empire and its fleet must hold to the joint British-French alliance. Churchill saw the war as a global conflict between democratic states like Britain and

Premier Reynaud greets
Churchill in Paris on
May 31, just as British
and French forces are
frantically evacuating
from Dunkirk.

France and the totalitarian aspiration to world dominance by the German dictator, with his expected allies, Italy and Japan. Victory, Churchill said, would come from the economic power of the British and French empires and ultimately from the United States.

Reynaud endorsed Churchill's view, and insisted that the war had to be carried on from the French colonies in North Africa—Morocco, Algeria, and Tunisia. But neither Reynaud nor Churchill could convince the French politicians. And time was growing short. Meantime, bitterness was waxing over the behavior of Britain—especially its rush to evacuate the BEF—and its inadequate military contributions. This bitterness was especially strong in the French military leadership. Pétain, already working for an armistice, disputed Churchill's right to join in the debate over the fate of France.

The French battle line was tremendously unbalanced. The Maginot Line was a solidly manned front, but the unfortified span between Montmédy and the mouth of the Somme was much less so, and it grew weaker as it went westward. Density of troops in the east was adequate, one infantry division per six miles of front. It was fairly satisfactory in the center, one infantry division per nine miles of front. But it was less so on the Somme, nine to ten miles per division, where there were few obstacles to passage over the river.

The German attack plan envisioned a three-step operation. Fedor von Bock's Army Group B was to break through the Weygand Line in the west. After that Gerd von Rundstedt's Army Group A was to destroy the French masses in Champagne. Finally, Wilhelm von Leeb's Army Group C had the task of speeding up the collapse of the Maginot Line, and hindering the withdrawal of its defenders.

The first attack began on June 5, 1940, only a day after the fall of Dunkirk by the assault of Panzer Corps Hoth. The French put up fierce resistance south of Amiens. But around Abbeville, Erich von Manstein's infantry 38th Corps tore open a break. Together the two corps split the 10th Army (Marie-Robert Altmayer) and on the third day crossed the Seine at Rouen and its vicinity.

Rundstedt launched his attack on June 9. Guderian broke out on both sides of Rethel, and kept going. Since this penetration was so successful, Kleist's Panzer Group was switched over to reinforce it.[3]

The first, and most decisive, breakthrough was made, not surprisingly, by Erwin Rommel's Ghost Division, the 7th Panzer.[4]

Hoth's 15th Panzer Corps was assigned the sector from Amiens to Abbeville. Rommel's portion was midway between these two cities, at Hangest. Here there was a flat and marshy stretch of about a mile between the 7th Division's position on the north bank of the Somme, and the French position on the slopes south of the river. Across this stretch ran two railway lines, carried on two separate bridges over the river, then on raised embankments along the soft riverside meadows, and finally over the Hangest–Longpré road by two more bridges.

The French had blown the highway bridges over the Somme at Hangest and nearby Longpré, but not the two railway bridges, nor even the two railway bridges that ran over the Hangest–Longpré road. Why the French failed to break these bridges is not known. But Rommel, seeing they were intact when he moved up, kept the bridges under constant artillery and machine-gun fire to deter any belated attempt to blow them up.

Early on the morning of June 5, 1940, while the 7th Panzer's artillery opened a barrage on the slopes just south of the river, the division's 6th Rifle Regiment crossed the bridges on foot, and Rommel's engineers went to work unbolting the rails and clearing away the sleepers on one of the bridges, leaving a solid structural surface underneath that could support his tanks and vehicles. Rommel left his signals vehicle on the north bank, with orders that it was to be the first vehicle over the river, then walked across himself. The vehicle and the first tanks of the 25th Panzer Regiment crossed at six a.m. It was an astonishingly easy transit, made more so by the ineffectual resistance on the south bank by two regiments of Senegalese troops of the 5th Colonial Division. The division's artillery was not in position, and served as no deterrent.

Rommel drove forward in his signals vehicle to a grain field where he could observe the advance of the rifle regiment. A French soldier's head suddenly appeared out of the standing grain in front of Rommel, then disappeared. Rommel's orderly went forward and found the Frenchman, who had been wounded. Close by were other wounded soldiers, and some dead. The barrage had dealt heavily with the enemy positions.

As Colonel Karl Rothenburg, commander of the panzer regiment, prepared to swing around a low elevation and strike for the village of Le Quesnoy (Quesnoy-sur-Airaines), five miles south of the river, all traffic stopped on the bridge. A Panzer IV had shed a track and was blocking passage. It took half an hour before the tank could be pulled and pushed across the bridge.

A whole panzer battalion was launched against Hangest, a mile and a half east of the bridge, to eliminate a worrisome enemy force there. The tankers' orders were merely to shoot up the place, and leave it for an engineer company being sent forward to clean out the village. The tanks did their job, then turned up a steep hill right above the village. Nearly every tank in the battalion got stuck. As Rommel observed, the route "was not very well chosen." When the crews got out of their tanks, machine guns in Hangest opened up on them, causing a number of casualties.

Rommel quickly sent a detachment of self-propelled guns to bombard the outskirts of Hangest and stop the fire. But this did not work, and Rommel was forced to detail his motorcycle battalion to go in on foot. As he was giving his orders, machine-gun fire from the village rattled against the armor plate of his signals vehicle, doing no damage. But an NCO in an armored truck just behind was slow in getting down, and was seriously wounded. Only after the motorcycle battalion assaulted the westernmost houses of the village one by one was the fire at last halted.

As the division was forming up to move south toward Le Quesnoy, French artillery at last found the range and began heavy bombardment of the entire crossing site. Though casualties were light, the effect on morale was great. About the same time, Rommel learned that the 5th Panzer Division would not make its scheduled assault crossing of the Somme nearby until four p.m., and that the 2nd Motorized Division, now part of Hoth's corps, had gained only 2,000 yards of ground at its crossing site. Rommel decided that 7th Panzer had to get out of this bombardment zone fast, and he ordered the attack to proceed.

He told 25th Panzer Regiment to set out straight for Le Quesnoy, while his recce battalion was to protect the panzers' rear and flanks, and to open fire on all suspicious woods on either side along the route. The infantry was to bring up the rear of the column. The artillery and flak battalions were to cover the division as it started forward, then leapfrog forward behind the moving attack.

Here was a vivid example of the German practice of leading from the front. Rommel was able to ascertain the situation with his own eyes and from the direct reports of the troops who were engaged. He could give his orders verbally, and his officers were able to move off at once. This was in total contrast to the long and labored method of command in the French army.

As part of Weygand's hedgehog defense system, the Senegalese troops were dug into the woods on the slopes of two small hills (116 and 104) between which the road ran to Le Quesnoy. They were armed with field guns and antitank guns. However, Rommel told the panzers and the recce battalion to pour hails of fire into both woods as they passed. This fire caused the colonial troops to withhold their own fire, so passage of the division was unhindered.

In the northern outskirts of Le Quesnoy a fierce battle developed. The enemy had installed themselves skillfully around the edges of the village as another hedgehog. Around the Château du Quesnoy on the edge of the village, held by a battalion of Senegalese troops, stones had been wrenched out all along the thick walls to make loopholes from which machine guns and antitank guns poured fire into the oncoming tanks. But the rapid fire of the tanks, especially the 75mm shells of the Panzer IVs, forced the enemy to stop firing. While one battalion of tanks moved around Le Quesnoy on the west, Rothenburg passed the main body of tanks alongside the wall of the château, and kept going. The armored cars, following behind, held the enemy in check long enough for the infantry to pass by as well.

In this fashion the whole division got through Le Quesnoy without having to assault either the château or the other defended places in the village. These could be left to troops coming after. The division emerged on a wide and open plain to the south.

Rommel ordered the division to keep on going, right through fields of growing wheat and barley. Any enemy troops sighted were either wiped out or forced to withdraw. Large numbers of colonial troops were brought in as prisoners, many of them hopelessly drunk.

The division's objective for the day was the country east of Hornoy, 14 miles south of the Somme. Accordingly, Rommel ordered the attack to continue through Montagne-Fayel and Camps-en-Amiénois, three and six miles south of Le Quesnoy, respectively. The panzers destroyed a large concentration of enemy troops in the Bois de Riencourt as they passed. Numerous saddled horses stampeded riderless across the plain. At last heavy artillery fire from the southwest began to land on the division, but was unable to stop the advance. Rommel had spread out his whole division over a broad front and in great depth. Tanks, flak guns, field guns, all with infantry mounted on them, raced across the open country.

A radio message from corps warned 7th Panzer to avoid Montagne-Fayel because an attack by Stuka dive-bombers was

Surrendered French Senegalese colonial troops, some wounded, are escorted to the rear by a German soldier.

scheduled on it. Rommel immediately gave orders by radio for the division to stop and all units to dig in where they were. The enemy took advantage of the halt to launch heavy fire from the west. Enemy tanks put in an appearance, but they were soon disposed of either by high-velocity 88mm antiaircraft guns or by tank fire. Rommel then brought up all of his field artillery and shelled enemy territory from where the artillery fire was coming. This, Rommel recounted, "took away their taste for attack."

During the night one antiaircraft battery lost a couple 88mm guns from strikes by French artillery. But by nine a.m. on June 6, action had quieted down, and Rommel was able to get his regimental and battalion commanders together to plan the day's operations.

Rommel did a remarkable thing. In order to avoid the defensive hedgehogs in the villages and the woods, and to keep away from expected blocks on the main roads, he formed the entire division in extended order over a 2,000-meter front and at a depth of several miles. He directed the division to roll over the open country. With the panzer regiment once more leading the way, the whole division moved as if on an exercise. "In this formation," Rommel wrote, "we advanced up hill and down dale, over highways and byways straight across country. The vehicles stood up to it well, even those which were not meant for cross-country work. With the tanks clashing every so often with enemy forces, the attack moved forward slowly enough for the infantry to follow up and maintain close contact."

The panzer regiment crossed the Caulières–Eplessier road, twenty miles beyond the Somme, without fighting. Immense dust clouds could be seen in the rear, a sign that the infantry troop carriers were coming up in the same extended formation.

On the morning of June 7 at Eplessier, Rommel had a brief meeting with Hermann Hoth, the corps commander, who gave Rommel permission to thrust forward at full speed. He and Hoth drove up to Hill 184 beyond Eplessier to view the terrain ahead. There Rommel had another brief discussion with panzer commander Rothenburg, and stressed the main points to be observed during the day's advance—avoidance of villages, most of which were barricaded, and avoidance of all main roads.

"The advance went straight across country," Rommel recounted, "over roadless and trackless fields, uphill, downhill, through hedges, fences, and high grain fields. The route taken by the tanks was so chosen that the less cross-country-worthy vehicles of the 37th Reconnaissance Battalion and the rifle regiments could follow in their track prints.

"We met no enemy troops, apart from a few stragglers, but plenty of indications in the shape of military vehicles and horses standing in open country that they had left shortly before our arrival. Four French soldiers were picked up near Feuquières. One of them, in spite of being severely wounded, maintained his fire on our tanks right up to close quarters. Fleeing civilians, and also

To avoid defended villages and roadblocks, Rommel spread out his 7th Panzer Division over a front of two thousand meters and a depth of several miles. Here they are seen advancing straight across country toward the Seine River and Rouen in early June 1940.

troops, were on all the roads. Sometimes we even surprised refugee lorries in open country, their occupants, men, women and children, underneath the vehicles, where they had crawled in mortal fear. We shouted to them, as we passed, to go back home."

From Bazancourt, 28 miles northeast of Rouen, the way led first along paths in the fields and then straight across country to the hills of Menerval, five miles to the northwest and 45 miles beyond the Somme, which the panzers reached at five thirty p.m.

"In farms which we passed," Rommel wrote, "the people were hastily packing up, throwing bedding out of upper story windows into the yards, and would soon have been on the road if we had not arrived. In other farms carts stood packed high and ready harnessed; in others again women and children took to their heels on sighting us and all our shouting could not persuade them to return home."

Rommel now drove to a panzer company that had been ordered to push into the wooded country near Forges-les-Eaux west of Saumont, some eight miles northwest of Menerval. By the time Rommel arrived, the company had picked up 40 vehicles and was stopping traffic in both directions. The company also had captured a large ammunition depot nearby, 100 trucks, and 300 prisoners, including the supply staff of a French army corps.

The news that the Germans had seized Forges-les-Eaux was shattering to the government in Paris. Many thousands of Parisians knew this pleasant, sleepy, old-fashioned watering place on the road to Dieppe, and only 40 kilometers northeast of Rouen. Its capture brought the immediacy of danger to the people of Paris. The growing apprehension was being fed by flights of cars and vehicles of all types from regions north of the capital.[5]

On this day, June 7, Rommel had swept forward more than 30 miles, a thrust that split the French 10th Army, defending the sector from Amiens to the sea. This move isolated the 9th Corps with four French divisions and the British 51st (Highland) Division on the coastal flank, and sent it in retreat toward the sea at St. Valéry-en-Caux, 50 miles southwest of Abbeville.

The Andelle River was being held, thinly, by British troops. To meet the emergency caused by the German breakthrough, an improvised force of nine infantry battalions, made up of rear-echelon troops, the "Beauman" Division under Brigadier A. B. Beauman, had been hastily stretched along a 60-mile line from Dieppe to the Seine, to cover Rouen. It had no artillery and few antitank guns. But portions of the British 1st Armoured Division, refitting in the rear, scraped together a brigade of 90 tanks to support the center of the line.

But Rommel struck the eastern sector around Rouen, where there were no British or French tanks. On the morning of June 8, Rommel pushed toward a point a few miles from Rouen. There he planned to mount an artillery bombardment to feign a direct attack on the city. Meanwhile the mass of 7th Panzer would switch 11 miles to the southwest and seize by a coup de main two bridges at a loop of the Seine River at Elbeuf. This would open the region south of the Seine to swift occupation.

To force the pace, Rommel took personal command of the leading battalion. All went quietly until the advance reached Sigy, on the Andelle River, eight miles west of Menerval, where the lead panzer company met British fire. During the brief engagement, the British blew up the bridge over the river. Rommel searched for a ford to get the tanks across, and found one a few hundred yards south of the village. Although the water was about three feet deep, the first tanks crossed without difficulty. But the engine cut out on the first Panzer II to cross, and it blocked all other vehicles. German soldiers threw pieces from the demolished bridge and cut willows from the banks to improve the passage, while a Panzer III that had already crossed came back and towed the Panzer II out of the water.

Just at that moment Rommel received a wireless message that

German soldiers move into a French town.

a recce troop had seized intact railway and road bridges at Normanville, only a couple miles downstream. Rommel immediately switched the vehicles to Normanville, and struck out straight for Rouen.

Once more Rommel directed his panzers and other vehicles to avoid all villages and main roads, and to drive across country. About eight p.m. a panzer company seized a crossroads five miles east of Rouen to provide protection for the artillery and flak units that were to come up and launch a long-range barrage. But the artillery and flak units had gotten involved in a firefight at a village along the way. Just before total darkness the guns finally arrived, and started the decoy attack.

Rommel now drove off quickly for Elbeuf with the panzer regiment and motorcycle battalion. It was totally dark. While crossing the main road near the village of Boos, just east of Rouen, an enemy antitank gun fired on the column from a distance of only a hundred meters. The panzer crews didn't notice and didn't hear the blasts above the roar of their engines. Fortunately for the panzers, the gun, although it fired about fifteen times, did not hit a single tank.

The Germans had great difficulty finding the way in the dark with their inadequate maps. The noise of their passage wakened people in the villages, and brought them rushing into the streets. They were sure the tanks were British, and were deeply disappointed to find they were German.

The tanks finally rolled close to Elbeuf. Rommel stopped the column and sent the motorcycle battalion, reinforced by five Panzer IIIs, ahead to storm the bridges before they could be blown, and to hold them for the panzers.

Rommel waited for a long time to get news of the storming parties. But it never came. At last, around two a.m. on June 9, Rommel gave up and started for Elbeuf with the panzers. The situation was getting dangerous. He did not want to have his panzer regiment standing in a column in the Seine valley when day broke. It would become a tremendous target for French artillery.

In Elbeuf, Rommel found wild confusion. Vehicles blocked the narrow streets. Rommel went forward on foot to find the storming parties, which had not yet done their job. They gave no valid reason for their failure. Rommel decided there still might be a chance, and he told the battalion commander to launch assaults at once. But the storming parties never reached the bridges. The French blew both spans before they had gone a hundred meters. Further heavy detonations sounded to the east and west, as the French blew all the bridges over the Seine in this sector.

Rommel was extremely angry. The only thing to do was to retreat out of the narrow peninsula. As day broke, the Seine valley was shrouded in mist that shielded the panzers as they retraced their path.

Rouen meanwhile fell to the 5th Panzer Division, which was following in the wake of 7th Panzer. Late in the afternoon of June 9, corps told Rommel to prepare to strike for the coast to cut off two or three French and British divisions trying to escape through the port of Le Havre. On the morning of June 10, a French-speaking German officer interpreted a report by a civilian who said he had left Le Havre at five a.m. He said that on the previous day he had seen only a few British soldiers in cafés, but no formations or units. Rommel concluded that the civilian was reliable, so there was no need to occupy Le Havre.

Shortly afterward a radio signal informed Rommel that a powerful enemy motorized force was moving out of the forest north of Saint-Saëns, 20 miles northeast of Rouen, and was heading to Yvetot, 25 miles west. Rommel ordered the recce battalion, already sent toward Yvetot, to block the Saint-Saëns–Yvetot road. Rommel also sent a heavy and a light flak battery toward Yvetot at top speed. Meantime, the panzer regiment set out for the town behind the flak batteries.

When the panzers reached Yvetot about ten thirty a.m., Rommel found that the recce battalion had already stopped the enemy column. It was men of the French 31st Division, with some British troops attached, who were supposed to embark from the port of Fécamp, east of Le Havre, that afternoon. The enemy column was quickly broken up, while the vanguard of 7th Panzer moved on at high speed along the one road in this area that accessed the sea, 18 miles away. Rommel and his signals section drove on ahead of the panzers through Les Petites Dalles down to the water, ten miles east of Fécamp.

"We climbed out of our vehicles and walked down the shingle beach to the water's edge," Rommel reported. "Close behind, Rothenburg came up in his command tank, and drove down to the water. Our task was over and the enemy's road to Le Havre and Fécamp was closed."

The recce battalion reported enemy pressure on the hill east of Fécamp. By the time Rommel arrived, the battalion had already captured a coast defense artillery battery there. From this elevated position Rommel could see that the town and harbor were empty of enemy troops and ships. His troops pushed to the hills south of town, and sealed off enemy access to the port.

The next day, June 11, the division moved along the coast to St. Valéry-en-Caux, 18 miles east of Fécamp, and 20 miles west of Dieppe. A few miles west of St. Valéry, 7th Panzer met heavy artillery and antitank fire, forcing it to veer off to the southeast. But the fire grew in violence, and all movement was stopped. Rommel used every lull in the fire to drive closer to St. Valéry. On the main road just west of the town the British had built a fortified line, and resistance was heavy. Meanwhile 25th Panzer Regiment pushed forward to high ground that overlooked St. Valéry just west of the town, and was using every gun to prevent the embarkation of enemy troops. Rommel drove up and could see British troops moving around the port.

Members of Rommel's staff tried to convince the nearby defenders to give up, and were able to persuade about a thousand to surrender. Most were French, and only a few British.

Among the British was a naval officer who had been lecturing his men on the mole of the port and succeeded in dissuading them from surrendering. The Germans finally opened up on this officer with machine guns from a cliff 200 meters away, but did not hit him. For half an hour he lay as if dead behind a heap of stones, but then finally decided to surrender. He spoke fluent German, and when an officer of Rommel's staff berated him for allowing so many of his men to be wounded, the officer replied: "Would you have acted differently?" This officer was Commander R. F. Elkins, naval liaison with the 51st (Highland) Division. He did not long remain a prisoner. He escaped four days later and was back in England by the end of June 1940.

That evening, Rommel sent several prisoners into St. Valéry to call on the garrison to surrender by nine p.m. and to march under cover of white flags to the hills west of town. The British and French turned down all idea of capitulation, and sent the negotiators back empty-handed. They kept their troops hard at work building barricades and bringing guns into position. It was evident to Rommel that the British were planning to resume embarkation of troops that night.

In these circumstances, Rommel ordered his tanks and recce battalion to open a strong barrage at nine p.m. A Panzer IV smashed a strong barricade on the mole where numerous guns were in position. Fires were soon blazing everywhere around the town. But the British did not yield.

Early the next morning, June 12, Rommel received reports that British troops were attempting to make their way out in small boats under cover of warships to a number of transports standing offshore. At ten a.m. two 88mm guns of an antiaircraft battery were lost by direct hits of a British warship's guns. About a thousand meters northeast of St. Valéry a British transport was just putting out to sea. The 88mm battery had ceased fire, but Rommel ordered one of the 88s to reopen fire. It no longer was standing stable on its four feet, but the gunners nevertheless were able to drop shells near the ship. The unstable footing prevented the gunners from making precise range corrections, however. Meanwhile the 88 came under fire from a British auxiliary cruiser lying a thousand meters offshore. Rommel ordered a smoke screen that hid the 88, but it was unable to hit the British transport, which got away.

Shortly afterward, Rommel directed a forward observer with a 100mm howitzer battery to take the auxiliary cruiser under fire. Rounds from this weapon set the ship afire and forced the crew to beach it.

Rommel now ordered the panzer regiment to advance into the western part of St. Valéry. Rommel came along on foot beside the tanks with Colonel Rothenburg and an aide. They reached the western mole of the inner harbor without fighting. A hundred meters away on the opposite side of the mole stood a number of British and French soldiers. They were irresolute, their rifles grounded. Nearby were a number of guns that had been damaged in the previous bombardment. Rommel and other officers tried to persuade the enemy troops to lay down their arms and walk across a narrow bridge to the Germans. It was some time before the British could bring themselves to do it.

While the panzers were moving around the southern side of the harbor toward the eastern part of town, Rommel followed his infantry across a narrow bridge into the market square. The infantry cleaned up the town street by street and house by house.

Shortly afterward an NCO told Rommel that a high-ranking French general had been taken prisoner on the eastern side of town, and was asking to see Rommel. Soon French general Marcel Ihler, commander of 9th Corps, appeared, and declared he was ready to surrender his force of five divisions, including two brigades of the British 51st (Highland) Division.

During the next few hours, twelve generals were brought in as prisoners, including Major General Victor Fortune, commander of the 51st Division. The 7th Panzer captured 46,000 men at St. Valéry, including 8,000 British.[6]

That night Rommel wrote his wife, Lucie-Maria, living at Wie-

ner Neustadt, Austria: "Dearest Lu: The battle is over here. Today one corps commander and four division commanders presented themselves before me in the market square of St. Valéry, having been forced by my division to surrender. Wonderful moments!"

The breakthrough of Rommel's 7th Panzer Division, followed by other advances to the lower Seine, led to swift decisions in Paris. Marshal Pétain, now vice premier, asked General Weygand on June 8 how long he thought the front along the Somme and Aisne could hold. Three days, he responded. "What do you expect to do, then?" Pétain asked. "Push the government to request an armistice," Weygand answered.[7]

The next day, June 9, Premier Paul Reynaud told Pétain that no honorable terms could be expected from Hitler, and it would be imprudent to separate from Britain. But Pétain scoffed. "The British have got us into this situation," he said. French interests should take precedence over British. When Weygand arrived soon thereafter, he said the army was fighting its last battle. If this battle was lost, the army would be broken into fragments and destroyed.

Reynaud proposed that the remaining French forces withdraw swiftly into the Breton peninsula of Brittany, and continue the fight from there. Weygand didn't like the idea, and said French forces were in no condition to withdraw into a Breton redoubt. The meeting broke up with no decisions. But Pétain immediately departed for Nitray, a château near Montrichard on the Cher River, a tributary to the Loire River in central France.

Meanwhile anxiety was sweeping Paris. While Rommel was driving toward Rouen and the Seine, there were reports that other German troops were almost in the suburbs. Special trains, 45 for passengers and 14 for archives, had been moving since June 6 on orders from Reynaud that all ministries inessential to battle were to retire to various towns and villages along the Loire that had been earmarked previously. This order created chaos in the capital, made worse by the failure of Weygand to say whether Paris was to become a battlefield or be declared an open city.

The government abandoned its offices in Paris on the afternoon and evening of June 10. Reynaud started off for Chissay near Montrichard on the Cher. En route at Orléans a message was waiting that Churchill wanted to meet with him and Weygand the following day. Reynaud turned off to Weygand's new headquarters, the Château du Muguet, near Briare, on the Loire about 60 kilometers southeast of Orléans. Churchill's party included Anthony Eden, his secretary of state for war; General Sir John Dill, who had replaced General Ironside as chief of the Imperial General Staff; and Churchill's representative to the French government, Major General Sir Edward Spears. Waiting on June 11 at the château were Reynaud, Weygand, Pétain, and de Gaulle.

The meeting brought no final answers. Churchill told the French leaders that Britain intended to fight on no matter what happened. He spoke of new British forces now reaching France, but it was clear they could make only a tiny contribution. Churchill expressed his strong desire that the French fleet should not be allowed to fall into German hands. Weygand's account was discouraging. There was nothing to prevent the enemy from reaching Paris, he said. He had no reserves. There were vague references to a Breton redoubt, but no agreement.

The next morning, General Georges, northeastern front commander, came over from his new offices near the Briare train station to say good-bye to Churchill. The battle, he said, was almost over and an armistice was inevitable.

That evening, the French leaders met again. Both Weygand and Pétain said an armistice was necessary. De Gaulle, on the other hand, pressed for a Breton redoubt. But Admiral François Darlan, the navy chief, had already declared such a bastion to be untenable without heavy aircraft protection, which was not likely to be forthcoming.

Marshal Henri-Philippe Pétain (*left*) meets with Admiral François Darlan. This photo was taken in January 1940.

Meanwhile on June 10, the Italian dictator Benito Mussolini brought Italy into the war against France, and Britain reciprocally declared war on Italy. Mussolini's armies did practically nothing, but United States president Franklin D. Roosevelt, speaking at commencement that day at the University of Virginia in Charlottesville, enunciated the disgust of the democratic world when he said: "The hand that held the dagger has struck it into the back of its neighbor." Roosevelt reversed his usual emphasis on avoiding American involvement in the war and promised to extend aid "full speed ahead."

Churchill met with Reynaud again on June 13 at Tours, on the lower Loire. Reynaud asked Churchill, if France were driven to ask for an armistice, whether Britain would agree to abrogate the March 28 agreement not to seek a separate peace. Churchill answered only that if France remained in the fight with her fleet and empire, and if the Germans did not destroy Britain, the Nazis would ultimately be swept away. He said he expected assistance from the United States. Reynaud replied that this was no help. But Churchill would not release France from its agreement, and flew back to London.

That evening at a cabinet meeting, Pétain read out a denunciation of propositions to carry on the war from North Africa. For his part, he said, he would not "abandon the soil of France but would accept the suffering which will be imposed on the country and its sons. In my eyes, the armistice is a necessary condition for the survival of eternal France."

The idea of a Breton redoubt was not abandoned, but nothing was done to implement it. The decision was made to transfer the government to Bordeaux. The next morning, June 14, Reynaud set off from Tours in a car down the main road that was swarming with refugees and vehicles. It took him ten hours to reach Bordeaux, 300 kilometers away.

Meanwhile in Paris, from June 11 on, the rail stations were besieged. On this and the next days doors to the stations were closed against crowds. Many trains marked for merchandise or military were actually for evacuees. But there were not enough of them. Mobs tried to escape by car until gasoline was exhausted, then by cart, bicycle, and on foot.

Not until June 13 was the flow of refugees turned off by Weygand's announcement that Paris was to be considered an open city—that is, it would not be defended. On this day the last train from the Gare Montparnasse left for the southwest at eight thirty a.m., and eventually reached Tours by roundabout ways. But thousands did not go anywhere. Scavengers and robbers appeared. But most of those who remained closed their shutters and retired indoors to wait for the enemy.

Georg von Küchler's 18th Army broke through the Paris defenses and entered the city on June 14. The 40th Corps (Georg Stumme) passed through the city from north to south without fighting. Lieutenant Colonel Hans Speidel, who was in advance, set up the first German offices there, as General Henri-Fernand Dentz capitulated. By June 16, the advanced forces reached Orléans and the Loire.

On the western wing, while Rommel's 7th Panzer was taking the surrender of thousands of French and British at St. Valéry, the remainder of 4th Army (Günther von Kluge) crossed over the Seine and kept going. On the left wing panzers of Ewald von Kleist and Heinz Guderian passed through Dijon and Besançon, almost to the Swiss frontier, and continued on toward the Rhône River valley. The 41st Corps (Hans Reinhardt) cut the communications of the Maginot Line. This line had been attacked by Army Group C (Wilhelm von Leeb) from the front. In the north, the 1st Army (Erwin von Witzleben) drove on Château Salines. Around Alt-Breisach the point of the 7th Army (Friedrich Dollmann) gained the west bank of the Rhine and the fortifications of Colmar. There was little resistance by any French forces anywhere.

On June 14, the day that Paris fell, the Soviet government of Joseph Stalin commenced collecting its spoils, as part of its pact with Germany in August 1939. It issued an ultimatum to Lithuania, and, over the next few days, to Latvia and Estonia, and quickly annexed these Baltic states. A few days later it demanded cession by Romania of Bessarabia (Moldova) and northern Bukovina. There was nothing anyone could do to save these regions from Soviet tyranny.

Abandoned British and French
equipment scattered on the beach at
Dunkirk after the evacuation ended.
This photo was taken by the Germans
in June 1940.

CHAPTER 13

ARMISTICE AT COMPIÈGNE

On the evening of May 30, 1940, Lieutenant General Alan Brooke, commander of 2nd Corps of the BEF, went down on the beach at Dunkirk, and was carried in an open boat to a destroyer, along with his military assistant, Lieutenant Colonel Ronald Stanyforth, and his aide-de-camp, Captain A. K. (Barney) Charlesworth.[1]

Fifty-seven years old, reared in France, and speaking the language like a native, Brooke had won distinction for getting the BEF to Dunkirk after the Belgian collapse opened a gaping hole in the Allied line. The War Office considered him invaluable for the future of the British army, and decided it was imperative to get him out of the cauldron. Brooke selected one of his division commanders, Major General Bernard Law Montgomery, to take over the corps and complete its evacuation.

The destroyer waited for five hours at anchor. It was a nerveracking evening for Brooke. The harbor was repeatedly visited by German bombers, and he watched the crash of numerous bombs on the sea and the continuous firing of antiaircraft guns. The day before, he had witnessed a Stuka dive-bomber score a direct hit on a destroyer amidships. The bomb had penetrated into the ammunition magazines. There was a terrific explosion and a column of smoke mushroomed over the ship. As the smoke cleared, the destroyer had completely disappeared.

Lieutenant General Alan Brooke, commander of 2nd Corps of the BEF.

The destroyer carrying Brooke got under way shortly after midnight. Less than three hours later there was a crash. Brooke felt certain the ship had hit a mine or been torpedoed. But the skipper had selected a route to avoid these dangers that was shallow at low water. He hit bottom, damaged the propeller slightly, but kept on going. The ship arrived at Dover at seven fifteen a.m. on May 31.

Brooke and party drove off to London by car. Brooke was shocked by the contrast of the peaceful Kentish countryside with the Belgian and French roads crammed with distressed and demoralized humanity, smashed houses, bombs, and aircraft that he had left only shortly before.

In London, Brooke reported to General Sir John Dill, chief of the Imperial General Staff, then caught a train down to his home at Hartley Wintney, near Farnborough in Hampshire.

General Sir John Dill became chief of the British Imperial General Staff in May and supervised the extraction of British forces from France.

"On the platform I found my wife and two children to welcome me," Brooke wrote. "It all felt like the most wonderful dream. I drove home with them where I had a nursery tea with them, after which I retired to bed and to one of the very deepest sleeps I have ever had."

On June 2, Brooke was back in the War Office and asked General Dill what he now wished him to do. "Return to France and form a new BEF," Dill answered. This, Brooke recalled later, was one of his blackest moments. "I knew only too well the state of affairs that would prevail in France from now onwards," he said.

Dill could offer few enough troops. The British forces south of the Somme were already in jeopardy, and some were going to be lost in just a few days. A modest number of units were being readied in England, and would be shipped to Cherbourg on the Cotentin Peninsula of Normandy and to Brittany shortly. Still in a black mood, Brooke went to an interview with Anthony Eden, the secretary of state for war. Eden made the mistake of asking whether Brooke was satisfied with what was being done for him.

Brooke answered that he was far from satisfied. He said the mission he was being sent on had no value and no possibility of accomplishing anything. Furthermore, he said, the army had only just escaped from a major disaster at Dunkirk, and now it was risking a second.

Brooke allowed that the mission might have some political value to give support to the French government, but he told Eden that the expedition promised no chances of military success and every probability of disaster.

Brooke and his party left Southampton on June 12 on a dirty little Dutch steamer capable of only 12 knots and with no food on board. The ship arrived at Cherbourg at nine thirty p.m., but was told by the harbormaster that it could not disembark until six a.m. the next day. At Brooke's insistence, the British officer in command at Cherbourg, Gervase Thorpe, arrived at midnight by launch and took him ashore. When Brooke reached France, he came under the orders of General Weygand.

Of the British forces in France, most of the 51st (Highland) Division had just been thrown away at St. Valéry-en-Caux. The 52nd (Lowland) Division was newly arrived. What was left of the so-called "Beauman" Division of rear-echelon troops under Brigadier A. B. Beauman and of the 1st Armoured Division had withdrawn south of the Seine River.

Meantime Churchill was meeting Premier Reynaud at Tours on June 13. Churchill saw little chance of saving the French army, but hoped to persuade the government to continue the fight in North Africa. But he returned to England knowing that powerful elements in the government were seeking a separate peace.

There had been talk about setting up an Anglo-French redoubt on the Breton peninsula, which, under cover of sea power, might hold a small corner of France. But though favored by Reynaud and de Gaulle, the idea had been dismissed by Weygand.

Early on June 13, General Brooke began a 340-mile journey from Cherbourg, first to Le Mans, the British headquarters, then to Briare, southeast of Orléans, still the headquarters of the French supreme command. The road to Le Mans was swarming with refugees. When Brooke arrived he discovered there were well over 100,000 British troops in France, along with vast dumps of supplies. Brooke told the British chiefs at Le Mans to begin immediately evacuating home all unarmed personnel.

Brooke now set off with Colonel Sir John Swayne, liaison officer with the French command, to Briare, 170 miles away. "When we arrived in the vicinity of Orléans," Brooke wrote, "we met the main stream of refugees fleeing from Paris. We had to do a long detour to avoid the town, which was a solid block of cars."

Brooke arrived at supreme headquarters at eight p.m., and was informed it was too late to see General Weygand that night. The war couldn't be allowed to interfere with Weygand's sleep. Next morning—June 14, the day the Germans entered Paris—Weygand told Brooke that the French army was disintegrating into disconnected groups. He then said that the Inter-Allied Council, the British-French group that supposedly was overseeing operations, had decided to hold a position covering Brittany east of Rennes—a subject that had never been mentioned to Brooke by the War Office. The two officers went to see General Georges, who showed him the current situation map. It depicted a line drawn in red chalk with several sausage-shaped indentations. Brooke asked what they signified. Georges answered that they were penetrations of German armored forces. He said there were no reserves. The map proved what Weygand had said: The French army was disintegrating. There was no hope of organized resistance.

Brooke now turned to the question of defending Brittany. The line Weygand called for, in front of Rennes, was 150 kilometers long from the north to the south shores of the Breton peninsula. This, Brooke said, would require at least fifteen divisions. Where would they come from? At most the British could muster four divisions, including a Canadian division now coming ashore at Brest in Brittany. Weygand said a few divisions of the 10th Army might possibly be found. Brooke responded that such a plan had no hope of success. Weygand and Georges agreed. Weygand said he had already informed the Inter-Allied Council that it was impossible, but had still been told to execute it. Therefore, Weygand said, setting up a line east of Rennes could be considered an order.

There was no hope whatsoever of holding such a line, and it was more than probable that the Germans would reach it long before the Allies could deploy forces along it. Brooke realized that immediate action was necessary to save the British forces in France. He prepared a message to be flown back at once to General Dill by Major General Sir Richard Howard-Vyse, head of the British military mission. The message read that the only course left was to stop sending any more troops and to instruct Brooke to evacuate the rest.

Brooke got back to Le Mans that afternoon, and put in a call to Dill, who told him the flow to troops to France had already been stopped. Brooke pressed for a decision to reembark all British troops at once. Dill said he would talk with Churchill, who had already told him there had been no agreement about holding a line east of Rennes, and for Brooke to ignore the order. Dill called Brooke back and told him to evacuate troops not under command of the French 10th Army.

Brooke sent orders for the Canadians who had already landed to return to Brest and reembark at once, and for the 52nd Division, less the 157th Brigade and the 3rd Armoured Brigade (of the 1st Armoured Division) with the French 10th Army, to proceed to Cherbourg and leave as soon as possible. Meanwhile all noncombat elements of the armored division, all rear-echelon troops, and any Allied soldiers trying to get away, notably some defiant Frenchmen and a large number of Poles, were to move to ports for departure at once.

Just before dinner with the commander of the 52nd Division, Major General James Drew, and his artillery commander, John Kennedy, Brooke got a call from Dill, who said he was with Churchill at 10 Downing Street and that the prime minister did not want Brooke to withdraw troops from France.

"What the hell *does* he want?" Brooke demanded.

"He wants to speak to you," Dill said, and handed the receiver over to Churchill, whom Brooke had never met nor talked to.

Churchill told Brooke he had been sent to France to make the French feel the British were supporting them. Brooke replied that it was impossible to make a corpse feel, and the French army was dead. When Churchill persisted, Brooke replied that Churchill was only throwing away good troops to no avail.

"Our talk lasted for close to half an hour," Brooke reported, "and on many occasions his arguments were so formed as to give me the impression that he considered that I was suffering from 'cold feet' because I did not wish to comply with his wishes. This was so infuriating that I was repeatedly on the verge of losing my temper. Fortunately, while I was talking to him I was looking through the window at Drew and Kennedy sitting on a garden seat under a tree. Their presence there acted as a continual reminder of the human element of the 52nd Division and of the unwarrantable decision to sacrifice them with no attainable object in view."

Finally, as Brooke was becoming exhausted, Churchill said, "All right, I agree with you."[2]

Early on June 15, Brooke was informed that Lieutenant General Sir James Marshall-Cornwall had arrived. Brooke told him to take command of British forces operating with the French 10th Army, and to direct their retreat on Cherbourg. Brooke allocated a motor transport column to render the British troops mobile.

Brooke, feeling too exposed at Le Mans, ordered his headquarters and rear-echelon forces back to Vitré, 20 miles east of Rennes. On his way to Vitré, Brooke went to the villages that elements of the Canadian division had occupied to make certain they had received orders to return to Brest and reembark. He found their rear parties just departing.

As this rush for the ports was under way, Brooke ran into a

new block from London. Dill informed him that the two brigades of the 52nd Division now in Cherbourg could not be embarked. This was entirely a political decision not to rile the French, and Brooke exploded both at Dill and at Anthony Eden. At last on June 16 London relented and allowed him to send off the two Scottish brigades. Half got away that night, and the remainder embarked the next day, June 17. But London required the 157th Brigade and the 3rd Armoured Brigade with 10th Army to remain until it began to disintegrate.

Brooke moved his headquarters once more, to Redon, north of the Breton port of St. Nazaire. By midnight on June 16, nearly 60,000 British troops had been embarked for home and port officials were hopeful of getting most of the remaining British and foreign troops away in the next twenty-four hours.

In Bordeaux on the morning of June 16, Marshal Pétain told the French government it was getting nowhere in deciding whether to transfer the war to North Africa or to ask for an armistice. He said he was resigning.

Late in the morning Premier Paul Reynaud got a message from Churchill that Britain would agree to France asking Germany for terms, if, and only if, the French fleet sailed for British ports immediately.[3] Reynaud remarked how silly this demand was. How could the French fleet quit the Mediterranean the very moment the government was being pressed by the British to go to North Africa?

A second message came in the afternoon from London. It was the duty of the French government to extricate Polish, Belgian, and Czech troops in France. Charles de Gaulle, in London to discuss plans for moving the government and troops to North Africa, called Reynaud and announced that Churchill was proposing a union between France and Britain.[4] Reynaud presented the proposal to the cabinet, but it was too much of an effort by men on the path to surrender to take up such a radical idea.

Reynaud put up for a vote a proposal to ask Germany for terms. The majority voted to do so. With that Reynaud resigned, and went to the president, Albert Lebrun, for advice. "Call Marshal Pétain," Lebrun said bitterly. "He has the majority of the cabinet with him."

Pétain accepted at once. The new government asked the Spanish ambassador to request his government to seek a cessation of hostilities and terms of peace from Germany.

Responding to the news, Churchill's representative to the French government, Major General Sir Edward Spears, told the prime minister on the phone on the night of June 16 that he did not think he could perform useful service any longer, and thought he should come home. Churchill agreed. Spears went on to say that he was anxious about the safety of General de Gaulle, and thought he should leave France. Churchill readily assented to a plan made for this.

The morning of June 17, de Gaulle went to his office in Bordeaux, made a number of engagements for the afternoon as a blind, and then drove to the airfield with his friend Spears to see him off. They shook hands and said good-bye, and as the plane began to move, de Gaulle stepped in and slammed the door. The machine soared off into the air, while the French police and officials gaped. Churchill wrote afterward: "De Gaulle carried with him, in this small airplane, the honor of France."[5]

At twelve thirty p.m. on June 17, Pétain broadcast to the nation: "Frenchmen, at the appeal of the president of the republic, I have today assumed the direction of the government of France. Convinced of the affection of our admirable army, convinced of the confidence of the whole nation, I gave myself to France to assuage her misfortune. It is with a heavy heart that I say we must end the fight. Last night I applied to our adversary to ask if he is

Marshal Pétain, a French hero of the First World War, took over the government on June 17 and immediately asked Hitler for terms.

prepared to seek with me, soldier to soldier, after the battle, honorably, the means whereby hostilities may cease."

That same evening Churchill broadcast the following statement:

The news from France is very bad, and I grieve for the gallant French people who have fallen into this terrible misfortune. Nothing will alter our feelings towards them or our faith that the genius of France will rise again. What has happened in France makes no difference to our actions and purpose. We have become the sole champions now in arms to defend the world cause. We shall do our best to be worthy of this high honor. We shall defend our island home, and with the British Empire we shall fight on unconquerable until the curse of Hitler is lifted from the brows of mankind. We are sure that in the end all will come right.

While General Brooke was moving British troops out of the ports of western France as quickly as possible, Erwin Rommel's 7th Panzer Division was bearing down on Cherbourg in hopes of capturing large elements of these forces.

After seizing St. Valéry, the division received a pause to rest and reorganize. Meanwhile the French 10th Army fell back westward, whereas the neighboring French 7th and 6th Armies retreated eastward. To exploit this split in the front, the leading German infantry corps pressed southward toward the Loire River, while the 7th Panzer was brought down behind them on June 16 and launched westward on June 17 for Cherbourg.

On the night of June 16, the 10th Army had begun a new retreat, leaving little in front of Rommel. He was eager to get going. "Air reconnaissance had reported the presence in Cherbourg of either warships or transports and it was therefore highly probable that embarkation was in progress there," he wrote.

First objective was L'Aigle, 55 miles south of Rouen and on the

— ROMMEL'S SWEEP FROM L'AIGLE TO CHERBOURG JUNE 17–19, 1940 —

25

25

0 Miles

0 Kilometers

Rouen

Elbeuf

Yvetot

Bernay

Fécamp

Seine R.

Le Havre

Lisieux

L'Aigle

F R A N C E

Trun

Falaise

Argentan

Montreuil

Caen

Flers

English Channel

Bayeux

N O R M A N D Y

Vire

St. Lô

Carentan

Coutances

Avranches

C. de la Hague

Pte. de Barfleur

St. Vaast

Querqueville

Ft. CENTRAL

Cherbourg

Ft. DU ROULE

Tonneville

Les Pieux

Sotteville

Valognes

St. Sauveur

Ste. Mère-Église

St. Sauveur-de-Pierre Pont

Bolleville

La Haye-du-Puits

Lessay

Barneville

Carteret

St. Lô d'Ourville

COTENTIN PENINSULA

Path of the 7th Panzer Division
June 17–18, 1940

Jeffrey L. Ward

eastern edge of Normandy. The division moved fast, with scarcely any obstructions. Some miles east of the town the recce battalion in advance ran into a column of French infantry. The captain in charge told Rommel through an interpreter that Marshal Pétain had proposed an armistice, and had instructed French troops to lay down their arms. Rommel answered that he had heard nothing of a cease-fire and his orders were to move on. The panzer division now ran along the road past the French column and kept going at a pace of 25 to 30 miles per hour.

The division met more French troops behind this column, and beckoned to them with white handkerchiefs, saying the war was over for them. The next villages were filled with French colonial troops. The panzers drove past at top speed, waving at the soldiers, but not otherwise bothering with them.

At five thirty p.m. the division reached Montreuil, 40 miles west of L'Aigle and 12 miles southwest of Argentan. There Rommel ordered an hour's rest for a meal and to refill fuel tanks. Since there seemed to be no worry about serious resistance, he decided to continue the advance, with Cherbourg, 130 miles away, as the objective.

He directed the rest of the journey to follow an indirect route by way of Flers—25 miles west of Argentan—to Coutances near the western coast of the Cotentin Peninsula, then north along the west coast to Barneville, then into Cherbourg from the southwest.

The division raced at top speed toward Flers. French troops were encamped on both sides of the road. The Germans waved at them as they drove by. The French stared in wonderment, but no one fired a shot. The division moved along at about 30 miles per hour, in perfect formation, through one village after another. On the western outskirts of Flers the column passed a large crowd of soldiers and civilians. Suddenly a civilian ran toward Rommel's car with a drawn revolver, intending to shoot, but French soldiers pulled him up short. The Germans rolled on.

Rommel was under no illusion that the whole division could maintain the speed of the advance, but reckoned that any laggards could catch up in a few hours. He had established a system of signs marked "DG 7" for *Durchgangstrasse* 7 or Through Route 7th Division, which was contrary to normal German practice and for which he was later taken to task. Night fell, revealing enormous fires on the right front, from gasoline and oil stores set alight at the airfield at Lessay, 30 miles north of Coutances and 34 miles south of Cherbourg.

About midnight the recce battalion in the vanguard rolled through La Haye-du-Puits, five miles north of Lessay, then turned off on the coast road to Bolleville, with Barneville a few miles beyond.

The head of the column suddenly ran up against a defended roadblock and came under heavy artillery and machine-gun fire. The leading armored cars were hit and three went up in flames. The roadblock appeared to be held by a considerable force. The moon was up and Rommel did not like the idea of attacking with tired troops and without artillery or tanks. He ordered action broken off and a wait until daybreak to move against the position.

Rommel's division had covered more than 150 miles since morning, and more than 100 miles since its early evening halt to refuel. This far exceeded any day's advance ever made in warfare.

At daybreak on June 18 Rommel drove forward with the 6th Rifle Regiment. He had already sent envoys to demand surrender of the position. The roadblock occupied a commanding spot. Shortly the envoys came back and reported that the French soldiers had no knowledge of Pétain's armistice proposal and did not believe it. Rommel sent an envoy back to tell the French soldiers that, unless they surrendered by eight a.m., he would attack.

At the appointed hour, the Germans found that the French defenders had disappeared. The Germans had to cut and drag away a barricade of poplar logs that had been placed on the bridge at a nearby stream on the road.

An hour later the leading elements of 6th Rifle Regiment in armored troop carriers moved off as vanguard toward Cherbourg.

The troops soon came under fire from a hill on the flank. German answering fire was slow to start, and, to get it going, Rommel ordered the machine-gun crew of his armored car to open into the bushes on the right of the road. At the same time, Rommel ordered a 37mm antitank gun to open on the nearest houses and bushes. While this was taking place, the first German field howitzers came into action, firing over open sights 150 yards behind the vanguard. The weight of this fire soon silenced the fire on the hill, and infantry of the rifle regiment assaulted the hill and captured it.

After this short but violent action, the column resumed its march. The pace was too slow for Rommel and he had to push the advance several times to speed it up. "The longer we took getting into Cherbourg, the more chance the enemy in the intervening territory or in the port itself had to prepare for our arrival," Rommel commented.

As the column dropped down into the valley at Barneville, the Germans could see the sea on the left and some buildings that looked like barracks. But they were unoccupied. At the entrance to the town the Germans found civilians clearing away some partially constructed roadblocks. Nowhere did the Germans have to go into action.

As the column neared Cherbourg, Rommel noted several captive balloons in the sky. Rommel was well aware of the formidable ring of forts around Cherbourg. Major construction had commenced in the 1770s, and the forts had been modernized in the last years of the nineteenth century. All the forts possessed casemated heavy cannon that could fire in all directions.

One of the forts began dropping shells on the rear of the column. The leading unit halted, though no firing had come from the front. Rommel drew up to the vanguard in his armored command car and found a strong roadblock where negotiations were in progress with the enemy forces, who gave every indication they were ready to surrender. Suddenly a 75mm shell landed among the Germans, closely followed by another.

The Germans dived for cover. The leading vehicles of the rifle regiment were in flames. In order to get fire to bear as quickly as possible, Rommel ordered the machine gunner of his armored car to open fire in the general direction of the enemy, and he directed the nearest infantry platoon commander to lead his troops in an immediate attack on the roadblock. But with shells falling all around and splinters whistling about everyone's ears, it was not easy to mount an attack.

Meanwhile Rommel called forward an artillery battery and ordered other infantry to push around the right flank of the roadblock and proceed toward Cherbourg. When the guns arrived, Rommel directed them to lay down the heaviest barrage possible on the heights around Cherbourg and on the port installations.

Around four p.m. many of the Cherbourg forts opened a tremendous barrage into the area the Germans were holding. British warships also joined in with heavy naval gunfire. The artillery and antiaircraft guns received special attention and casualties began to mount.

Rommel decided to launch a formal attack with the 7th Rifle Regiment, supported by tanks, through Hainneville to Querqueville, on the north coast, three miles west of Cherbourg. Once the Germans could seize the hills south of Querqueville, it would be easy to command the port and the city of Cherbourg with artillery.

When Colonel Karl Rothenburg, commander of the panzer regiment, saw the attack route, he pointed out that the terrain was crisscrossed with hedges and sunken roads, and was very unfavorable for tanks. Despite this Rommel ordered the tanks to proceed with the infantry. Just at this time, some officers presented Rommel with maps found in a château where they had taken up quarters. The maps showed fields of fire of all the batteries making up the Cherbourg fortress. The route Rommel had selected for assault was right in the center of where the heaviest French firing would come. Accordingly, he called off the attack.

Shortly thereafter an infantry battalion announced that it had seized a hill just west of Redoute du Tot on the western edge of the fortress ring. This opened a way to avoid the northern approach toward Querqueville and to advance farther south. The attack got under way at nine p.m. and moved forward quickly. Rommel went with the leading elements. His dispatch rider led Rommel up to the just-seized hill, where he could see the naval dockyards about 2,000 meters away.

Rommel hoped to see British troops trying to get away from the harbor. But Cherbourg was not going to be a repetition of St. Valéry.

General Marshall-Cornwall, ordered by Brooke to take command of the two British brigades with the French 10th Army, had arrived on June 15 at the army south of L'Aigle, on the eastern edge of Normandy. There he learned that 10th Army was withdrawing toward Brittany the following night. He ordered the two British brigades to pull out immediately.

The motorized British troops set off at midnight and reached Cherbourg within twenty-four hours, after moving 200 miles by roads encumbered with columns of troops and refugees. The direct road through Carentan had been mined, so the British column was diverted to the west coast through Lessay, La Haye-du-Puits, and Barneville, the very route Rommel took the next day.

General Marshall-Cornwall began evacuating his force at eleven thirty a.m. on June 18, as Rommel was approaching Cherbourg. A covering battalion on the coast road was withdrawn between noon and three p.m. that day, and the last troopship carrying this battalion left Cherbourg at four p.m.

"In the last gleam of daylight [of June 18]," Rommel recounted, "we saw the defense works on the outer and inner moles, and the naval harbor, which contained many small ships. The rest of the harbor was empty, the British having apparently already gone."

It had been that close.

The next morning, June 19, Rommel's artillery was disposed all around the harbor. Civilians streamed down every road out of Cherbourg to escape the approaching battle. Rommel issued orders by radio to halt the exodus and send the civilians back into the town. He had no intention of bombarding the town, only the military targets such as the forts and the fortified naval dockyard.

Rommel got word that one of his officers had just been killed by fire from Fort Central, and he issued orders for concentrated fire on this fort, located on the outer roadstead of the harbor, due north of the city. Rommel had excellent observation from his high command post, and was able to send small corrections that directed the fire into the center of the fort. Soon three out of four rounds were direct hits, and the fort ceased fire. Rommel pulled up a high-velocity 88mm antiaircraft gun and directed it to destroy Fort Central's superstructure by direct fire.

Rommel now learned that the Redoute des Couplets had just surrendered. This redoubt, also on the west, offered an excellent view over the Cherbourg defenses, and he hurried to it. Rommel ordered fire to open on anything moving in the naval dockyard. By this time all fire had ceased from the forts out to sea.

At one fifteen p.m. Stuka dive-bombers, punctual to the minute, swooped down and released their bombs on the forts fronting the sea and scored a direct hit on Fort Central. The artillery also opened up. Rommel watched the effect of the fire from the Redoute des Couplets. A storm of shells descended on the dockyard. Flames were soon shooting up from its arsenals and sheds. Tremendous clouds of smoke rose over the forts. Meanwhile the German rifle regiments occupied the town during the bombardment.

A number of French naval officers appeared to negotiate surrender. Rommel had the officers brought up to his observation post, mainly to show them the tremendous effect of the German artillery fire. One naval officer was horrified to see that Fort Querqueville was shrouded in smoke, and asked why the Germans

German infantry in action. The soldier in the foreground carries an MG-34 machine gun.

were bombarding it—it had already ceased fire. "That may be," Rommel replied, "but it has not surrendered."

Negotiations now moved quickly. Rommel ordered a cease-fire, and the French naval personnel gave up. But not a single British soldier was there. They had all gotten away.

While the drama was being played out at Cherbourg, General Brooke, at Redon, near the Breton port of St. Nazaire, concluded that there was nothing the British could do in France, and told responsible officers to move every Briton out. He himself got permission from General Dill to leave, and he notified the navy to have a destroyer in St. Nazaire ready to take him and his corps headquarters out on June 17.

On that day he learned by a phone call from Dill of Pétain's broadcast calling for a French cease-fire. The French high command had told him nothing. Later, Brooke wrote: "Throughout that last trip to France I had the unpleasant feeling that the French high command knew only too well that the French forces in France were doomed, and that it was a matter of very little concern to them how many of the British troops were sucked down with them in the whirlpool of this catastrophe."[6]

Brooke sent his naval liaison officer on ahead to St. Nazaire to find out when the destroyer would be available. He returned with the news that the *Lancastria* had just been sunk with some 6,000 men on board. The destroyer had gone to the rescue and was no longer available. Brooke could choose between the destroyer *Ulster Sovereign,* sailing the next morning, or an armed trawler, *Cambridgeshire,* capable of taking only his headquarters and a few others. It could sail at once but would be required to escort a convoy. Brooke selected the trawler.

At St. Nazaire, Brooke and his party of thirteen had to wait for the trawler, as it had also gone to assist in the *Lancastria* rescue. It had saved 900 men from swimming in fuel oil, and conveyed them to another transport. While on the trawler, the rescued men had stripped off their oil-soaked clothing. The whole trawler was covered with heaps of foul-smelling garments.

The *Lancastria,* a 16,000-ton Cunard liner pressed into service as a troopship, had been struck by two bombs from a German Junker 88 bomber, and had sunk in fifteen minutes. Only the men on the decks and in exterior cabins with portholes had any chance of survival. Only about 2,500 were rescued. It was the worst one-day loss of British troops since the battle of the Somme in 1916.

The trawler lay at anchor until four a.m., during which time there were several air raids. To avoid the smell as much as possible, the soldiers slept on deck. Throughout June 18, the trawler steamed slowly with its convoy around the Brittany peninsula.

"We spent the whole of this day on the trawler, mostly lying on the deck in the sunshine and thanking God we were safely out of France for a second time," Brooke wrote in his diary.

In Compiègne, France, inside the same railway car used to sign the 1918 armistice that ended the First World War, French and German officials review the terms of the French surrender.

The trawler drew into Plymouth at six p.m. A barge came out to meet them. They went to Admiralty House, where the admiral of the port gave them tea and provided them with baths and dinner. Brooke called up Dill, and caught the midnight train for London.

When he got there he went straight to the War Office, where he was greeted with an inquiry as to why he had not saved more vehicles and equipment. But his prescience, decision, and moral courage had saved 150,000 British troops, as well as 18,200 French, 24,300 Poles, 5,000 Czechs, and 162 Belgians, who also were evacuated to England. Brooke's insistence on getting the troops out, and the determination of Admiral William James to put ships into any port with waiting soldiers, constituted a second "Dunkirk." The rescued French and Poles provided the nucleus for Free French and Polish forces that gave splendid service later in the war.

Adolf Hitler resolved that armistice terms would be severe, but not harsh enough to jeopardize French acceptance. On June 19 he announced he was ready to propose conditions. France appointed a delegation headed by Léon Noël, former ambassador to Poland, and on June 20 it set out north up a cease-fire corridor to Paris. On June 21, under German escort, the delegation was driven to Compiègne, a few miles north of Paris. There in the clearing at Rethondes was the identical railway carriage that had been the scene of the German surrender in 1918. To the Germans, the selection of the railway carriage was poetic justice. To the rest of the world, it was rubbing salt in the wounds.

After a rude and unnecessary harangue by General Wilhelm Keitel, the Germans presented their terms. They were less harsh than many expected, caused by Hitler's wish to come to terms with Britain. The French fleet was not to be handed over to the Germans, and northern but not southern France was to be occupied. After long telephone talks with the government in Bordeaux, the delegates signed the armistice early on June 22, 1940.

General de Gaulle inspects Free French troops in Britain shortly after the surrender of France in 1940.

In unoccupied southern France, centered around the watering spot of Vichy, a government under Marshal Pétain was set up. "Vichy France" became a collaborator with Nazi Germany. The oppressive heel of Adolf Hitler bore down on the people of both occupied and unoccupied France.

On June 18, in reply to Pétain's broadcast and in defiance of Germany, a French voice broadcast to the world over BBC: "I, General de Gaulle, at this moment in London, invite French officers and soldiers at present on British territory, engineers, and skilled workers, to get in touch with me. Whatever happens, the flame of French resistance must not be quenched. Nor shall it be."[7]

While Vichy France descended into degradation and shame, the Free French—their symbol the Cross of Lorraine, borne by Joan of Arc—restored the honor of France in heroic battles against the Nazis in the years to come. De Gaulle himself became a great French president. The archcollaborator Pétain ended his life in prison.[8]

Adolf Hitler, with Rommel at his right hand, is greeted by cheering German soldiers of the 7th Panzer Division in France.

EPILOGUE

WHAT MIGHT HAVE BEEN

Of the myths that sprang up in the wake of the 1940 campaign in the West, the one propounded by Winston Churchill has become the orthodox story of what it all meant. It was put before the House of Commons in all of its eloquence on June 18, on the morrow of the collapse of the French government:

> What General Weygand called the Battle of France is over. I expect that the Battle of Britain is about to begin. Upon this battle depends the survival of Christian civilization. Upon it depends our own British life, and the long continuity of our institutions and our Empire. The whole fury and might of the enemy must very soon be turned upon us. Hitler knows that he will have to break us in this island or lose the war. If we can stand up to him, all Europe may be free and the life of the world may move forward into broad, sunlit uplands. But if we fail, then the whole world, including the United States, including all that we have known and cared for, will sink into the abyss of a new Dark Age, made more sinister, and perhaps more protracted, by the lights of perverted science. Let us therefore brace ourselves to our duties, and so bear ourselves that, if the British Empire and its Commonwealth last for a thousand years, men will say, "This was their finest hour."[1]

In this summer of 1940 when Britain indeed did stand alone, when the aerial Battle of Britain indeed did erupt in unprecedented ferocity, violence and destruction, and when Britain indeed not only did survive but emerged triumphant and undefeated, few persons anywhere doubted that this had, in fact, been Britain's finest hour.

But what took place *after* the surrender of France and in the months and years to come was made possible only because of what Adolf Hitler had failed to *accomplish in the days before* the surrender of France. Winston Churchill noted that his cabinet never entertained any possibility other than complete and total resistance to Nazi Germany. He attributed the world's wonder at what happened to "foreigners who do not understand the temper of the British race all over the globe when its blood is up." But if Hitler had made a different decision at Dunkirk, the bravery and defiance of Churchill and his government might have gone for naught.

Alistair Horne, in his book *To Lose a Battle*, wrote: "Had the BEF been wiped out in northern Europe, it is difficult to see how Britain could have continued to fight, and with Britain out of the battle, it is even more difficult to see what combination of circumstances could have aligned America and Stalin's Russia to challenge Hitler."[2]

The almost inconceivably bad news coming out of Europe had propelled the United States back into an extreme form of isolationism. This position had been enunciated in George Washington's farewell address of 1796 when he warned against "permanent alliances" with foreign countries. But it had become American doctrine after Thomas Jefferson's inaugural address in 1801, when he told his "fellow citizens" he thought it "proper you should understand what I deem the essential principles of our government," among these, "peace, commerce, and honest friendship with all nations, entangling alliances with none."[3]

The visceral response of the United States in 1940 was to withdraw into a "Fortress America" as a defense against the world.

Franklin D. Roosevelt was seeking any way possible to support Britain's war against Hitler, but he was helpless in the face of the overwhelming resolve of the American people to protect the nation's sea frontiers, not embark on adventures in Europe.

Thus, after Churchill appealed to the United States on May 15 for "forty or fifty of your older destroyers," to help defend against Germany and Italy, Roosevelt complied, but he exacted a telling price—long-term leases of bases on eight British colonies along the endangered Atlantic coast from Newfoundland to British Guiana (Guyana).[4] Thus, if Britain fell and the Royal Navy vanished from the seas, the United States would still possess an outer band of defenses that could shield the East Coast from German attack.

Before the summer was out, Roosevelt had taken immense steps to strengthen the United States, but not necessarily to help Britain. He had signed a law to create by far the greatest navy on earth (doubling the fleet), begun building an air force of 7,800 combat aircraft, called the National Guard into federal service, and passed the first peacetime draft in American history.

Therefore, Britain could not rely on the United States for any significant help in the period of its greatest weakness, the summer and fall of 1940.

Dunkirk had been the chance for Hitler to inflict a decisive and permanent defeat on Britain. When he failed to do so, he changed the entire course of history. His rescue of the BEF not only vastly increased British resolve to continue the war, but also vastly improved chances that democracy would prevail over fascism.

Until the 1940 campaign, Britain had been considered to be unassailable. Amphibious attack was infeasible, since the Royal Navy ruled the narrow seas. Britain had not been successfully invaded since the Norman Conquest of 1066. But airpower had made possible another way of reaching Britain. And if Britain had no longer possessed an army, the chances for successful aerial invasion—like that which brought down Holland in days—increased dramatically.[5]

The BEF was almost identical to the regular peacetime standing

Churchill, alongside a young woman from the Observer Corps, watches the English skies for German bombers in August 1940.

army. In it were almost all of its experienced soldiers. If this army had been lost, there would have been few persons who could train new recruits for a new army. The most irreplaceable were the commissioned officers. Almost all the truly qualified leaders in the British army were at Dunkirk—in fact, all of those who became top commanders in the years ahead, Bernard L. Montgomery, Harold Alexander, Kenneth Anderson, and others. Alan Brooke, who commanded a corps at Dunkirk and who became chief of the Imperial General Staff, wrote: "Had the BEF not returned to this country it is hard to see how the army could have recovered from the blow. The reconstruction of our land forces would have been so delayed as to endanger the whole course of the war."[6]

A loss of the BEF would have crippled land defense in southern England, leaving only the Royal Air Force and the Royal Navy to keep out invaders. But, more important, the loss of the BEF would have had a perhaps decisive effect on the willingness of the British people to continue the war at all. The main thought of most Britons would have been how to get those 247,000 men home again.

The imprisoned Britons would have been the ace that Hitler could have played to bring peace. Churchill already was confident Hitler would allow Britain to keep its empire and its navy, and wanted in exchange a free hand in eastern Europe. The German foreign minister Joachim von Ribbentrop had conveyed to Churchill in 1937 that this was Hitler's heart's desire.[7] Returning the imprisoned soldiers to their homes would have most probably been the decisive factor in convincing the British people to end hostilities.

Churchill maintained that his government would have continued the war under any circumstances, even from the colonies, and presumably even if the BEF had been captured. But the question must be asked, how long could that government have survived after a disaster at Dunkirk? It is very likely that a new government would have come in and the new leaders would have been willing to negotiate with Hitler.

Therefore, in allowing the BEF to escape, Hitler gave up his greatest chance of bringing Britain to the peace table. This shows that Hitler was profoundly irrational and incapable of looking at alternative means of achieving his goals. This same fatal flaw was manifested in his fixation on the actual, physical destruction of the Soviet Union, as opposed to its neutralization, and in his murderous desire to eliminate all the Jews in Europe. The inability of Hitler to perceive rational, attainable solutions saved the BEF and in the end saved the world.

The litany of Hitler's blunders does not end with the rescue of the BEF, however, for Erich von Manstein's plan, and Guderian's and Rommel's exploitation of his plan, also opened up a fantastic opportunity to create a virtually invincible German empire that did not depend upon the surrender of Britain. What it did depend upon was vision. In a dictatorship, the only vision that matters is that of the dictator. If he does not possess vision, even the most brilliant plans can turn to dust. Hitler had shown his lack of vision in failing to see what was being accomplished by the panzers and at Dunkirk. He was now going to show this lack of vision on a world stage.

Shortly after the armistice with France, the German navy commander Erich Raeder proposed a way to take advantage of the victory by seizing the Suez Canal and overrunning the Middle East. Several of Hitler's senior army advisers—notably Wilhelm Keitel and Alfred Jodl—also saw the opportunity. But, afraid of Hitler's explosive and unpredictable anger and knowing that he was determined to attack the Soviet Union, they were not as emphatic as Raeder.

The British had just 36,000 men in Egypt, including one incomplete armored division. Italy's entry into the war had closed off Britain's supply line through the Mediterranean except by means of heavily guarded convoys. The main British route now had to go

12,000 miles around the Cape of Good Hope in South Africa and up through the Red Sea.

It would take Britain months and perhaps a year to substantially reinforce the Western Desert Force in Egypt, and this was not going to happen, because Britain had to devote most of its strength to defense of the homeland.

Admiral Raeder weighed in to Hitler at conferences on September 6 and 26, 1940. At the second conference Raeder cornered Hitler alone and showed him step by step how Germany could defeat Britain elsewhere than over the English Channel. Doing so would put Germany in a commanding position against the Soviet Union.[8]

Raeder's main argument was that Germany with Italian help should capture Suez. This would force the Royal Navy to abandon the eastern Mediterranean. In October 1940, the army high command sent a panzer expert, Major General Wilhelm von Thoma, to North Africa to find out whether German forces should be sent to help the Italians. Thoma reported back that four German armored divisions could be maintained in Africa and these would be all the force necessary to drive the British out of Egypt and the Suez. At the time, Germany had 20 panzer divisions, none being used.[9] After Suez, German panzers could advance quickly through Palestine, Syria, and Iraq as far as Turkey.

"If we reach that point," Raeder told Hitler, "Turkey will be in our power. The Russian problem will then appear in a different light. It is doubtful whether an advance against Russia from the north [that is, Poland and Romania] will be necessary."

Pressing on the southern frontier of Turkey would put the Turks in an impossible position. Hitler was already gaining Hungary, Romania, and Bulgaria as allies. Therefore, Turkey could be approached both by way of Bulgaria at Istanbul, and by way of northern Iraq and Syria. Turkey would be forced to join the Axis or grant passage for Axis forces and supplies. A defiant stance would result in the swift defeat of the Turkish army and disaster.

German forces could occupy French North Africa with or without Vichy France's cooperation. From French Morocco, the Germans could approach from the *south* the small strip of Morocco along the Strait of Gibraltar ruled by Spain. Spain would be forced to grant transit rights or stand aside if German forces occupied the strip without permission. Spain could not resist for fear of German attack into the heart of Spain from France. As a result, German airfields and batteries could be set up along the south shore of the strait—which is only 8 to 27 miles wide.[10] This would close it to Britain. Sealing the Strait of Gibraltar would force the British to abandon the western Mediterranean and their base of Malta, because they could not supply it.[11]

With the Royal Navy out of the Mediterranean, it would become an Axis lake. Having no hope of help from Britain, Greece and Yugoslavia, the only nonaligned countries in the Balkans, would be forced to come to terms. German forces also could occupy all of western Africa, including the French base of Dakar in Senegal. Aircraft, ships, and submarines from Dakar could close down much of Britain's convoy traffic through the South Atlantic.

In the Middle East the payoff would be much greater. Germany would gain unlimited supplies of oil, its single scarcest commodity. German forces could move easily into Iran and block that country as a route for supplies to the Soviet Union from Britain and the United States. Russia would be left with only the ports of Murmansk on the Barents Sea and Archangel on the White Sea through which goods from the west could be funneled.[12] This would require dangerous passages in atrocious weather, with constant danger of attacks by German ships and aircraft stationed in Norway.

More important, the Soviet Union's major oil fields were in the Caucasus and along the western shore of the Caspian Sea, just north of Iran. Germany could threaten not only an attack directly from Poland and Romania in the west but also from the south through the Caucasus to the Soviet oil fields. The danger of envelopment and quick loss of oil would immobilize Joseph Stalin, and force him to provide Germany with whatever grain and raw materials it might need.

Germany, without the loss of a single soldier, would have the benefits of the Soviet Union's immense materials storehouse, as well as delivery of tin, rubber, nickel, and other goods from Southeast Asia by way of the Trans-Siberian Railway.

A German position in Iran would also pose a huge threat to British control of India, which was agitating for independence under Mohandas K. Gandhi and other leaders. From Iran, Germany could reach India through the Khyber and other passes, invasion routes used long before and long after Alexander the Great made passage in 326 B.C. Germany would not really have to do anything. The threat alone would force Britain to commit every possible soldier to defend its crown jewel.

In possession of the Middle East, all of North and West Africa, and Europe west of Russia, its armed forces virtually intact, its economy able to exploit the resources of three continents, Germany would be virtually invincible. Britain's defiance on the periphery of Europe would become increasingly irrelevant. Germany would not have to inaugurate an all-out U-boat war against its shipping. Britain's remaining strength would have to be expended in protecting its empire and the convoys to and from the home islands.

The United States would have no hope of invading mainland Europe against an undefeated and waiting German army, unless it spent years building a gigantic navy, army, and air force, transports, landing craft, vehicles, and weapons. The United States might possibly have decided to undertake such a mission. But far more likely the American people would turn first to protect the Western Hemisphere and to counter the expansion of Japan in the Pacific.

Meanwhile Germany could consolidate its empire, create a mammoth common market in Europe, and grow more powerful economically, militarily, and politically every day.

Adolf Hitler, however, rejected the proposal of Admiral Raeder. He had been obsessed for years with destroying the Soviet Union, starving millions of Slavs in the east, and populating the region with Germans. This lust after *Lebensraum*, or living space, for the German people—along with his malignant desire to eliminate the Jews of Europe—consumed his mind and made him oblivious to reasonable solutions.

He decided, instead of neutralizing the Soviet Union by an indirect strike through the Middle East, to attack Russia head-on in the summer of 1941. He refused to consider any other course. But this direct approach, combined with the enormous size of Russia, required far greater resources than he possessed, and doomed him to failure.[13]

In February 1941 he sent Erwin Rommel to assist the Italians in Libya. But his aim was not to capture Suez but to keep Mussolini in the war. Despite the few resources Hitler gave him, Rommel came close to carrying out Raeder's dream. But Hitler never shared it. His headlong assault on Russia consumed Germany's strength and led straight to defeat, degradation, and the shattering of the German nation.

Fortunately for the world, Adolf Hitler possessed none of the military insight of the officers—Manstein, Guderian, and Rommel—who made his stunning battlefield victories possible. And he possessed none of the strategic vision of Admiral Raeder, who could have translated the great military victories into an enormous German empire.

ACKNOWLEDGMENTS

I am most grateful to my editor, Brent Howard, for his wise advice and tremendous contributions to bringing order and clarity to this book, and especially for his enthusiastic support of our plan to reproduce so many authentic photographs of the campaign and the leaders who guided it.

In addition, I want to thank the rest of the team at New American Library for working so hard to see this book into final form. The cover design and typography are quite dramatic, and for that I wish especially to thank Anthony Ramondo and Brad Foltz.

A military history is only as good as the maps that accompany it, and I am most fortunate in having Jeffrey L. Ward as my cartographer. His maps are beautiful, accurate, and focused on the essential geographical elements that define the campaign.

I wish to give special thanks to picture editor Zachary Bathon, who searched diligently through the National Archives for authentic pictures of the 1940 campaign.

I wish to thank my agent, Agnes Birnbaum, for her friendship, her faith in me, and her unerring counsel.

Finally, I wish to thank my sons, Bevin Jr., Troy, and David, and my daughters-in-law, Mary and Kim, for their continuous encouragement and their unflagging support of my work.

SELECTED BIBLIOGRAPHY

Addington, Larry. *The Blitzkrieg Era and the German General Staff.* New Brunswick, N.J.: Rutgers University Press, 1971.

Alexander, Bevin. *How Hitler Could Have Won World War II. The Fatal Errors That Led to Nazi Defeat.* New York: Crown, 2000.

——. *How Wars Are Won. The 13 Rules of War—From Ancient Greece to the War on Terror.* New York: Crown, 2002.

Barnett, Corelli. *Hitler's Generals.* New York: Grove Weidenfeld, 1989.

Bartov, Omer. *Hitler's Army.* New York, London: Oxford University Press, 1992.

Bauer, Eddy. *Der Panzerkriege.* 2 vols. Bonn: Verlag Offene Worte, 1966.

Benoist-Méchin, Jacques. *Sixty Days That Shook the West: The Fall of France, 1940.* New York: G. P. Putnam's Sons, 1963.

Bloch, Marc. *Strange Defeat. A Statement of Evidence Written in 1940.* New York, London: 1968.

Bryant, Arthur. *The Turn of the Tide, 1939–1943: A History of the War Years Based on the Diaries of Field Marshal Lord Alanbrooke.* Garden City, N.Y.: Doubleday, 1957.

Bullock, Alan. *Hitler, a Study in Tyranny.* London: Harper Perennial, 1971, 1991.

Chapman, Guy. *Why France Fell.* New York: Holt, Rinehart and Winston, 1968.

Churchill, Winston S. *The Second World War.* 6 vols. Vol. 2, *Their Finest Hour.* Boston: Houghton Mifflin, 1948–1954; London: Cassell, 1948–1954.

Cooper, Matthew. *The German Army 1933–1945.* New York: Stein and Day, 1978.

Corum, James S. *The Luftwaffe: Creating an Operational War, 1918–1940.* Lawrence: University of Kansas, 1997.

Craig, Gordon A. *The Politics of the German Army 1640–1945.* New York: Oxford University Press, 1964.

Dahms, Hellmuth Günther. *Die Geschichte des Zweiten Weltkrieges.* München, Berlin: F. A. Herbig, 1983.

Dallek, Robert. *Franklin D. Roosevelt and American Foreign Policy, 1932–1945.* New York: Oxford University Press, 1979.

Das Deutsche Reich und der Zweite Weltkrieg, vol. 2. Produced by *das militärgeschichtlichen Forschungsamt.* Stuttgart: Deutsche Verlags-Anstalt, 1979–1983.

Ellis, L. F. Major. *The War in France and Flanders, 1939–1940. History of the Second World War.* London: HMSO, 1953.

English, John A., and Bruce I. Gudmundsson. *On Infantry.* Westport, Conn.: Praeger, 1994.

Finney, Patrick, ed. *The Origins of the Second World War.* New York: Oxford University Press, 1997.

French, David. *The British Way of War.* London: Unwin Hyman, 1990.

Frieser, Karl-Heinz, with John T. Greenwood. *The Blitzkrieg Legend. The 1940 Campaign in the West.* Annapolis, Md.: Naval Institute Press, 2005. Copyright *Militärgeschichtlichen Forschungsamt* (of the German Army) 2005. Originally published as Karl-Heinz Frieser, *Blitzkrieg Legende. Der Westfeldzug 1940.* Munich: Oldenbourg (2nd edition), 1996.

Fuller, J. F. C. *A Military History of the Western World.* 3 vols. Reprint of 1956 edition. New York: Da Capo Press, n.d.

Gilbert, Martin. *The Second World War.* New York: Henry Holt, 1989.

Goerlitz, Walter. *History of the German General Staff.* New York: Praeger, 1953.

Goutard, Adolphe. *The Battle of France, 1940.* New York: Ives Washburn, 1959.

Guderian, Heinz. *Panzer Leader.* New York: E. P. Dutton, 1952.

Gudmundsson, Bruce I. *On Artillery.* Westport, Conn.: Praeger, 1993.

———. *Stormtroop Tactics.* Westport, Conn: Praeger, 1989, 1995.

Halder, Gen. Franz. *Diaries.* Privately printed. Copyright Infantry Journal (U.S.A.), 1950.

Hinsley, F. H., et al. *British Intelligence in the Second World War.* London: HMSO, 1979.

Horne, Alistair. *To Lose a Battle: France 1940.* Boston: Little, Brown, 1969.

Jackson, Julian. *The Fall of France. The Nazi Invasion of 1940.* New York: Oxford University Press, 2003.

Kiesling, Eugenia C. *Arming Against Hitler: France and the Limits of Military Planning.* Lawrence: University of Kansas Press, 1996.

Kimball, Warren F. *Forged in War: Roosevelt, Churchill and the Second World War.* New York: William Morrow, 1997.

Krausnick, Helmut, and Hans-Heinrich Wilhelm. *Die Truppe des Weltanschauungskrieges.* Stuttgart: Deutsche Verlags-Anstalt, 1981.

Liddell Hart, Capt. Basil H. *The Other Side of the Hill.* London: Cassell, 1951. Published in the U.S. as *The German Generals Talk.* New York: William Morrow, 1948.

von Manstein, Erich. *Lost Victories.* Chicago: Henry Regnery, 1958.

May, Ernest R. *Strange Victory. Hitler's Conquest of France.* New York: Hill and Wang, 2000.

von Mellenthin, F. W. *Panzer Battles.* Norman: University of Oklahoma Press, 1956.

Messenger, Charles. *The Art of Blitzkrieg.* London: Ian Allen, 1976.

Overy, Richard. *The Air War 1939–1945.* London: Papermac, 1980.

Powaski, Ronald E. *Lightning War. Blitzkrieg in the West, 1940.* Hoboken, N.J.: John Wiley & Sons, 2003; Edison, N.J.: Castle Books, 2006.

Rommel, Field Marshal Erwin. *The Rommel Papers.* Ed. B. H. Liddell Hart. New York: Harcourt, Brace, 1953; London: Collins, 1953.

Rottman, Gordon L. *World War II Infantry Anti-Tank Tactics.* New York, Oxford: Osprey, 2005.

Shirer, William L. *The Rise and Fall of the Third Reich.* New York: Simon & Schuster, 1960.

Spears, Sir Edward L. *Assignment in Catastrophe: Prelude to Dunkirk, the Fall of France.* New York: A. A. Wyn, 1955.

Taylor, A. J. P. *The Origins of the Second World War.* New York: Touchstone, 1986.

Die Truppenführung, Ein Handbuch für den Truppenführer und seine Gehilfen. Seventh edition. An official German Army field manual for troop leaders. Berlin: E. S. Mittler & Sohn, 1933.

Williams, Charles. *The Last Great Frenchman. A Life of General de Gaulle.* New York: John Wiley and Sons, 1993; London: Little Brown, 1993.

Zabecki, David T., ed. *World War II in Europe: An Encyclopedia.* 2 vols. New York: Garland Publishing, 1999.

ENDNOTES

Chapter 1: Breakfast at Hitler's

1   Manstein, 111.
2   Frieser, 80.
3   Ibid., 67.
4   Ibid., 76.
5   *Das Deutsche Reich und der Zweite Weltkrieg*, vol. 2 (Hans Umbreit), 250.
6   May 17–19. The OKH operation order of October 19, 1939, described the aim of the offensive as follows: "To defeat the largest possible elements of the French and Allied armies and simultaneously to gain as much territory as possible in Holland, Belgium and northern France as a basis for successful air and sea operations against Britain and as a broad protective zone for the Ruhr [the main German industrial region just east of Holland around Düsseldorf, Essen, and Dortmund]." See Manstein, 97.
7   *Das Deutsche Reich und der Zweite Weltkrieg*, vol. 2 (Hans Umbreit), 239–40.
8   Nothing was hidden in Germany about laws against Jews or government-sponsored persecution of them. The Nuremberg Laws of September 15, 1935, deprived Jews of German citizenship, turning them into "subjects." The law forbade marriage or extramarital relations between Jews and "Aryans," a category defined by the Nazis as Caucasian gentiles, especially of the Nordic type. This was a descent of the German state into total barbarism. As the German Jewish political theorist Hannah Arendt (1906–75) writes in *The Origins of Totalitarianism* (1951): "The Rights of Man, after all, had been defined as 'inalienable' because they were supposed to be independent of all governments, but it turned out that the moment human beings lacked their own government and had to fall back upon their minimum rights, no authority was left to protect them and no institution was willing to guarantee them." In *Origins*, Arendt points out that the first step of the Nazis'

destruction of the Jews was to make them stateless, in the knowledge that people with no stake in the political community have no claim on the protection of its laws. See Adam Kirsch, "Beware of Pity: Hannah Arendt and the power of the impersonal," in *The New Yorker*, January 12, 2009. When the American correspondent William L. Shirer came to Germany in the summer of 1934, he found that the majority of Germans did not mind having their personal freedom taken away, so much culture destroyed, replaced by barbarism, and life and work regimented to a degree never seen by a people accustomed for generations to control. Part of the reason was that the Gestapo or secret police lurked in the background. Another was fear of the concentration camp for those who got out of line or who were Jews, Reds, or Socialists. The Blood Purge of June 30, 1934, when Hitler killed all of his own followers whom he distrusted, warned everyone how ruthless the Nazis could be. Yet Nazi terror in the early years affected few, and people did not feel they were being cowed by the dictator. On the contrary, they supported Hitler's regime with enthusiasm. It imbued them with a new hope, confidence, and faith in the future of Germany. The majority of Germans felt that Hitler was liquidating the past—with its disappointments. He was freeing them from the severe restraints of the Versailles treaty, and making Germany strong militarily. The Germans wanted this, and were willing to make sacrifices to achieve it. See Shirer, 231.

9   Here, as in many instances in the future, Hitler's obsessive hates and his inability to see nonviolent or alternative ways of achieving his goals prevented him from adopting policies that would have pacified other countries and still given Germany dominance on the Continent. Hitler was incapable of compromise and of any strategy that gained his ends indirectly. Hitler's entire approach was a headlong assault on anything or anyone that opposed him. Although his own chief leaders did not realize it at the time, his decision to attack in the West in 1939 was therefore entirely consistent.

10 May, 314–20; Shirer, 671.

11 Manstein, 103.

12 Chapman, 18.

13 Frieser, 139.

14 Guderian, 89.

15 Manstein, 104.

16 Shirer, 718–19.

17 Alexander, *How Wars Are Won*, 19; Bruce Gudmundsson, *Stormtroop Tactics* (Westport, Conn.: Praeger, 1989). The idea of holding the enemy in place by a frontal attack or threat and sending a movement around the enemy's flank or to his rear is an ancient tactic, of course. It is mentioned in the Bible (2 Samuel 5:23–25), and has been used in many variations over the centuries. The German storm troop or infiltration tactics were a brilliant solution to a specific problem in World War I, since they overcame the

severe limitation on movement imposed by trench warfare, machine guns, and long-range artillery.

18 Frieser, 334–36.

19 Sheibert, Horst, *Das war Guderian. Ein Lebensbericht im Bildern* (Friedberg: Podzun-Pallas Verlag, 1980), 173.

20 For a recent analysis of the impact of these two English intellectuals on military thought, see "'Young Turks, or Not so Young?': The Frustrated Quest of Major General J. F. C. Fuller and Captain B. H. Liddell Hart," by Brian Holden Reid, in the January 2009 issue (vol. 73, no. 1) of *The Journal of Military History* (147–75), published by the Society for Military History, Lexington, Virginia.

21 Rommel, 124.

22 Alexander, *How Hitler Could Have Won*, 7–8.

23 Guderian, 90.

24 In this book some distances are given in miles and others in kilometers. To convert kilometers into approximate miles, multiply by 0.6. To convert miles into approximate kilometers, multiply by 1.6.

25 Manstein, 104. Manstein saw that, if panzers rushed to the English Channel and cut off Allied forces in Belgium, the mobile Allied troops remaining in the interior of France could set up a strong defensive line along the Somme and Aisne rivers to link up with the Maginot Line to the east. To prevent this from happening, Manstein called for an offensive movement southward with German infantry formations striking toward Reims and Soissons immediately after a breakthrough was obtained at Sedan. The aim would be to destroy the cohesion of enemy forces in this region by turning the western flank of the Maginot Line later, and attacking it from the rear. Manstein's book has a map showing this proposed advance on page 103. Thus Manstein's plan called for both a strike westward with panzers to the channel, and a simultaneous strike southward into the French interior. OKH refused to implement this "offensive-defensive" movement to the south, however, and the French were in fact able to set up a defensive line that had to be cracked later with substantial casualties.

26 Frieser, 69–70.

27 Frieser, 95–98; May, 283.

Chapter 2: Uproar in the North

1 Chapman, 67, 83; Shirer, 720–57.

2 Frieser, 92.

3 The Maginot Line was the most massive monument to static warfare ever conceived. This line fronted the French frontier toward Germany. The Great Wall of China was longer, but it was designed as a barrier, not as an

active defensive system like the Maginot Line. Built in the 1930s and named after André Maginot, minister of war in 1930, who had been severely wounded in the war, the Maginot Line consisted of elaborate clusters of fortresses, deep in the ground, joined by tunnels, with storerooms, engine rooms, and living quarters, and with cannon and machine guns that rose up to fire and sank back into the ground when silent. In front of these fortresses were fields planted with heavy antitank rails and laced with barbed wire to deter infantry.

The Maginot Line ran from the Swiss frontier at Basel to Luxembourg, although some lighter and less formidable defenses were built along part of the Belgian frontier. In March 1934 Marshal Henri-Philippe Pétain, then minister of war, told the Senate it was unnecessary to extend the Maginot Line to cover the Belgian frontier. With a few demolitions the densely forested Ardennes low mountain range of eastern Belgium and Luxembourg could be made impenetrable, he said. And if the Germans attacked by way of Belgium, Pétain emphasized, "one must go into Belgium." This made some sense in 1934 because Belgium was an ally. But on October 31, 1936, King Leopold III of Belgium, beginning to fear German aggression, declared neutrality. Yet a neutral stance by Belgium would count for little, for the Maginot Line made it certain that any German attack would go through the Low Countries. This led to clandestine talks between Belgians and French.

4   Churchill, 35.

5   For a detailed analysis of how linear battles were fought, see "The Battle of Cantigny," by Paul Herbert in the Spring 2008 issue (vol. 13, no. 4) of *On Point: The Journal of Army History*, published by the Army Historical Association. The article describes the first offensive of the United States Army in World War I at the village of Cantigny, 70 miles north of Paris, on May 28, 1918. The 1st Infantry Division's 28th Infantry Regiment carried out the attack. It followed precisely the doctrine of linear warfare that had been worked out by the French. To seize the Cantigny plateau, the division attacked with a single regiment, its three battalions advancing abreast, each in its own zone. The American line was just beyond the village of Villers-Tournelle, and the Americans had to cross a "no man's land" of 1,500 yards to reach Cantigny. The center battalion was reinforced by twelve French Schneider tanks, and had the primary job of clearing the village of Cantigny of German troops. The attack was preceded by a heavy bombardment by 75mm guns and 155mm howitzers. Then the Schneider tanks crossed the American trenches at preselected places. The barrage of 75mm guns shifted from the village to the line of departure for the American infantry, blasted there for three minutes, then moved forward in a "rolling barrage" that stayed ahead of the infantry, who came out of their trenches and

advanced more or less abreast at a fixed distance behind the shell blasts. The aim of the rolling barrage was to force the enemy to keep under cover and not be able to arrest the advance of the infantry. To everyone's surprise, the attack met spotty German resistance, and the Americans were able to capture the village. The French tanks could not enter the village because of rubble from explosions, and were soon withdrawn. The success of the attack depended upon the weight of the artillery barrage on German positions, and surprise.

6　Frieser, 326.

7　Rommel, 184.

8　Manstein, 63.

9　The 1933 edition of the German field manual on leadership, *Die Truppen führung*, in the chapter on the troop leader and his helpers, gives the following definition of a proper military leader (page 25): "Willpower, strength of character, and military skills are mandatory attributes for a troop leader. Clear principles must guide him. These principles can be discerned only through constant work, the study of military history, and thinking deeply about the nature of war. Clarity of judgment acquired in this way will enable the leader to take appropriate action in all situations, even the most difficult ones. The most important dimensions of leadership are readiness to take responsibility and initiative. Every leader must always be conscious that inaction is more dangerous than failure to select the best means of carrying out an action. Constant personal contact with the troops is especially important, so the leader can evaluate their needs and their abilities with his own eyes. If the troops know that their leader lives for them and shares joys and sufferings with them, they will expend their last strength to achieve victory and also to bear failure. The troop leader must lead his troops personally and he must think through all situations his troops are likely to encounter. He must make positive decisions and give explicit orders. He must show himself to be superior to his subordinates both intellectually and in strength of character. He must never allow himself to become dependent on them, or to sink into a purely representative or superficial role with them. If he does these things, he will discover, in [the nineteenth-century German chief of staff] Alfred von Schlieffen's words, a 'god-like spark' within himself. This will allow him to lead his troops to victory in some cases, and to avoid collapse in others."

10　Frieser, 337–38.

11　This concept grew out of a theory espoused after World War I by an Italian, Giulio Douhet. His argument was that a nation could be forced to its knees by massive bombing attacks against its centers of population, government, and industry. Such attacks would destroy the morale of the people and war production, and achieve victory without the use of ground forces. This theory won wide acceptance in the years leading up to World War II and during the war itself. As examples, the American four-engine Boeing B-17 Flying Fortress and the B-24 Liberator bombers and the later Boeing B-29 Superfortress were all designed as "strategic bombers" to strike at the enemy heartland. The counterargument gave rise to the modern fighter plane or interceptor to shoot down the strategic bombers before they could penetrate into one's own heartland. In the event, strategic bombing was not decisive in World War II, except for the atomic bombs dropped on Hiroshima and Nagasaki, Japan, August 6 and 9, 1945. The enormous destruction of these blasts forced the Japanese government to surrender. The extensive strategic bombing of Germany in 1944 did not destroy German morale, and military production did not decline, but actually rose. See Alexander, *How Hitler Could Have Won*, 41–42.

12   Despite the fact that the French and British armies remained committed to static warfare, the French in particular made great progress in building outstanding tanks. By spring 1940 French tanks not only outnumbered German tanks 3,254 to 2,439, but they were generally more heavily armored and carried better guns.

Only 1,006 of the German tanks could engage in battle. These were the Panzer IIIs and the Czech-built Škodas, which mounted 37mm cannons, and the Panzer IVs, which carried short-barreled, low-velocity 75mm cannons. The remaining German tanks, Panzer Is and IIs, carried only machine guns or 20mm cannons and could not challenge other tanks.

The French, on the other hand, had 2,489 battle tanks. Some had 37mm cannons, but most mounted a high-velocity 47mm gun, the best tank cannon in the world at the time, while the heavy Char B tank also carried a powerful 75mm gun. However, only about 900 of the French battle tanks were in three "light armored divisions," *divisions légères mécanisées*, and three regular armored divisions—*divisions cuirasses*, or D.C.R—plus about 150 more in the fourth armored division (commanded by Colonel Charles de Gaulle) that was formed after the campaign started. The remainder were parceled out in separate tank battalions attached to infantry divisions.

Two light armored divisions were organized in a "Cavalry Corps" under General René-Jacques-Adolphe Prioux. These divisions were quite powerful formations, having combined 239 Hotchkiss tanks mounting 37mm guns and 176 Somua tanks carrying 47mm guns, along with a battalion riding motorcycles, a reconnaissance group in armored cars, and three battalions of motorized infantry called dragoons. Thus Prioux's corps was actually more powerful than Hermann Hoth's two-division panzer corps, with which it collided, and, properly employed, might have played a major role in the campaign.

The three armored divisions also were powerful and, if deployed together, might have made a great difference. Each armored division had 62 Char B tanks with 47mm and 75mm guns, and 84 Hotchkiss tanks, plus a battalion of infantry in armored troop carriers, two motorized artillery battalions, and an engineer unit.

13 Chapman, 38–39.

14 May, 130.

15 Ibid., 336.

16 Chapman, 87.

17 Panzer Group Kleist, for example, had five panzer and three motorized divisions, totaling 134,370 men, 41,140 vehicles, and 1,222 tanks (or half of the total panzer force). See Frieser, 102.

18 The Germans used shaped or hollow-charge explosives to blow the Eben Emael defenses.

   The hollow-charge principle was discovered in 1888 by an American, Charles Edward Munroe. A solid cylinder of explosive is formed with a metal-lined conical hollow at one end. When detonated, the enormous pressure generated drives the liner into this hollow space, melts it, and projects forward a high-velocity jet of molten metal that can penetrate armor and other solid objects. The principle was later used to create the German Panzerfaust and the American bazooka handheld antitank weapons in World War II, and rocket-propelled grenades today. A full story of the Eben Emael attack is presented by Simon Dunstan, *Fort Eben Emael* (Oxford, England: Osprey Publishing, 2005).

19 The French, thinking as always of a stable front line and a long war, withheld the majority of their aircraft in the south to be used at some indeterminate later time when they might be decisive. The result was to render the vast bulk of French airpower null and void, and to surrender the air over the battlefields to the Germans. The French air force also worked out no system to assist the French army on the battlefield. There was no program of cooperation between the two branches, neither liaison staffs nor radios.

20 Chapman, 101; Goutard, 111.

21 Although Hoepner was attacking, his was the weaker force. He had 623 tanks (280 in the 3rd Panzer Division and 343 in the 4th Panzer). But only 73 of these were Panzer IIIs, with 37mm guns, and 52 were Panzer IVs, with short-barreled 75mm guns. The vast majority of Hoepner's tanks, 498, were Panzer Is and IIs, light-skinned, armed either with machine guns or inadequate 20mm guns. These tanks could not challenge other tanks. In fact, they were weaker than the French Renault reconnaissance vehicles and the 90 Panhard 178 armored scout vehicles, whose 25mm cannon could penetrate even the Panzer IVs.

22 Frieser, 332.

23 Frieser, 241–46; Chapman, 100–01.

Chapter 3: Attack in the South

1   Chapman, 115–16.
2   Frieser, 119–36.
3   Ibid.,142–44; Dahms, 170; Goutard, 115.

Chapter 4: Crossing the Meuse at Sedan

1   German aerial reconnaissance photos noted in the spring of 1940 that the steeply sloped heights of the Bois de la Marfée rose only two and a half kilometers south of Sedan, and dominated the entire potential battlefield. The photos showed that Marfée was studded with extremely strong bunkers made of reinforced concrete and housing powerful cannon. In light of this evidence, General Rundstedt and his army commanders doubted whether it was correct to put the main effort at Sedan. This put in grave doubt the entire attack plan of Manstein and Guderian. To make sure of the findings, however, Rundstedt's intelligence chief summoned one more expert to look at the pictures. He was Major Max von Stiotta, an Austrian engineer. Stiotta showed Rundstedt and the other army chiefs that the bunkers were actually construction sites that were mere shells, not anywhere near half finished. Stiotta provided Guderian with the decisive counterargument to keep the *Schwerpunkt* at Sedan. See Frieser, 146.
2   May, 427–28.
3   Frieser, 159–61.
4   Frieser, 155, cites Paul Deichmann, *Der Chef im Hintergrund* (Munich and Hamburg, 1979, 100). See also Guderian, 104.
5   A shaped charge consists of a hollow liner or cone of metal backed on the convex side by explosive. When the explosive is detonated, it collapses the metal cone, melts the metal, and propels a jet of molten metal into the target, producing very high stresses that can penetrate armor or crack open reinforced concrete.
6   Chapman, 119–21; Goutard, 136–37; Frieser, 175–78.
7   The failure of Britain and France to produce a dive-bomber contributed greatly to their air forces' inability to hit the pontoon bridge. Allied bombers were designed primarily to fly level over a target area and drop bombs to cover it. Unlike the Stuka dive-bomber, Allied bombers found it extremely difficult to drop a bomb on a pinpoint target, like a bridge. The United States Navy, on the other hand, developed the Douglas SPD Dauntless dive-bomber that could do precisely what the Stuka could do: hit a specific small target by diving straight at it. The Dauntless was designed in 1939, began manufacture in 1940, and went into service in 1941. It was responsible for most of the sinkings of Japanese ships in the Pacific War.

The key to the success of the dive-bomber was its ability to aim at a target and drop a bomb on it. More recent developments of laser, radar, infrared, the Global Positioning System (GPS), and other methods to guide "smart" bombs to targets eliminated the need for an aircraft to do the job of aiming "dumb" or unguided gravity bombs.

8   Frieser, 178–83; Guderian, 102–05.

Chapter 5: The French Try to Destroy the Bridgehead

1   This remarkable action demonstrates the different doctrines of the French and German armies, as skillfully explained by Karl-Heinz Frieser, author of the official German history of the 1940 campaign. French doctrine considered the tank to be a supporting weapon of the infantry. It had to move at the tempo of a walking soldier. German doctrine, designed by Guderian, considered the tank the main weapon and obliged other arms to adjust to its speed. In reaching Bulson Ridge, Kirchner did not follow Guderian's doctrine that tanks must be employed in large compact formations (his mantra was, *Klotzen, nicht kleckern!* Hit with the fist, don't feel with the fingers!). Kirchner sent his tanks forward *kleckerweise*, or in penny packets. Since every minute counted, he could not wait to assemble a large concentration of tanks, and the panzer company attacked unsupported into the unknown. See Frieser, 189–90.

2   Chapman, 122; Goutard, 125–37; Frieser, 183–93; Guderian, 104–05.
3   Guderian, 105–06.
4   Frieser, 193–94.
5   Ibid., 222–23.
6   Ibid., 252–53.

Chapter 6: The Incredible Fight for the Stonne Heights

1   Frieser, 214.
2   Ibid., 199–214; Chapman, 139–40, 143–44; Goutard, 139–44; Jackson, 30.

Chapter 7: Rommel Opens the Floodgates

1   Rommel, 8.
2   Ibid., 7.
3   The precarious position that the 1st Rifle Regiment had been left in after crossing the Meuse at Sedan on May 13 and the morning of May 14— without artillery or tank protection—led Guderian to abandon his previous

policy of keeping tanks separate from infantry, engineers, and artillery. He now formed *Kampfgruppen*, or mixed battle groups, consisting of armor, guns, infantry, and sometimes engineers. These were precisely the formations that Rommel used from the outset, and that permitted him to have such quick success. The great advantage of *Kampfgruppen* was that they could take on any enemy force. For the rest of the war the Germans routinely formed ad hoc battle groups as needed, and dissolved them when the task was completed. Allied forces were much more hidebound, and were much less flexible in forming battle groups. For example, the British armored division consisted of tank brigades and a "support group" of artillery and infantry. This led to many awkward situations in the desert war in North Africa in 1941–42, when support groups encountered German panzers. The support groups had to depend upon a few 25-pounder (87.6mm) gun-howitzers and two-pounder (40mm) antitank guns, which were not always sufficient.

Chapter 8: The Strike for the English Channel

1   Chapman, 170–71.
2   Churchill, 45–49.
3   Ibid., 75.
4   Ibid., 49–51.
5   Chapman, 142.
6   May, 389.
7   Goutard, 195; Chapman, 163.
8   Frieser, 193.
9   Guderian, 67.
10   Guderian, 107–8.
11   Frieser, 217.
12   Guderian, 108.
13   Ibid., 108–09.
14   Ibid., 109–10.
15   Frieser, 253–54.
16   Ibid., 257.
17   Chapman, 150; Frieser, 263.
18   Williams, 91.
19   Frieser, 264–65; Chapman, 176–78; Goutard, 191–92.

Chapter 9: The Ghost Division

1   In this fast, unsupported advance to Cerfontaine, Rommel wanted to use his divisional artillery to curtain off both flanks from any possible attack.

To simplify wireless traffic and to avoid having to encode messages, Rommel set up a "line of thrust" with his operations officer and the artillery regiment. The line ran straight between the church in the village of Rosée, 11 kilometers northeast of Philippeville, and the church at Froidchapelle, 16 kilometers southwest of Philippeville. All officers marked the line on their maps. It was set off in numbered sections. Thus, if Rommel wanted to call artillery fire on, for instance, Philippeville, he simply radioed: "Heavy artillery fire immediate round eleven," which was the number for this town. The system worked perfectly. See Rommel, 14–15.

2   Rommel, 14–17.

3   Frieser, 266.

4   Rommel's account of this conversation with Kluge is remarkable for what it does *not* say. It goes as follows: "The intention was first to gain the frontier near Sivry, while, at the same time, the Reconnaissance Battalion reconnoitered the Maginot Line over a wide front and the mass of the artillery moved into position around Sivry. Then the Panzer Regiment, under powerful artillery cover, was to move in extended order up to the French line of fortifications. Finally, the Rifle Brigade, covered by the tanks, was to take the French fortifications and remove barricades. Not until all this was accomplished was the breakthrough to Avesnes to be made, with the armor in the lead and the mass of the division following closely behind. General von Kluge gave complete approval to our plan." See Rommel, 17. Rommel did not say what became apparent soon thereafter: He intended all the time to advance not only through the Maginot Line and on to Avesnes, but to keep on going.

5   Frieser, 268–69.

6   Ibid., 271.

7   Ibid., 272.

Chapter 10: The British Attack Rommel at Arras

1   Rommel, 29.

2   Churchill, 59–60. Churchill's recommendations to the French on how to deal with the *chars allemands* were unrealistic. He telegraphed Premier Paul Reynaud on May 21, 1940: "Undue importance should not be attached to the arrival of a few tanks at any particular point. What can they do if they enter a town? Towns should be held with riflemen, and tank personnel should be fired upon should they attempt to leave vehicles. If they cannot get food or drink or petrol, they can only make a mess and depart. Where possible, buildings should be blown down upon them. Every town with valuable crossroads should be held in this fashion. Secondly, the tank columns in the open must be hunted down and attacked in the open country by numbers of small mobile columns with a few cannon. Their tracks must

be wearing out, and their energy must abate." See ibid. Erwin Rommel and other panzer leaders had already figured out effective ways of neutralizing attempted attacks by enemy forces, whether units in the field or saboteurs in towns, as Churchill was recommending. If enemy fire fell on them, or even if it had not fallen but was suspected of being likely, tank commanders were instructed to open up with all weapons, cannon and machine guns, spraying a wide area around them with heavy fire. This had the effect of suppressing virtually all enemy fire, and of inhibiting the French from initiating fire in the future for fear of being struck down in a hail of German counterfire. The only effective means of attack by individual soldiers was to sneak up on stationary tanks and place a satchel charge of explosives under them. This, however, could be carried off only when tank crews were distracted by other events, because an individual soldier approaching a tank was an easy target. Soldiers throwing what later in Russia were called "Molotov cocktails" (gasoline sealed inside a wine bottle with an igniter attached) at tanks gained a lot of popular attention in newspapers, but they rarely had much effect on tanks—and then only if a bottle struck an air vent, and even this seldom knocked out a tank.

3   The Germans sent two infantry battalions and two artillery groups to form a bridgehead south of the Somme at Abbeville. Charles de Gaulle's 4th Armored Division was ordered to destroy this bridgehead. The division now had 160 tanks, including 33 Char Bs. Although the division gained some ground and captured a few German prisoners, it was stopped almost entirely by the fire of a few high-velocity 88mm AAA or flak guns. At the end of the engagement, de Gaulle had only 24 tanks left, and withdrew. Weygand rejected a proposal by de Gaulle to concentrate the remaining armored and tank-armed cavalry divisions in a corps under his command. De Gaulle wrote a blistering letter to Premier Paul Reynaud attacking him for abandoning France to "men of yesteryear"—referring to Pétain and Weygand—and exhorting Reynaud to stand up and play the man. On June 5, 1940, Reynaud invited de Gaulle to join his government as undersecretary of state for war. See Williams, 92–93.

4   Guderian, 110–13.

5   Frieser, 278.

6   May, 131.

7   Chapman, 179–80.

8   Churchill, 58–59.

9   Ellis, 87–88.

10   Frieser, 286.

11   Rommel, 33.

12   Frieser, 276–77; Goutard, 95–96; Chapman, 216–18.

13   Bryant, 92.

14 Chapman, 219–20.

15 Captain Marc Bloch, an officer of the French 1st Army, described how the British came to lose their confidence in French leadership. "French officers as a whole were convinced that our staff training was the best in the world," he wrote, "and I have a feeling that they may have been a little too vocal about it. What happened was that, in the course of a few days, the entirely unexpected collapse of our armies on the Meuse suddenly threatened all the elements farther to the north with encirclement. Faced by a disaster which might well have involved the loss of the whole of their Expeditionary Force, the British felt that they had a right to be consulted. Their faith in us had already been shaken. The slowness and ineffectiveness of our movements did the rest. Our prestige was a thing of the past, and our Allies made no bones about not concealing the fact. Can one blame them?" See Bloch, 74–75.

Chapter 11: The Miracle of Dunkirk

1 The narrative on Dunkirk is drawn from the following sources: Frieser, 287–303; Chapman, 200–09; Goutard, 224–44; *Das Deutsche Reich und der Zweite Weltkrieg* (Hans Umbreit), vol. 2, 292–98; Dahms, 176–83; Churchill, 74–118; Guderian, 114–20.

2 Guderian, 117–18.

3 Frieser, 295.

4 Liddell Hart, *The German Generals Talk*, 132, 134–35.

5 Frieser, 295.

6 Guderian, 117.

7 One of many disastrous headlong attacks was Hitler's insistence on seizing the city of Stalingrad on the Volga River in Russia in the summer of 1942. His aim, he said, was to stop the flow of oil tankers up the Volga to supply the Red Army in the interior of Russia. The principal aim of the 1942 offensive was to gain the oil fields of the Caucasus and along the western shore of the Caspian Sea. By striking at Stalingrad, Hitler more than cut in half the forces that could be used in the Caucasus, and this weakness caused the offensive to fail. However, if Hitler had used all of his strength to seize the oil fields, the movements of the tankers up the Volga River would have been stopped in any case. Without oil the Red Army could not have continued the war. Therefore, seizure of Stalingrad was not necessary. Here is a clear instance of Hitler's total inability to see strategic opportunities and potential strategic consequences. His forces at Stalingrad were also too weak to capture the city. Instead of withdrawing, he insisted on holding on, allowing the Russians to surround and destroy the German 6th Army, a

loss of 250,000 men. This defeat threw Hitler onto the strategic defensive. From the moment of the surrender of the 6th Army in February 1943, Hitler was headed straight for defeat. See Alexander, 145–63.

8 Goutard, 229, cites Bernard von Lossberg, *Im Wehrmachtsführungsstab. Bericht eines Generalstaboffiziers* (Hamburg: Nölke, 1950), 82.

9 Frieser, 298.

10 Chapman, 210.

11 Churchill, 101.

12 Ibid., 104.

13 Bloch, 15–21.

14 Goutard, 229.

15 Churchill, 77.

16 Liddell Hart, *The German Generals Talk*, 134–35.

17 Churchill, 142–43.

Chapter 12: The Fall of France

1 Chapman, 346–47, Appendix B. Armor was reorganized into five panzer corps, each of two panzer divisions and one motorized division or regiment. 19th Panzer Corps was dissolved. 1st and 2nd Panzer Divisions, with 29th Motorized Division, went to 39th Panzer Corps commanded by Rudolf Schmidt. Wietersheim's 14th Corps was converted to panzer by the introduction of the formerly independent 9th Panzer Division and 10th Panzer from 19th Corps, and the Grossdeutschland motorized regiment. To 15th Corps (Hoth), 16th Corps (Hoepner), and the 41st Corps (Reinhardt) were added the 2nd, 13th, and 20th Motorized Divisions. 15th Corps became independent under 4th Army, 14th and 16th remained under Kleist, while the 39th and 41st were grouped under Guderian in 12th Army.

2 Goutard, 247–49.

3 Dahms, 184–85.

4 This section of the narrative is drawn primarily from Rommel, 44–67.

5 Chapman, 257.

6 The 154th Brigade of the 51st Division had been detached earlier in June to form a mobile battle group, "Arkforce," and was able to escape from northern France while the rest of the division withdrew to St. Valéry.

7 This section of the narrative is drawn chiefly from Chapman, 257–92.

Chapter 13: Armistice at Compiègne

1 This section is mainly drawn from Brooke's own account in Bryant, 114–47.

2 Churchill's own account of the phone conversation (Churchill, 192–93) was that Brooke rang him up, not the other way around, and that "after ten minutes I was convinced that he was right and we must go." Brooke commented that it was impossible for him to initiate a call to the prime minister, since he didn't have his number. He also said Churchill did not disclose "that, without sufficient knowledge of conditions prevailing on that front at that time, he was endeavoring to force a commander to carry out his wishes against the commander's better judgment. With all his wonderful qualities, interference of this nature was one of his weaknesses. The strength of his powers of persuasion had to be experienced to realize the strength that was required to counter it." See Bryant, 137.

3 The Royal Navy and Churchill were terrified that the French fleet, fourth-largest in the world and brought to a high degree of efficiency by Admiral François Darlan, would be used against the British. The only two major assets that Britain now possessed were its control of the seas and the air over southeastern England and the channel. Were either to be lost, Britain's position would become almost hopeless. If the German and French fleets were combined, they would be more than a match for the Royal Navy. See Williams, 99.

4 Williams, 100–06, 110–14. On the morning of June 14, Premier Reynaud sent for Admiral Darlan to discuss logistics of moving the army and the government to North Africa, and told General de Gaulle to go to London to ask for British assistance. Unable to secure an airplane, de Gaulle set out northward in a car for Brittany. He stopped at Paimpol, on the north coast, where he gave his last respects to his dying mother, then made for Carantec, a small port farther west along the north Breton coast. There, the place of refuge for his wife, Yvonne, and two daughters, he gave instructions for them to be ready to move at a moment's notice, then drove on thirty miles southwest to Brest. There he boarded the French destroyer *Milan* and landed at Plymouth. In London on June 16, Jean Monnet, chairman of the Franco-British Economic Coordinating Committee, and Charles Corbin, the French ambassador, burst into de Gaulle's room at the Hyde Park Hotel. They told de Gaulle they had been discussing a proposed union between Britain and France with the foreign secretary, Edward Lindley Wood, the Earl of Halifax, and with his chief diplomatic adviser, Sir Robert Vansittart. There was to be a federal constitution, one Parliament, one government, and common citizenship. The British leaders saw it as the only way to keep France in the war. De Gaulle agreed and undertook to bring Churchill around to the scheme.

After talking to de Gaulle, Churchill accepted the plan and got the accord of the War Cabinet. De Gaulle called Reynaud, who assembled his cabinet to hear the British proposal. Winston Churchill wrote (Churchill, 207–13) that de Gaulle had told him that some dramatic move was essential to give Reynaud the support he needed to keep the government in the war. He said a proclamation of indissoluble union of the French and British peoples would serve the purpose. Accordingly, the War Cabinet drew up a proposed declaration that France and Britain would no longer be two separate nations, but one Franco-British Union, with citizens of each country becoming citizens of the other. Both countries were to share responsibility for repairing war damages, and for the continued conduct of the war under a single War Cabinet. Reynaud was excited by the proposal and believed he would be able to gain approval with it to carry the war to North Africa. However, the proposal received a hostile reception in the French cabinet. Opposition was so great it was never put to a vote. All further discussion turned on asking the Germans what their terms for an armistice would be. De Gaulle returned to Bordeaux on the night of June 16 by air. The next day he flew back to London. His wife, Yvonne, following instructions de Gaulle had given her, made contact with the British consul in Brest, and secured passage on a Polish freighter bound for Plymouth. As the German tanks moved into the Breton peninsula, she and her daughters fled from Carantec. But the car taking them broke down, and, when they finally arrived in Brest, the ship had sailed. Luckily, they were able to board a British tramp ship still in the harbor. It was the last ship out. The Polish freighter they were to have taken was sunk by German torpedo boats with the loss of all hands. On her arrival in Plymouth, Yvonne telephoned her husband. "Ah," he replied, "it's you? I am in London. I am waiting for you."

5   Churchill, 217–18.

6   Bryant, 143.

7   This statement was carefully contrived not to offend the British government, which was still trying to negotiate with the new Pétain government. Two days later de Gaulle showed his true intent. He broadcast over the British Broadcasting Corporation once again. He proclaimed that he was now speaking in the name of France. "I announce formally the following: any Frenchman who still has weapons has the absolute duty to continue the resistance; to lay down arms, to abandon a military position, to accept the surrender of any piece of French land to the enemy, would be crimes against the nation." He went on to instruct the resident generals in the French Empire on their duty to refuse to obey any instructions coming from the enemy. See Williams, 114.

8   Chapman, 311–17; Churchill, 199–223.

Epilogue: What Might Have Been

1   Churchill, 225–26.

2   Horne, 525.

3   Alexander, *How America Got It Right* (New York: Crown, 2005), 253 n.5.

4   These bases were in Newfoundland, Bermuda, the Bahamas, Jamaica, Antigua, St. Lucia, Trinidad, and British Guiana. See Churchill, 414.

5   The combination of the Royal Air Force's splendid Spitfire and Hurricane fighters and two radar nets—one to spot high-flying incoming enemy aircraft, and the other to pick up low-level flights—permitted Britain to defend itself from Luftwaffe attacks, which began in earnest on August 13, 1940. However, Britain was dependent on its sector stations, nerve centers that guided fighters into battle using the latest intelligence from radar, ground observers, and pilots in the air. Seven sector stations around London were crucial to the protection of southern England. Hermann Göring learned about the sector stations on August 24, and switched his emphasis to their destruction. From that day to September 6, the Luftwaffe sent over an average of a thousand planes a day. They damaged five fighter airfields in southern England badly, and hit six of the seven key sector stations so severely that the communications system was on the verge of being knocked out. The RAF began to stagger. Between August 23 and September 6, 466 fighters were destroyed or badly damaged (against 352 German losses). More important was the loss of pilots. During the period 103 RAF pilots were killed and 128 seriously wounded, one-fourth of those available. A few more weeks of such losses and Britain would no longer have an organized air defense. At this moment, Adolf Hitler intervened with an incredibly stupid order. Because a flight of German bombers had struck central London by mistake on August 24, RAF Bomber Command launched a reprisal raid on Berlin the next night, the first time the German capital had been bombed. Bomber Command followed up with several more raids in the next few days. Hitler was enraged, and shifted the Luftwaffe away from destruction of the sector stations to terror bombing of London and other British cities. It was this colossal blunder by Hitler himself, more than the magnificent opposition of the RAF, that saved Britain from being unable to defend itself in the air. See Alexander, *How Hitler Could Have Won*, 38–41.

6   Bryant, 124.

7   Churchill, 226.

8   *Das Deutsche Reich und der Zweite Weltkrieg*, vol. 3, 191–200; Shirer, 813–15. A German Navy memorandum of a meeting with Hitler on November 14, 1940, contained the following observations: "Italy will never carry out the Egyptian offensive. The Italian leadership is wretched. They have no understanding of the situation. The Italian armed forces have neither the leadership nor the military efficiency to carry the required operations in the Mediterranean area to a successful conclusion with the necessary speed and decision." Therefore, the task must be carried out by Germany. "The fight for the African area is the foremost strategic objective of German warfare as a whole. . . . It is of decisive importance for the outcome of the war." But

Hitler was not convinced. He had never been able to envisage war in the Mediterranean and North Africa as anything but secondary to his main objective. As Raeder elaborated in the meeting, Hitler retorted that he was "still inclined toward a demonstration with Russia." Hitler said: "In view of the present political developments and especially Russia's interference in Balkan affairs, it is necessary to eliminate at all costs the last enemy remaining on the Continent before coming to grips with Britain." From this point on, Hitler stuck fanatically to this fundamental strategy of attacking the Soviet Union. See *Fuehrer Conferences on Naval Affairs*, mimeographed, London: British Admiralty, 1947, shown as FCNA, 1940, 124–25; Shirer, 815–19.

9   When General von Thoma reported his findings to Hitler, the führer responded that he could spare only one panzer division for Africa, whereupon Thoma replied that it would be better to give up the whole idea. Thoma's comment angered Hitler, and he told Thoma his concept of sending German forces to Africa was narrowly political, to keep Benito Mussolini from changing sides. The evidence is clear that in the Mediterranean, Hitler's interest focused on keeping Mussolini happy and on wild schemes like getting Spanish dictator Francisco Franco's permission to send German troops through Spain to assault Gibraltar. His mind remained fixed on a direct assault on Russia. He was hoarding his tanks to use there. See Alexander, *How Hitler Could Have Won*, 46–47, 53.

10   The famous Pillars of Hercules of ancient times have been identified as the Rock of Gibraltar on the northern, Spanish, shore, and the Jebel Musa at Ceuta on the southern, Moroccan, shore. Here the strait is fourteen miles wide.

11   Heinz Guderian believed that Hitler made a grave mistake in giving France such favorable armistice terms. He said France should have been presented with the alternatives of either accepting occupation of the entire country and handing over of the French fleet and colonies, or of maintaining the independence and integrity of the country, its colonies, and its fleet in exchange for French assistance in securing a rapid peace with Britain. If the Germans had occupied or had access to the French Mediterranean bases, Guderian wrote, they could have landed in Africa, while German parachute troops could have seized the British base of Malta. "Should the French be willing to participate in these operations, so much the better," Guderian wrote. "Should they refuse, then the war must be carried on by the Italians and ourselves on our own, and carried on at once." The weakness of the British in Egypt was known. The Malta defenses were inadequate. "The presence of four to six panzer divisions in North Africa would have given us such overwhelming superiority that any British reinforcements would inevitably have arrived too late." Guderian wrote that General Franz Ritter von Epp, the Nazi governor of Bavaria, independently came

to the same conclusions as Guderian did, and laid them before Hitler. But the führer was not interested. See Guderian, 136–37.

12 This is assuming that Japan would take advantage of the opportunity and seize the Philippines and British, French, and Dutch colonies in southeast Asia, as, in fact, it did do in 1941. This would have brought the United States, Britain, the Commonwealth, and the Dutch East Indies into conflict with Japan and closed off Western access to Soviet ports in Siberia, notably Vladivostok, terminus of the Trans-Siberian Railway.

13 William L. Shirer, in his *Rise and Fall of the Third Reich* (Shirer, 757), reasons that the German military leadership, as well as Adolf Hitler, lacked any grand strategic concept. Their horizons were limited. The German military had always restricted its aspirations to land warfare against the neighboring nations on the European continent. Hitler himself had a horror of war at sea. And his land-minded great captains were almost totally ignorant of it. The Dover Straits loomed in their minds as an obstacle that they could not overcome. An alternative strike across the Mediterranean would have necessitated vast operations overseas at distances from home bases. In 1940 and 1941 this seemed beyond the scope of the German imagination. Admiral Raeder felt that the senior army leaders had a "purely continental outlook," and did not understand the war-winning opportunities that had opened up on the south shore of the Mediterranean. He was certain they would never counsel Hitler correctly. See Alexander, *How Hitler Could Have Won*, 49.

INDEX